PRAISE FOR *THE FORGOTTEN RECIPE*

"Clipston delivers another enchanting series starter with a tasty premise, family secrets, and sweet-as-pie romance, offering assurance that true love can happen more than once and second chances are worth fighting for."

—RT BOOK REVIEWS, 4½ STARS, TOP PICK!

"In the first book in her Amish Heirloom series, Clipston takes readers on a roller-coaster ride through grief, guilt, and anxiety."

—BOOKLIST

"Clipston is well versed in Amish culture and does a good job creating the world of Lancaster County, Penn. . . . Amish fiction fans will enjoy this story—and want a taste of Veronica's raspberry pie!"

—PUBLISHERS WEEKLY

"[Clipston] does an excellent job of wrapping up her story while setting the stage for the sequel."

—CBA RETAILERS + RESOURCES

PRAISE FOR AMY CLIPSTON

"Clipston brings this engaging series to an end with two emotional family reunions, a prodigal son parable, a sweet but hard-won romance and a happy ending for characters readers have grown to love. Once again, she gives us all we could possibly want from a talented storyteller."

—RT BOOK REVIEWS, 4½ STARS, TOP PICK! ON *A SIMPLE PRAYER*

". . . will leave readers craving more."

—RT BOOK REVIEWS, 4½ STARS, TOP PICK!
ON *A MOTHER'S SECRET*

"Clipston's series starter has a compelling drama involving faith, family and romance . . . [an] absorbing series."

—*RT BOOK REVIEWS*, 4½ STARS, TOP PICK! ON *A HOPEFUL HEART*

"Authentic characters, delectable recipes and faith abound in Clipston's second Kauffman Amish Bakery story."

—*RT BOOK REVIEWS*, 4 STARS ON *A PROMISE OF HOPE*

". . . an entertaining story of Amish life, loss, love and family."

—*RT BOOK REVIEWS*, 4 STARS ON *A PLACE OF PEACE*

"This fifth and final installment in the 'Kauffman Amish Bakery' series is sure to please fans who have waited for Katie's story."

—*LIBRARY JOURNAL* ON *A SEASON OF LOVE*

"[The Kauffman Amish Bakery] series' wide popularity is sure to attract readers to this novella, and they won't be disappointed by the excellent writing and the story's wholesome goodness."

—*LIBRARY JOURNAL* ON *A PLAIN AND SIMPLE CHRISTMAS*

"[*A Plain and Simple Christmas*] is inspiring and a perfect fit for the holiday season."

—*RT BOOK REVIEWS*, 4 STARS

THE COURTSHIP
BASKET

ALSO BY AMY CLIPSTON

THE AMISH HEIRLOOM SERIES

The Forgotten Recipe
The Courtship Basket
The Cherished Quilt (available
November 2016)

THE HEARTS OF THE LANCASTER GRAND HOTEL SERIES

A Hopeful Heart
A Mother's Secret
A Dream of Home
A Simple Prayer

THE KAUFFMAN AMISH BAKERY SERIES

A Gift of Grace
A Promise of Hope
A Place of Peace
A Life of Joy
A Season of Love

YOUNG ADULT

Roadside Assistance
Reckless Heart
Destination Unknown
Miles from Nowhere

NOVELLAS

A Plain and Simple Christmas
Naomi's Gift included in
An Amish Christmas Gift
A Spoonful of Love included
in *An Amish Kitchen*
A Son for Always included
in *An Amish Cradle*
Love Birds included in
An Amish Market

NONFICTION

A Gift of Love

THE COURTSHIP
BASKET

AMY CLIPSTON

ZONDERVAN

The Courtship Basket
Copyright © 2016 by Amy Clipston

This title is also available as a Zondervan e-book.
Visit www.zondervan.com

Requests for information should be addressed to:
Zondervan, *3900 Sparks Dr. SE, Grand Rapids, Michigan 49546*

Library of Congress Cataloging-in-Publication Data

Names: Clipston, Amy, author.
Title: The courtship basket / Amy Clipston.
Description: Nashville: Zondervan, [2016] | Series: An Amish heirloom novel
Identifiers: LCCN 2016002207 | ISBN 9780310342014 (softcover)
Subjects: LCSH: Amish--Fiction. | Man-woman relationships--Fiction. | GSAFD:
  Love stories. | Christian fiction.
Classification: LCC PS3603.L58 C68 2016 | DDC 813/.6--dc23 LC record
available at http://lccn.loc.gov/2016002207

Scripture quotations are taken from the Holy Bible, New International
Version®, NIV®. Copyright © 1973, 1978, 1984, 2011 by Biblica, Inc.® Used by
permission of Zondervan. All rights reserved worldwide. www.zondervan.
com. The "NIV" and "New International Version" are trademarks registered in
the United States Patent and Trademark Office by Biblica, Inc.®

Interior Design: James Phinney

Printed in the United States of America

16 17 18 19 20 21 22 RRD 17 16 15 14 13 12 11 10 9 8 7 6 5 4 3 2 1

For Nyeisha and Eric with love

GLOSSARY

ach: oh
aenti: aunt
appeditlich: delicious
Ausbund: Amish hymnal
bedauerlich: sad
boppli: baby
brot: bread
bruder: brother
bruderskinner: nieces/nephews
bu: boy
buwe: boys
daadi: granddad
daed: dad
danki: thank you
dat: dad
Dietsch: Pennsylvania Dutch, the Amish language
  (a German dialect)
dochder: daughter
dochdern: daughters
dummle!: hurry!
Englisher: a non-Amish person
fraa: wife
freind: friend
freinden: friends

froh: happy

gegisch: silly

gern gschehne: you're welcome

grossdaadi: grandfather

grossdochder: granddaughter

grossdochdern: granddaughters

grossmammi: grandmother

Gude mariye: Good morning

gut: good

Gut nacht: Good night

haus: house

Ich liebe dich: I love you

kaffi: coffee

kapp: prayer covering or cap

kichli: cookie

kichlin: cookies

kind: child

kinner: children

kumm: come

liewe: love, a term of endearment

maed: young women, girls

maedel: young woman

mamm: mom

mammi: grandma

mei: my

mutter: mother

naerfich: nervous

narrisch: crazy

onkel: uncle

Ordnung: The oral tradition of practices required and
    forbidden in the Amish faith.

schee: pretty

schmaert: smart
schtupp: family room
schweschder: sister
schweschdere: sisters
Was iss letz?: What's wrong?
willkumm: welcome
Wie geht's: How do you do? or Good day!
wunderbaar: wonderful
ya: yes

AMISH HEIRLOOM FAMILY TREES

Martha "Mattie" m. Leroy Fisher
Veronica (m. Jason Huyard)   Rachel   Emily

Vera (deceased) m. Raymond Lantz
Michael ("Mike") (mother—Esther—deceased)   John

Timothy m. Sylvia Lantz
Samuel (m. Mandy)   Marie   Janie

Annie m. Elam Huyard
Jason (m. Veronica)   Stephen

Tillie m. Henry (Hank) Ebersol

Margaret m. Abner (deceased) Lapp
Seth (deceased)   Ellie

Fannie Mae m. Titus Dienner (bishop)
Lindann

Susannah m. Timothy Beiler
David   Irma Rose Beiler Smucker

Irma Rose m. Melvin Smucker
Sarah

NOTE TO THE READER

WHILE THIS NOVEL IS SET AGAINST THE REAL BACKDROP OF Lancaster County, Pennsylvania, the characters are fictional. There is no intended resemblance between the characters in this book and any real members of the Amish and Mennonite communities. As with any work of fiction, I've taken license in some areas of research as a means of creating the necessary circumstances for my characters. My research was thorough; however, it would be impossible to be completely accurate in details and description, since each and every community differs. Therefore, any inaccuracies in the Amish and Mennonite lifestyles portrayed in this book are completely due to fictional license.

PROLOGUE

RACHEL FISHER SMILED AS SHE STEPPED OUT ONTO THE PORCH of her parents' large farmhouse. The crisp February air caressed her cheeks as a breeze brushed her blue dress against her legs, and she reflected on the day. Her older sister, Veronica, had married Jason Huyard while Rachel and her younger sister, Emily, stood by as attendants and more than two hundred members of their community filled the congregation gathered in her father's largest barn.

The wedding service had been perfect, and Rachel was bursting with joy and excitement for Veronica, who had lost her former fiancé in an accident nearly a year ago, but then met and fell in love with Jason.

As she moved to the porch railing, Rachel's thoughts turned to David Beiler, and she smiled. She'd been dating him for four years now, and she was certain their wedding would be next. Rachel had already started a mental list of everything she needed to do to prepare for the ceremony. She dreamed of marrying in November, the busiest wedding season.

Like Veronica, Rachel wanted to have the service in her father's large barn. She imagined her sisters and herself wearing hunter green dresses she would sew. Rachel would smile with happiness as she and David stood before their community and took those sacred vows that would join them together for life.

If only he'd propose to me . . .

Rachel tucked an errant strand of dark brown hair behind her

1

ear and leaned against the railing. Loud voices sounded from the house behind her as well as from the barn and pasture, signaling that the celebration continued despite a cloudy sky and dropping temperature. She breathed in a faint aroma of threatening rain and rubbed her arms where gooseflesh appeared, grateful that a late-winter snowstorm they'd feared had never materialized.

She searched the pasture where young people gathered and tried to find David's handsome face. She had seen him after the service, but then he disappeared into the crowd. After she helped deliver the food to the tables, she started looking for him. Her search led her to the house, where she thought he might be lounging in the family room, talking to her father. Instead, she'd found only a few women working in the kitchen.

When her ears caught the sound of soft voices around the corner of the house, Rachel moved to the far end of the porch to see who was there. She stopped short when she realized she could be interrupting a private conversation.

"I know," a feminine voice said. "I was wondering if we were going to be able to talk alone."

The voice was familiar, but it was too low for Rachel to place it. It was rude for her to listen in on the conversation, and she knew she should walk away. Yet something kept her cemented in place. She leaned against the corner of the house and listened more intently.

"I told you I would get away as soon as I could," a masculine voice responded. His voice was hesitant. "I just had to find a way to be discreet. I left when she wasn't paying attention."

Rachel gnawed her lower lip. That voice was so familiar too. Who was it?

Then it hit her like a thousand bales of hay falling from the loft in the barn. That voice belonged to David. An icy chill shimmied up her spine.

"So when are you going to tell her?" the young woman asked,

her voice holding a hint of a whine. "I'm tired of sneaking around. I'm ready to let the world know we want to be together."

Rachel shook her head. Surely she was wrong about the voice. David would never cheat on her or sneak behind her back. Yes, she should just walk away and stop behaving like a voyeur.

"I promised you I'd tell her, and I will. I just need to find the right time," the man said. "Don't you trust me?"

"Of course I do, David."

Rachel swallowed a whimper. Who was the young woman stealing her dreams? She leaned forward on the railing and peered around the house. Her best friend, Sharon, was standing beside David.

Rachel's world tilted and a gasp escaped her mouth.

As if startled by the sound, David and Sharon spun, turning their gazes to Rachel.

"Rachel?" Panic flashed in David's eyes as he took a step toward her, then froze. "I was looking for you."

Sharon gaped, then spoke. "Rachel?"

Rachel shook her head. This had to be a nightmare. How could the two people she loved like members of her own family betray her like this? Anguish at this treachery stole her words and nearly suffocated her. "How-how could you?" she stammered. She took a step back, turned, and ran toward the front door.

"Rachel, wait!" Rachel could hear Sharon coming around the corner, shouting, "It's not what you think!"

Rachel rushed through the front door of the house and raced up the stairs to her bedroom as Sharon's voice chased after her, begging her to stop. She stepped into her room, closed the door, and locked it before sinking down onto the corner of her double bed.

Grief choked her and tears trickled down her hot cheeks. All the plans she'd made for her life with David disintegrated into a distant memory as knocks sounded on her door.

"Rachel?" Sharon's wobbly voice sounded through the door. "Rachel, please let me in. Let me explain, okay?"

"Go away." Rachel's words were muffled as she covered her face with her hands.

"Rachel, please listen to me. I never meant to hurt you." Sharon's voice quavered. "We've been best *freinden* since first grade. I can't imagine losing your friendship."

Rachel swiped her hands across her face and tried to clear the lump from her throat. "Just leave."

"No." Sharon's voice was determined. "We need to talk about this."

"There's nothing to talk about. You and David betrayed me. It's over."

"We were going to tell you. We were waiting for the perfect time to let you know."

"That's why you were sneaking around." Rachel shook her head as if Sharon could see her through the door. "I was so naïve. I thought you were my best *freind*."

"I *am* your best *freind*," Sharon insisted. "This wasn't planned. It just sort of happened." She sniffed. "Please let me in. I want to tell you how sorry I am."

"Just go away." Rachel stretched out on her bed, resting her cheek on her cool pillow.

Closing her eyes, she allowed her tears to finally flow, washing away her fantasy of marrying David and raising a family with him. For four years she'd believed he'd one day be her husband. Now she was alone. She was twenty-two and didn't have a boyfriend with whom to plan a future.

"Rachel?" Sharon's voice asked from the hallway. "Rachel, please let me in."

Rachel pulled a pillow over her head to shield herself from Sharon's pleading voice. She longed for Sharon to leave. There was nothing her former best friend could say to make this better. Rachel's whole world was falling apart.

The hallway outside her room grew silent, and Rachel breathed a sigh of relief. She just wanted to be alone. As a fresh rush of tears filled her eyes, Rachel turned and buried her face in her pillow.

A few minutes later, another knock sounded on her door.

"I said go away!"

"Rachel?" It was Emily. "Are you all right?"

Rachel climbed from the bed and unlocked the door.

"*Ach*, no. What happened? I've been looking for you and someone said she saw you run upstairs." Her younger sister's pretty face clouded with concern as she stepped into the room. At twenty, she was the shortest of the Fisher sisters, and like their sister, Veronica, she had the same blue eyes and blonde hair as their mother.

"David and Sharon have been seeing each other behind my back." Rachel sat on the corner of her bed.

Emily sat down beside her and shook her head. "I can't believe it."

As Rachel recounted the conversation she'd overheard, she felt her hopes and dreams shredding into a million pieces. Her life would never be the same. But as Emily stroked her arm and listened, Rachel was grateful she still had her sisters.

CHAPTER 1

RACHEL STOOD AT THE FRONT OF THE CLASSROOM AND WROTE the day's schedule on the dry-erase board. She breathed in the sweet aroma of the marker as she worked.

Today is the day!

The small trailer that housed the school was on the same property as a larger, traditional, one-room school building. She turned to glance around the small classroom and butterflies fluttered in her stomach.

The trailer was spacious enough for their needs. It had an area in the center of the room for the students' desks, and learning stations were situated around the room. Brightly colored photos of farm animals featuring the names of the four students hung on the wall in one corner. A colorful alphabet, complete with a pictured item illustrating each letter, was displayed on the wall above the dry-erase board. Large, open windows lined each wall, and an unusually warm, late-March breeze filled the room with the smell of spring and new beginnings.

It had been only two weeks since she'd accepted her cousin Malinda's invitation to start teaching there. After speaking to the parent committee and then observing the class, Rachel was finally ready to take her place at the front of the classroom with Malinda. Although she'd never imagined herself working as a teacher, Rachel quickly poured herself into learning the teaching techniques Malinda used for the students at this special school, which offered more one-on-one attention than the larger, one-room schoolhouses could offer.

Rachel looked at the five small desks in the center of the room. A new student was going to join their class today, and she couldn't wait to meet him. The school was for students who needed extra help, including children from different school districts in all of the Lancaster County Amish community, so Rachel wasn't acquainted with the new student or his family.

"I'll have to make a name sign for John Lantz," Rachel said. "Do we have more of those farm signs?"

"*Ya*, we do." Malinda pointed to a drawer unit near the desk. "You can write his name on one and his parents' names on another picture. His parents' names are in the file by our desk. I'll get the animal pictures out for you." She paused, frowning. "I wonder if you should only write his *dat*'s name. His *mamm* passed away."

"*Ach*, no." Rachel shook her head. "That's so *bedauerlich*."

"I know." Malinda nodded. "His *dat* is very ill. His older *bruder*, Mike, is raising him."

"That has to be difficult for him." Rachel crossed the room to the desk, picked up John's file, and placed it on the table near the front of the room before flipping it open. She leafed through, finding each of his work papers from his previous teacher covered in red ink. "He's really been struggling with reading and math."

"*Ya*, he has. I spoke with his former teacher, and she was hoping he could finish first grade with her. But she said he was struggling, and it was becoming a behavior issue. That's why Mike and his father made the decision to move him to this school. John needs a lot of extra help." Malinda took two farm animal pictures from the storage unit and then a black Sharpie from the cup on the desk. "Here. You can write the names."

"*Danki*." Rachel found John's parents' names on the front of the folder. She wrote *John Lantz* on the picture featuring a cow and then stared at his mother's name. She looked at the wall at the far end of the room where the other students' and parents' names were displayed. "I'm going write his mother's name. I'm certain her memory is still a part of his life."

"I agree." Malinda stood, and her gaze moved to the back of the room. She was a couple inches shorter than Rachel. Like Rachel, she had brown hair and brown eyes. "And we don't want him to feel left out when he sees both of the other scholars' parents listed there."

"Exactly." Rachel wrote out *Vera and Raymond Lantz* as she pondered John. Her prayers went out to the little boy, who was only six years old. He didn't have his mother, and his father was ill. No wonder he struggled in school. She silently vowed to be the best teacher she could be for him.

Rachel took the tape dispenser from the desk and went to the back of the room. She taped the two farm pictures near the others. "I think we're all set for his arrival now. I'll make sure we have his books together."

"*Danki.* I'd like to try having the scholars read aloud today," Malinda said as she organized a stack of papers on the large desk they would now share at the front of the room. "I think Lizzie is ready to read in front of the class. She's becoming much more confident since I started working with her more. She showed a big improvement last week."

"I'm not surprised she's improving so much. I could tell when I visited your class that you're a really *gut* teacher," Rachel said. Concern suddenly filled her. "I hope I will do as well as you do with the *kinner.*"

Malinda gave Rachel an encouraging smile. "I have complete faith that you will be a *wunderbaar* teacher. I'm so thankful you agreed to come and help me with this school."

"*Danki* for asking me." Rachel moved to the front of the

classroom and arranged a stack of books for John as Malinda began to place math worksheets on the students' desks.

"How is Veronica doing?" Malinda asked.

"She's doing well." Rachel set the dry-erase marker on the ledge in front of the board. "She and Jason moved into their new *haus* last week and she's really *froh*. He's going to build her a bake stand by the road so she can sell her pies when it warms up."

"That's *wunderbaar*." Malinda's smile faded. "How are you doing?"

"I'm fine." Rachel needed to change the subject. She didn't want to think about David or Sharon. Although it had been a month since the breakup, it was difficult enough seeing them together at church services and youth gatherings. Their happiness was apparent in their shining smiles and intimate whispers. Rachel's belief that David loved her and was going to marry her had been nothing but a childish fantasy. He had been in love with her former best friend all along, or at least for a while now. The thought still caused her chest to ache, but the sting of the breakup had softened slightly.

She turned toward the windows and saw a white van with an unfamiliar driver parked behind the schoolhouse. "I think our new student is here."

"Oh?" Malinda turned toward the window. "*Ya*, I think so. Would you like to go meet him? I met with his family last week, so he's already met me. You can go introduce yourself, and I'll get the other scholars ready for the day."

"That's a *gut* idea."

Rachel stepped outside the trailer and walked down the steps to the small rock driveway where the van was parked. The back door slid open revealing a small, blond boy with bright blue eyes sitting by a man with the same blond hair and blue eyes. Rachel realized he must be Michael Lantz, John's brother. A young woman with brown hair and brown eyes was with them, and Rachel wondered if she was a member of the family too.

Rachel was ready to greet all of them, but the boy and man were engrossed in a conversation and were oblivious to Rachel's presence.

The young woman climbed from the van and smiled. *"Gude mariye."* She gestured for Rachel to step away from the van so they could talk. "You must be Rachel. Malinda told me about you. I'm Marie, John's cousin. I help take care of John and his *dat*." She nodded toward the van. "John is a little *naerfich*. He wasn't *froh* when Mike told him he had to come to another school, but we've been doing our best to encourage him."

"We'll take *gut* care of him," Rachel said. "Malinda and I are excited for John to join our class."

A flurry of activity and noise filled the air as children entered the schoolyard and filed into the two schoolhouses. Rachel nodded greetings at students before turning her attention back to Marie. She looked past her into the van, where John and his older brother were still talking. John's little face contorted with a frown as he stared up at his brother. The boy looked determined to stay in the van.

"Do you think I should help get John from the van?" Rachel offered. "Maybe I can coax him to meet the other *kinner*?"

Marie craned her neck to look into the van. *"Ya,* that's a *gut* idea. John argued with Mike and me during the drive here. It's not just that he doesn't want to go to this school. He thinks he should stay home and take care of his *dat*. I told him that's my job, but he won't listen."

Rachel shook her head as empathy washed over her. "That poor *bu*. I promise I'll do my best to make him feel comfortable."

"Danki." Marie touched her arm. "Things have been difficult for him."

"I understand. Let's see if I can help." Rachel moved to the van. "Hi, John. I'm Rachel."

Mike and John both turned toward her, and she forced a smile despite their frowns.

"I'm a new teacher," Rachel said. "Today is my first day here, just like it's yours. We can help each other. Would you like to be my helper today?"

John looked skeptical, but Mike's frown eased slightly. She studied his tense expression, and his eyes seemed to plead with her to help him get John out of the van.

She looked back at John. "Would you like to walk in with me and meet the other students?"

John gnawed his lower lip.

"They can't wait to meet you. Malinda told them you were coming this week, and they're very excited." Rachel held out her hand, and John stared at it. "I promise we'll have fun today."

John turned to Mike. "You come too."

Mike pressed his lips together. "John, I told you. I'm already late for work."

John's face crumpled, and alarm rang through Rachel. He was going to cry. She had to do something to encourage him to join the class—fast!

"I have an idea," Rachel chimed in. "What if Mike came to the door and watched you step into the classroom? He could see you walk to your desk and then say good-bye."

John thought about the suggestion and then nodded. "*Ya, that's gut.*"

"*Wunderbaar.*" Rachel held out her hand again. "Let's go inside."

John took her hand and jumped out of the van. But then he unexpectedly released her hand and rushed toward the trailer.

"Don't run," Marie warned. "You might fall." She jammed her thumb toward the van. "I'll wait here. *Danki*, Rachel."

"Ya, danki." Mike sidled up to Rachel. "I didn't know what to do. But he suddenly seems eager to see what's going on inside."

Rachel looked up at him as he towered over her. He was taller than David, and she surmised he had to be close to six foot two. He was handsome with a long, thin nose and clean-shaven face. His eyes reminded her of bright blue hydrangeas she'd once seen at the grocery store, but they held both sadness and tension.

"Gern gschehne." She shrugged. "I'm just glad it worked."

"We had a rough start to the day," Mike continued, cupping his hand to the back of his neck. "He fought with me all morning when I tried to get him ready, and then he begged me to ride in the van with him. He doesn't understand that I have to get to work."

"I'm sorry to hear that," Rachel said. "Marie told me John wanted to stay home with your *dat.*"

Mike sighed. *"Ya."*

"Mike!" John called from the doorway to the trailer. "Come see my desk." He waved and then disappeared into the schoolhouse again.

Mike gestured toward the door. "We'd better go."

Rachel followed him up the steps, and as they entered the schoolroom they found John already standing by his desk.

"Teacher Malinda says this is my desk," John said. He pointed at Peter King standing beside him. "This is Peter. He sits next to me."

"That's *gut.*" Mike smiled and relief sparkled in his eyes. "I need to go now. I'll see you tonight."

John nodded and then waved, for the moment at least, all hesitation gone. "Bye!"

Mike turned to Rachel. *"Danki."* His eyes held her gaze for a few moments before he nodded. "I really appreciate it."

"Gern gschehne," she said. "I'll write in his daily journal and let you know how each day goes."

Rachel watched him walk toward the door. As he stepped

out into the sunlight, she turned toward her class and took a deep breath. Her teaching adventure was about to begin.

"HOW WAS YOUR FIRST DAY?" MAMM ASKED AS RACHEL STEPPED into the kitchen later that afternoon.

"It was *gut*." Rachel dropped her tote bag and lunch pail on a kitchen chair and sat down on the chair beside it. "It was very busy."

Mamm brought a plate of rolls to the table, along with a butter dish. "Supper will be ready in about thirty minutes. Emily and I made a chicken casserole."

Rachel inhaled the aroma, and her stomach gurgled. "I worked up an appetite." She grabbed a roll, pulled it apart, and began slathering it with butter.

"Rachel!" Emily rushed into the kitchen from the stairwell. "I was just wondering how your day went. How do you like teaching?"

"I liked it." Rachel bit into the warm roll and considered the children. "A new student joined the class today. His name is John Lantz. His *mamm* passed away, and his *dat* is very ill. He's only six years old and his *bruder* is raising him."

"*Ach*, no." Emily's eyes quickly shimmered with tears. "That's so sad."

Rachel nodded. "His *bruder* and cousin told me John didn't want to come to school today, so Malinda and I tried to make it fun for him."

"How did he do?" *Mamm* asked.

Rachel frowned. "He had a difficult time focusing. I had to keep reminding him to stay in his seat and to follow instructions. I can see why his former teacher struggled." Her thoughts turned to what Marie had told her. "His cousin said he wanted to stay home so he could help take care of his *dat*."

Emily sighed and shook her head. "Poor *bu*."

Rachel smiled determinedly as she remembered the sadness in Mike's eyes. "Malinda and I will take *gut* care of him."

"I'm so *froh* you're teaching," *Mamm* said. "I know you'll do a *wunderbaar* job. Malinda was so *schmaert* to ask you to help her with her class."

"And it came at the right time for you," Emily chimed in as she swiped a roll from the plate. "You can focus all your energy on those *kinner* and give them the extra attention they need."

"Right." Rachel took another bite of her roll and wondered how she could help John and his family.

MIKE CLOSED THE BARN DOOR AND STARTED FOR THE LARGE, whitewashed farmhouse he'd lived in since birth. His boots crunched on the rock path leading to the house as he reflected on the day. His muscles ached from his long shift at Bird-in-Hand Builders creating wooden lawn ornaments, and he couldn't shake the bleak mood that had been resting on his shoulders from the time he'd awoken this morning. He couldn't stand arguing with his baby brother, but he had to get John to school.

Why did John have to make things so difficult?

Because he's only six and doesn't understand what's going on.

Mike's inner voice stopped him in his tracks. He asked God daily for patience and strength while he carried the burden of raising his brother and caring for his father. He needed to continue to pray for both.

His boots clomped up the back porch steps. He pulled open the door and entered the house through the mudroom, where he yanked off his boots and set them beneath the bench.

"Mike?" Marie poked her head into the mudroom, her face filled with concern. "I was starting to get worried. You're usually home an hour before this."

"I had some work to finish up since I was late this morning." He stepped into the kitchen and inhaled the delicious aroma of meat loaf, which caused his stomach to rumble.

Marie frowned. "Did you skip lunch again?"

He shook his head as he sat down at the kitchen table. "I ate an apple and a couple of *kichlin* one of the other workers brought in."

She clicked her tongue like an irritated mother. "You need your strength, Mike. Have a seat and I'll fix you a plate." She crossed the room to the oven and pulled out a plate with a large piece of barbecue meat loaf, mashed potatoes, green beans, and a roll. She placed the plate in front of him and then brought him a glass of water.

"*Danki.*" He closed his eyes for a silent prayer and then smiled up at her. "I appreciate that you stayed late tonight. I don't know what I'd do without your help."

"Don't be *gegisch.*" Marie waved off his words. "I'm *froh* to help."

"How's *mei dat?*" Mike asked before forking a hunk of meat loaf.

When Marie's frown returned, his stomach clenched with apprehension. "He didn't do well with the treatment today. The nurses said his blood pressure dropped, and they had to elevate his legs."

Mike dropped his fork with a clatter. "Why didn't they call me? I would've rushed to the dialysis center to be there with him."

"Everything is okay." Marie held up her hands as if to calm him. "When I went to pick him up, the nurse said he was okay. He just had to rest."

Mike pushed back his chair and stood. "I'll go check on him."

"Mike, he's fine," Marie insisted. "He ate a little bit of meat loaf and then asked me to help him get ready for bed. He's tired, but I really think he'll be fine. You should finish your supper before you check on him. He's sleeping. I just checked on him a few minutes before you got home."

Mike forked more meat loaf into his mouth. Although it was

delicious, he wasn't enjoying it. His stomach was too tied up in anxious knots. "How's John?"

"He's *gut*." Marie fingered a paper napkin. "He did his chores and then took his bath. He's looking at books in his room."

"Did he say anything about school?" Mike pressed on between bites of mashed potatoes.

"He didn't seem to want to talk about it." Marie stood and walked to the sink. "I'm certain he'll be fine." She lifted a dish from the drainboard. "It will take him a few days to adjust to the new school, but it will be fine. Rachel seems like a *wunderbaar* teacher."

Mike thought about the pretty brunette teacher as he speared a few green beans with his fork. She had treated John with patience and understanding, and she'd known exactly what to say to get him out of the van and into the classroom. So he was sure she could help his brother adjust to the new school and get him caught up with his reading and writing.

He finished eating his supper and then placed the dish, utensils, and glass in the side of the sink holding the frothy water. "It was *appeditlich. Danki* again."

"*Gern gschehne.*" Marie started washing Mike's plate. "I'm going to head home after the dishes are done. I'm not certain if I'm coming tomorrow or if Janie is. I need to see if she plans to go to the market."

Gratitude swelled inside of him as he watched her work at the sink. What would he do without his cousins?

"I can't thank you enough. I don't know how I could handle my *dat*'s dialysis treatments and failing health without you and Janie." Mike rubbed his temples where a headache brewed. "When he was diagnosed three years ago, I never imagined his kidney failure would progress so quickly. I could never care for my *dat*, work at the shop, run the household, and care for John by myself. You and Janie have been a blessing to us."

Marie smiled. "That's what family is for. You go on and get your rest. I can tell you've had a tough day."

"*Danki.*" Mike paused and studied his cousin. "You've noticed how much worse my *dat* is getting too, haven't you?"

Marie sighed as a frown stole her smile. "*Ya*, I have."

"I can't stand the thought of losing him." His voice hitched on the last word.

"Don't worry about that right now." Her eyes were full of determination. "Trust God."

He nodded and went down the hallway, stopping when he reached the door to his father's bedroom. Loud snores rumbled. Mike pushed the door open and peered into where *Dat* lay on his right side, facing the door. The snores echoed throughout the large room that included a double bed, two dressers, and a plain, tan wing chair. A wheelchair sat in the corner, awaiting his father's next trip to the kitchen for a meal.

It seemed as if it were just yesterday that his father was working beside him at Bird-in-Hand Builders, teaching him how to create wishing wells and large wooden baskets that served as planters. His father had built the company with his brother, Timothy, and opened the doors before Mike was born. Now it was up to Mike to keep the business going for his *dat*, but he was thankful his uncle and cousin were there too.

What would I do without my family? The question echoed through his mind again.

Mike backed out the door and pulled it shut with a quiet click. As he moved to the stairs, he found John sitting on the bottom step.

"Johnny?" Mike asked. "What are you doing down here?"

"Waiting for you." John's voice was small and his blue eyes were hesitant. Mike hoped John hadn't been eavesdropping as he shared his deepest fears with Marie.

"Would you like me to read to you tonight?" Mike offered.

"*Ya.*" John's eyes brightened with excitement. "May I pick the book?"

"Of course you may." Mike started up the stairs behind his little brother. Daily, Mike struggled to be the father figure John deserved, but he always doubted himself. He was only twenty-four, and he had no parenting experience. At the same time, he had memories, and some of his favorites were of when his parents read to him. Mike had lost his mother, Esther, when he was only ten. Still, Mike would never forget the nights when she read to him until he fell asleep.

Mike's stepmother, Vera, who had been John's mother, had also passed away, and now Mike was the only immediate family member who could read to him. Their father was too ill most of the time.

Mike followed John to the second floor, where his bedroom and John's were both located. They made their way to John's room, and John rushed to his bookshelf and picked a book. Then he snuggled under the covers on his bed as Mike sat down on its edge.

As Mike opened the book, he again thought of his mother and stepmother. John's mother should be the one reading to him, or at least his father, but Mike would do his best to take care of his precious brother. He missed his stepmother, but his worry for his father ran deep into his soul. Nightly he prayed for his father's health, and also prayed that his brother would do better in school. God would see him through this difficult time in his life, but Mike also had to do his part of playing mother and father to his brother.

CHAPTER 2

"OKAY, SCHOLARS. IT'S TIME FOR THE FIRST GRADERS' READING time," Rachel said as she stood at the front of the classroom the following morning. "We're going to read aloud today. It's Lena's turn to choose the book. The rest of the class can work on math. Teacher Malinda is going to hand out the math sheet, and I want the first graders to come to the front of the room."

Lena and Luke hopped up from their chairs and hurried to the front. Lena retrieved three reading books from the first-grade shelf behind the teacher's desk and then they both stood in front of Rachel with their books open. John, however, remained in his seat, staring down at the wooden top of his desk.

Rachel turned toward Malinda, who shook her head after she gave the other students their math sheet to complete.

"John," Malinda said. "Did you hear Teacher Rachel? It's time for the first graders to read. Please get your book. Lena has it at the front of the classroom for you."

John continued to stare down at the desktop.

"John?" Rachel moved to his desk. "Did you hear us?"

John didn't look up.

"John?" Rachel squatted down next to him and gently touched his little leg. "Are you all right?"

The boy turned toward her and frowned.

"It's time to read aloud. Can you read?"

John shrugged.

Rachel turned toward Malinda, who also shrugged. Should she allow him to disobey her or should she insist he follow the class rules? Her inner voice told her to order him to obey, but her intuition advised her to let him stay in his seat. After all, it was only his second day in class.

What if John can't read at all and his former teacher embarrassed him by pushing him to read aloud in her class? Rachel couldn't risk humiliating him and ruining any chance of earning his trust. She wanted to help him, encourage him, and protect him. She thought of Mike's sad eyes. She had to keep her promise to him and take good care of his younger brother. Having him read along with the class was the best solution.

"Will you go get your book from Lena?" Rachel asked him.

John shook his head.

Rachel pressed her lips together while contemplating how to handle this boy. She couldn't allow him to break the rules, but she also had empathy for his family situation.

She turned toward the other students. "Lena," she said. "Would you please bring me John's book?"

The blonde six-year-old took the book from the shelf and brought it to Rachel, who placed it on the desk in front of John.

"*Danki*, Lena," Rachel said. "John, we're going to start with page one of this book. You may follow along." She turned to page one and then walked to the front of the room. "Lena, would you like to start?"

For the next thirty minutes, Lena and Luke took turns reading a paragraph aloud while Malinda graded math papers at her desk. Rachel frequently glanced toward John and found him still staring at the first page of the book. She began to wonder if he could read at all. Malinda hadn't mentioned that he was illiterate, but the idea gripped her.

When the reading time was over, Rachel rang a small bell indicating it was time to sing. While the students fetched their song binders and gathered at the front of the room, John remained in his chair.

Malinda touched Rachel's arm and leaned over to her. "Are you going to make John sing?" she whispered in her ear.

"Let's see if he'll join us." Rachel turned toward John. "Are you going to sing with us, John?"

John met Rachel's encouraging smile with a frown and then shook his head.

Rachel paused and assessed the situation. Her instinct told her to let the boy remain at his desk. "Fine. We'll miss having your voice in our small choir, but you can stay in your seat."

Rachel and Malinda led the students in singing four songs while John continued to study his desktop. Then Rachel rang the bell, dismissing them for lunch. The students retrieved their lunch pails from a shelf at the back of the room and then rushed out the door for the playground where the students from the larger schoolhouse were starting to gather in a large circle to eat their lunches. It was still warm enough today that the teachers did not have to insist on jackets.

John rose from his seat and slowly moved to the back of the room to retrieve his lunch pail. Rachel stood at the window and watched as he joined the other children outside. She pondered how he'd been excited when he first found his desk on Monday, and he had participated with the class to some degree, but today he refused to participate at all.

"Why didn't you punish him?" Malinda asked as she sidled up to Rachel. "I never allow one of the *kinner* to disobey instructions like that."

"I know." Rachel scowled as she faced her. "I just don't understand why he was so *froh* yesterday but today he's like a different *kind.*" Concern nipped at her as she pondered the boy's ill father. "Do you think something happened at home last night?"

Malinda frowned. "We have to insist the scholars follow the classroom rules, no matter what. Part of our job is to teach the *kinner* that they have to do as they're told."

"I understand that, but I can't help feeling like something is wrong." Rachel shook her head. "It's only his second day at our school. We can ease him into the rules."

"Ease him into the rules?" Malinda raised an eyebrow. "You know that's not how it works. You must insist on discipline."

Maybe I'm not cut out to be a teacher. "You're right," Rachel conceded. "I'll mention this when I write in his journal. I'll let his *bruder* know what's going on."

"That's a *gut* idea." Malinda crossed the room and fetched their lunch pails from under the desk. "Let's go eat with the *kinner.*"

Rachel followed Malinda out to the playground where they ate their lunches while sitting on their lunch pails. Teachers and children alike sat in a large circle that included everyone from both schoolhouses. After lunch the students set their lunch pails aside to play. They formed softball teams and then a game began in the center of the large playground. A smaller group gathered around the swings.

Rachel stood with Malinda by the fence while the children played. She turned and found John standing by himself near the swing set. The swings flew through the air as children screeched with delight.

"I don't think John knows how to interact with the other *kinner,*" Rachel said. Sympathy overcame her as John kicked a stone with the toe of his shoe.

"He'll be fine." Malinda turned toward the swing set. "We'll just keep encouraging him."

"*Ya,* I suppose so. I just can't stand to see a *kind* sad and lonely."

Rachel shook her head. "I always had a *freind* to talk to on the playground." Her thoughts turned to Sharon, and her stomach twisted. She never imagined her best friend since first grade would betray her the way Sharon had.

A small girl in the center swing lowered her feet until her shoes scraped the ground, sending an explosion of dust up into the air around her. She stopped the swing and said something to the girl swinging beside her. John walked over to her and pushed her, knocking her from the swing to the ground, where she landed on her bottom.

Rachel gasped, then rushed over to swing set, where the little girl sat stunned. The swing moved back and forth, smacking her in the side of the head twice before she burst into tears and crawled away from it.

"Naomi!" Mary, the teacher's assistant from the larger schoolhouse, called. "Are you all right? What happened?"

Rachel sidled up to Mary at the swing set. "John pushed her off the swing." She took John's arm. "You need to apologize right now, John."

John muttered something that sounded like "I'm sorry," but Naomi continued to wail as Mary lifted her into her arms.

Rachel frowned at Mary. "I'm going to talk to him."

Mary responded with a stiff nod as Naomi sobbed into her shoulder.

Rachel grasped John's arm, retrieved his lunch pail, and steered him toward the trailer while mentally debating if the boy was screaming for attention or if he was just a bully.

"Why did you push that little girl off the swing?" she asked him when they reached the privacy of the schoolhouse.

John stared at the toes of his shoes.

"Do you understand that you could have hurt Naomi badly?" Rachel continued. "How would you have felt if she'd broken her arm or leg?"

John lifted his gaze and his blue eyes sparkled with tears.

Rachel gaped. John wasn't a cruel boy if he felt remorse. His behavior had to be a cry for attention. Was he ignored at home? She cleared her throat.

"You have to be punished for your behavior, John," she said, hoping she sounded authoritative instead of emotional. "You need to sit at your desk quietly while the rest of the class enjoys recess. If you want to be outside with the rest of the class, then you need to learn how to behave. You can't go around pushing other *kinner*. You need to wait your turn for the swing set."

John lowered his small body into the seat and sniffed.

Rachel picked up his reading book and then remembered she wasn't certain if he could read. "Can you read, John?"

He shrugged, once again studying the top of his desk.

She decided the shrug was close enough to a yes, and she placed it on the desk in front of him. "You can read while you wait for the class to return." Then she picked up John's daily journal from the pile of journals on the desk and began to write.

Dear Mike,

 I want to make you aware that we've had problems with John at school today. He refuses to participate in class, and he pushed a girl off a swing during recess. I believe we need to schedule a conference to discuss this. I need your help working with John to improve his behavior. Please stop by the school as soon as possible.

Thank you,
Rachel Fisher

Rachel knew it was against the rules to request a conference with a parent or guardian since only the school board chairman was supposed to arrange conferences. At the same time, she felt this was important enough to request a conference herself. She only had John's best interests in mind, and the sooner they addressed his needs, the better.

She closed the journal and placed it back on the pile. At the end of the day, she would put the journals in the students' bags so they could take them home. She hoped she could find a way to help this boy who so desperately needed guidance and love.

MIKE DESCENDED THE STAIRS LATER THAT NIGHT. HE'D read to John and then said prayers with him before tucking him into bed. The day had been another long and tiring one as he built planters and took orders from customers. He looked forward to unwinding, and he finally had that chance.

He pulled a pot from a cabinet, added milk, and then set it on the burner of the propane stove. When he was little, his mother had taught him to drink warm milk when he couldn't sleep, and it had become a habit over the last six months when his father's health had taken a turn for the worse. He needed all the help he could get turning off his thoughts and finding rest at night.

Mike found John's bag on the counter and pulled out his daily journal. He opened it, but before he started to read, a thud sounded from the other end of the house.

"Michael!" *Dat's* voice called. "Michael! *Dummle!*"

Mike's adrenaline spiked with fear as he dropped the journal into the tote bag and rushed toward the back of the house. He found *Dat* sprawled on the floor of his bathroom.

"*Dat.*" Mike leaned down, feeling as though his heart had lodged in his throat. "Don't move. Does anything hurt? Should I call nine-one-one?"

"No, no." *Dat's* voice was thin, and his skin was pale. "Just help me get up."

Mike took *Dat*'s arm and gently lifted him to his feet. *Dat* was thin and frail, seeming to weigh only half as much as he had before he started dialysis treatments three times a week.

"Why didn't you ask me to help you to the bathroom?" Mike asked after his father was safely seated on the commode. "You know I'll always come and help you. I'd rather be certain you're safe."

Dat sighed, his tired blue eyes shimmering with tears. "I thought I could do it myself."

Mike noticed a stream of blood moving down his father's right arm. "You scraped yourself. I'll get a bandage." He searched the storage space under the sink and pulled out a box of Band-Aids and some antiseptic cream. Then he wiped his father's arm, applied the cream, and affixed the bandage over the small scrape. It seemed strange to take care of the man who had cared for him when he was a small boy. How had the tables turned so quickly?

"I thought I could go to the bathroom by myself, but I fell after I washed my hands. I can't pull myself up," *Dat* suddenly said, breaking the silence. "I don't have the strength anymore."

"It's all right." Mike touched his father's thin arm. "That's what I'm here for. It's my job to take care of you and John."

Dat's lower lip quivered. "That was supposed to be my job."

A lump constricted Mike's throat. He couldn't stand seeing his father emotional. Where was the strong man who had chased after eleven-year-old Mike when he'd set the chicken coop on fire? That had been an accident, but Mike had acted guilty by running away. In truth, he just hadn't wanted to face his *dat*'s disappointment.

"Let's get you back to bed." Mike's voice sounded thin and foreign to him. He supported his father's arms and gently lifted him to his feet. "Do you want me to sleep on the sofa so you can call me if you need anything during the night?"

"No, no." *Dat* waved off the question with his free hand as they moved slowly to his room. "You go to your room. I'll be just fine."

"No, I'll be on the sofa. That way I can get here quickly if you need me." Mike touched the small bell on the nightstand beside the bed. "You ring this as loud as you can if you need me. I'm a light sleeper, so I will come to help you."

Dat nodded. "*Ya*, I will. *Danki*. You go get some sleep. You look exhausted."

"*Gut nacht*." Mike tucked his father into his bed while considering the irony that he had put both his young brother and his father to bed in the same night.

Mike rubbed his temple as he padded back to the kitchen. He gasped when he remembered the pot of milk on the burner. He rushed to the stove and found that the milk had evaporated and the bottom of the pot was black. He flipped off the burner and moved the pot to the back of the stovetop.

Mike slumped against the counter and covered his face with his hands as the anxiety of the day overwhelmed him. He needed sleep, and he needed strength. How could he carry this load alone? His cousins couldn't be here all the time.

The question lingered in the back of his mind as he walked up the stairs to his bedroom to dress for bed and get his pillow and blanket. His thoughts moved to his mother. *Mamm* had an unfailing faith. At times like this, she would tell him he needed to pray more.

As Mike savored the memories of his beautiful mother, he walked back downstairs, dropped onto the sofa, and took her advice.

CHAPTER 3

"HOW WAS JOHN LANTZ TODAY?" MAMM ASKED AS SHE TOOK a roast out of the oven. "Was he better than yesterday?"

"*Ya*, he was a little better." Rachel set the dinner plates on the table. "He didn't bully anyone on the playground, but he's still not participating in class. He won't read aloud or sing with the other *kinner*. He also doesn't talk to them. Luke King asked John if he wanted to help him sweep the floor, and John didn't answer. He just kept staring at his desk."

"*Ach*, no." *Mamm* turned around. "That's so sad."

Rachel nodded. "*Ya*, I know." She set the last dinner plate at the head of the table for her father. "I don't understand why John went from being a little excited to be at school on Monday to being so unhappy. I feel bad for him, and I want to help him."

"It sounds like he needs some attention and love." *Mamm* frowned. "You can try to get him to talk to you. Maybe he'll tell you what's wrong."

"I've tried that, but he won't talk. I tried to get him alone again today before his driver came to get him, and he only stared down at his shoes. He's a very sad little *bu*." Rachel shook her head. "His *bruder* didn't respond to my journal entry about John's behavior. I'm really concerned about John, but I don't know what to do."

"You mentioned that their *dat* is ill, so maybe the older *bruder* didn't have time to write back last night," *Mamm* said as she peeled a potato.

"*Ya*, you're probably right." Rachel pondered her mother's thought and an idea struck her. She should try to give Mike Lantz a call. She had the class roster in her bag. Although it was against the school board rules to contact a parent or guardian directly, she couldn't stop herself from worrying about John. "I'm going to make a quick phone call. I'll finish setting the table when I get back." She retrieved her tote bag from the mudroom, pulled out the class roster, put on her sweater, and went out to the phone shanty next to the barn.

She dialed the number, and after a few rings a masculine voice sounded. "You've reached the Lantz farm. Please leave a message and we'll call you back."

Rachel cleared her throat. "Hello, this is Rachel Fisher. I'm a teacher at John's school. I wrote in John's daily journal about his behavior, and I didn't hear from you. I need to speak with you as soon as possible. John hasn't been participating in class, and he pushed a *kind* off a swing yesterday. I'd like to discuss this with you, so please write in the journal or call me." She rattled off her home number and then hung up. She hoped she'd hear from John's brother soon so she could figure out a way to help the boy.

THE DOCTOR'S WORDS ECHOED IN MIKE'S MIND AS HE SAT beside his father in the van that evening. *Dat's* lab work looked terrible, and he was lethargic. The doctor had shared the obvious: his father was getting weaker and weaker. His fall in the bathroom last night had illustrated this point.

Mike stared out the van window as the lush fields of neighboring farms rushed by in a blur of greens and yellows. His back was sore from sleeping on the old, lumpy sofa. He'd tossed and turned most of the night, trying in vain to get comfortable, but he'd only managed a few hours of sleep before it was time to do chores before going to work.

He had left the shop early to go with *Dat* to his doctor's appointment, and he could immediately tell by the doctor's expression that the news wasn't going to be what he'd hoped. The treatments weren't working as well as the doctor had anticipated, and his father's lab results weren't where they should be.

Mike's stomach tightened with anxiety. He couldn't bear the thought of losing *Dat* after tragically losing his mother and then his stepmother. He couldn't imagine the thought of John growing up an orphan. He and John both needed their father.

"I want to stop the treatments." *Dat*'s voice was grave as he sat beside him in the seat.

"What?" Mike's eyes widened as he studied *Dat*. Had he heard him correctly?

"I want to stop the dialysis." *Dat*'s expression was blank, void of emotion. "I don't want to go through this anymore."

"*Dat*." Mike lowered his voice, hoping the driver couldn't hear them over the sound of the country music pouring through the speakers at the front of the van. "You know what will happen if you stop dialysis, right?" His words came in a rush as fear crawled up his neck and dried his throat. "Your body will fill up with toxins, and you'll die. You need dialysis to filter your blood the way your kidneys can't."

"I know." Weariness contorted *Dat*'s gaunt features. "I'm tired, Michael. I don't know how much longer I can do this. All I am is a burden to you. You carry too much of a load as it is. You don't need me falling."

"You're *not* a burden." Mike emphasized his shaky words. "You're *mei dat*. John and I need you."

Dat nodded and turned his attention toward the window on the opposite side of the van.

"I need you to be strong, *Dat*," Mike continued. "You need to be strong for John and also for me. Do you want John to grow up an orphan?"

"He has you." *Dat's* voice was suddenly strong and clear as he met Mike's gaze with determined eyes. "You're a better *dat* than I can be right now."

"But I'm not his *dat*," Mike insisted. "You are." He placed his shaking hands in his lap.

Dat nodded. "I'm doing the best I can."

"That's all we can ask." Mike touched his father's arm.

DAT'S WORDS ECHOED THROUGH MIKE'S MIND AS HE ATE supper with *Dat*, John, and Janie, Marie's younger sister. Mike's stomach remained knotted with the thoughts of his father passing away. He couldn't allow himself to think about life without his father. It was just too painful.

When supper was over, John insisted on pushing their father's wheelchair into the family room before he rushed upstairs to take his bath. Mike helped *Dat* move to his favorite recliner and handed him his Bible and the latest issue of the *Budget*. Then he returned to the kitchen, where Janie was filling one side of the sink with sudsy water.

Mike thought once more how interesting it was that while Marie and her brother, Sam, had dark hair and eyes, Janie's hair was red and her eyes were bright blue.

"I need to go take care of the animals," Mike said as he walked toward the mudroom to retrieve his boots and jacket.

"Why didn't you ask John to help you?" Janie turned toward him. "He usually helps you with the chores, doesn't he?"

"He does, but tonight I just want to be alone with my thoughts." He continued toward the mudroom.

"Wait, Mike." Janie called after him. *"Was iss letz?"*

Mike stopped in the doorway and leaned against the woodwork. He silently debated how much to tell his cousin. Did she need to carry the burden of his father's health? He always felt guilty for dumping his troubles on his cousins when they already did so much to help him.

"Marie told me your *dat* had a doctor's appointment today after his dialysis treatment. Did you go with him?" Janie took a step toward him as he nodded. "Did something happen?"

"The doctor didn't have *gut* news," Mike began. *"Dat*'s lab work showed that his levels aren't where they should be. His calcium, phosphorus, and albumin levels aren't looking good."

"Oh." Janie nodded, but her eyes told him she didn't understand him.

"That means he's not doing well. The appointment didn't upset me, but our conversation in the car afterward did." Mike tried to steel himself against his flaring emotions as he shared what *Dat* had said to him in the van about wanting to stop the treatments and how Mike had responded to him. Janie gasped and covered her mouth with her hand as he spoke. "I can't imagine losing him. Do you think I said the right things to him?"

Although he was older than Janie, he desperately craved her approval. He needed someone to tell him he was doing a good job caring for his father and his brother.

"Ya, I do." Janie sniffed and wiped her fingers across her eyes. "I think you said the best things you could. We'll just continue to take care of him and pray that he gets stronger."

"Right." Mike cleared his throat as ongoing anxiety swirled inside of him. "I need to go take care of the animals." He slipped on his boots and jacket and started toward the door.

"Oh, and please check the messages," Janie called after him. "I meant to check them earlier, but I forgot."

Mike descended the back steps and walked to the barn. After taking care of the horses, he went to the phone and dialed the voice mail number. He found two messages from family members checking on *Dat's* health. The third and final message was from John's teacher Rachel.

While he listened to her message detailing his brother's problems in school, something inside of him snapped, and all his bottled-up frustration bubbled to the surface. He'd had enough stress for one day, and this message was the last straw. He slammed the phone down and marched into the house, where he found Janie wiping down the stovetop.

"I've had it," Mike announced, his voice booming louder than he'd expected.

Janie jumped with a start as she faced him. Her eyes were wide with surprise.

"I just got a message from John's teacher complaining about him. I don't think I can take much more of this." He slumped into a kitchen chair and rested his elbows on the table as his anger and frustration boiled through him.

"What happened?" Janie sat down across from him.

"His teacher Rachel left me a message saying he's not participating in class, and he pushed a *kind* off a swing on the playground yesterday." The palms of his hands blocking his face muffled his voice. "I'm not sure I can deal with this today. I hardly slept last night. I stayed on the sofa to make sure *Dat* didn't fall again."

"He fell last night?" Janie asked with surprise.

"*Ya*, he did. He fell in the bathroom." Mike shoved his fingers through his hair. "Rachel asked me to write in the daily journal. I was going to write in it last night, but after *Dat* fell, I totally forgot about it."

"You have too much on you." Janie's smile was supportive. "Why don't I write in it for you? I'll send a note saying you're going to talk to John. Marie and I can take care of the journal for you, so you can concentrate on other things. Will that help you?"

Mike cleared his throat. It was time for him to stop whining and take care of things. After all, that's what *Dat* would do. "No, but *danki*. I'll take care of it." He pushed back the chair and stood. "I'll write a note and then go check on John."

"All right." Janie hesitated. "You know Marie and I don't mind helping you. That's what family is for, Mike."

"I know. *Danki*." He located John's tote bag on the floor of the mudroom and retrieved the journal. "John is my responsibility since *Dat* can't care for him."

"Really, Marie and I can handle the journal with the teacher for you," Janie said. "I can't stand seeing you so upset about this."

"It's fine." Mike read Rachel's note and a frown formed on his lips. Her notes for the past two days were a summary of everything his brother had done wrong in the classroom. He hadn't sung with the class, he refused to read aloud, he pushed a girl off the swing, and he ignored a boy named Luke when he asked John if he wanted to help him sweep. Mike stared at Rachel's perfect handwriting while mentally debating what to write in the journal.

Finally, he wrote:

Received your notes and voice mail. Will be in touch.
—Mike Lantz.

"What did you write?" Janie appeared beside him and craned her neck to read the page, then turned a confused expression on him. "All you wrote is that you'll be in touch?"

"That's right." He closed the journal and shoved it back into the tote bag. "I'll be in touch when I figure out what to say to her."

"But, Mike," Janie began, "Rachel is only doing her job. The parents and teachers are supposed to work together, especially in a special school."

"I know." Mike started toward the stairs. "I'm going to talk to John, which is doing my part."

"But why didn't you tell her that?" Janie followed him. "Rachel is going to think you don't care or you're not taking her concerns seriously."

"I do take them seriously." Mike stepped onto the stairs. "I'm going to handle them in my own way."

"She's going to be upset with you," Janie warned as she stood at the bottom of the steps. "You really should write a note and tell her you're going to talk to John."

Mike continued up the steps, ignoring his well-meaning cousin.

"Mike, wait," Janie called after him.

When he reached the top step, he looked down at her.

"You should just write her a note telling her you're talking to John and working with him. That's all she wants to hear." Janie pointed in the direction of the kitchen. "I'm going to finish the dishes and then head home. Marie will be here tomorrow."

"*Gut. Danki.*" Mike said good night and then ambled down the hallway toward John's room. He found his younger brother sitting on his bed, playing with a metal toy tractor. He knocked on the doorframe, and John looked up.

"How are you, John?"

"Fine." John placed the tractor on the bed and gave Mike a puzzled expression. "Why didn't you want me to help with chores tonight?"

"I thought I would give you a break since you looked tired." Mike lowered himself onto the corner of John's bed, which creaked under his weight. "How was school today?"

John shrugged as he ran his small fingers over the metal truck.

"Do you like school?" Mike prodded.

John shrugged again and continued to avert his eyes from Mike's by studying the toy, which had been Mike's favorite when he was John's age.

"Johnny?" Mike asked, touching his brother's arm. "Is there something you want to tell me?"

John shook his head without looking up.

Mike gently placed his finger under John's chin and tilted his face so their eyes met. "John, your teacher wrote in your journal to tell me about your behavior. Why haven't you been participating in class like you're supposed to?"

John's lower lip quivered, and his eyes glistened with tears. "I don't want to go to school."

Mike's insides twisted with grief. "Why don't you want to go to school? Don't you like being with the other *kinner*?"

John sniffed as a tear trickled down his pink cheek. "I need to be home with *Dat* and you."

"No, no." Mike brushed the tear away with the tip of his finger. Seeing his little brother cry was nearly his undoing. He took a deep breath and pressed on, hoping his voice didn't quaver with his emotion. "You need to be in school with the other *kinner*. Janie and Marie take care of *Dat* during the day while I work and you're in school." He sighed as more tears escaped his little brother's sad blue eyes. "Are you misbehaving in school because you're worried about *Dat*?"

John shrugged while staring at the tractor. A teardrop traced his cheek and then dripped onto the worn metal toy.

"John," Mike said, his voice thick with emotion. "You don't need to worry about *Dat* while you're at school. You only need to follow the rules and do what your teachers tell you to do. You have to participate in class and be nice to the other *kinner*. Marie, Janie, and I will make sure *Dat* goes to the doctors and gets what he needs."

"What if he dies like *Mamm* did?" John's voice was so soft that Mike nearly missed the question.

The lump in Mike's throat choked back his words. Instead of speaking, he pulled John into his arms and held him close.

"It's all right," Mike finally whispered. "We'll be fine. I need you to do your best in school and follow the rules. I'll take care of us, all right?"

John nodded and sniffed.

"It's almost bedtime. Go brush your teeth."

John hopped up from the bed and rushed down the hallway toward the bathroom. Mike's fingers sought the cool metal tractor while he waited for John to return. He reflected on Janie's advice as he spun the tractor's tires. Janie was right when she suggested he write a note to Rachel, but he was too mentally and physically exhausted right now. He just wanted to say good night to his brother, take care of his father, and go to sleep. He would write a longer response to Rachel tomorrow if he felt more mentally capable to form a coherent thought.

After tucking John into bed, Mike made his way down the stairs to the family room, where he found *Dat* snoring in his recliner. Mike couldn't bring himself to move *Dat* when he looked so comfortable and peaceful.

Instead, Mike sank onto the end of the sofa as John's worried words about losing their father echoed through his mind. He couldn't stand to see John cry, and he longed to take away his little brother's worries and fears. He didn't know how to erase John's fears when they were the same ones that haunted him.

A yawn overtook him, and he slowly stretched his long body out on the sofa and positioned the pillow he'd left there the night before under his head. He had to do his best to keep John calm. He had to be the strength John needed and deserved. And he had to learn how to be a good father.

Another yawn gripped Mike as his father's snores rumbled from across the room. Mike closed his eyes, and soon he was asleep.

CHAPTER 4

RACHEL PERUSED THE STACK OF JOURNALS WHILE THE STU-
dents quietly worked on their math worksheets. She fished John's
journal from the pile and flipped to her last note. She was relieved
to finally find a response from John's guardian. Her eyes widened
and she read:

> Received your notes and voice mail. Will be in touch.
> —Mike Lantz.

It had been written in neat cursive penmanship.

Frustration surged through her. She scowled and looked across
the room to where Malinda had been helping Luke King with a
math problem.

"Malinda," Rachel said softly, hoping not to disturb the students who were working hard. "Would you please come here?"

Malinda raised her eyebrows with curiosity as she walked
over to the desk. "What's wrong?"

Rachel pointed to the note from Mike Lantz. "I can't believe
that's all he wrote in the journal," she whispered.

Malinda read it and frowned. "Well, at least he finally responded.
Maybe he'll write you a longer note tonight."

Rachel crossed her arms over her chest. She glanced across the
room and found John staring at his blank math paper.

"It's not enough," Rachel seethed through clenched teeth. "I'm going to call him again." She shook her head. "No, instead I'm going to go see him and demand a real response."

"You *called* him?" Malinda frowned as she turned toward the class. "Teacher Rachel and I need to speak outside for a moment. Please continue to work on your math worksheets." Then she took Rachel's arm and propelled her to the small porch behind the trailer as if Rachel were a petulant child. They stood just outside the opened door so they could still keep an eye on the students while they worked.

Malinda gave Rachel a weary expression. "You have to let this go." Her words were soft but deliberate. "It's not your place to call or go visit Mike. It's the school board chairman's job to handle parents and ask the parent or guardian to meet for a conference. If you and I both agree that the issues with the student need to be elevated, then we contact the chairman. I don't believe we're at that point. John hasn't been here a week yet." She stepped closer to Rachel and lowered her voice. "He needs time. He's still adjusting to this school. This is all new to him, and you're expecting too much."

Rachel shook her head and then shivered as the cool early-spring breeze seeped through her dress. "I disagree. I can tell he needs help. His behavior today was just as bad as it was on Tuesday. He pushed Luke off his chair during reading time, and he still refused to participate in singing. Something needs to be done."

"No, it doesn't." Malinda jammed her hands on her small hips. "You've always been stubborn, but I thought you would be a more supportive teacher."

"I am a supportive teacher." Rachel pointed to her chest as irritation coursed through her. "I'm worried about him. I know John is crying out for help. Something is going on at home, and it needs to be addressed. I want to work with his guardian to help him. That's our job, Malinda. We're supposed to take care of these *kinner*." She pointed toward the classroom.

"I'm aware of that, Rachel. I know you have a *gut* heart and want to help people, but you have to follow the rules. You can't let your stubbornness take over in this situation." Malinda pinched the bridge of her nose. "I can't allow you to elevate this. You know I've been teaching for two years now. I've been at this school since the fall, so I'm the senior teacher. I have the authority to make the decisions that affect this class. I don't want you to contact Mike in person. You may write him a note in the journal, but no more phone calls." She turned toward the class. "We need to get back inside. You handle the journals, and I'll continue with the math work."

Malinda stepped into the classroom and crossed the room to John's desk, where she began encouraging him to work on his math sheet.

Rachel slowly walked to the front of the classroom and sat down on the chair behind the desk. She thought of Malinda's warning while she studied a blank page in John's journal. Then she glanced across the room. Malinda was whispering to John, but he kept his eyes focused on top of the desk.

Deep down, Rachel believed this child needed help, and she couldn't stand back and wait for his brother to respond to her. Writing notes wasn't working, and she had to talk to him in person. Despite what her cousin said, she was going to talk to Mike. In fact, she was going to see him today.

Rachel closed the journal and placed it at the bottom of the pile. She picked up Luke King's journal and turned to a blank page. She held the pen in her hand while considering what she would say to Mike when she met him. She looked up as Malinda approached and hoped that her cousin would forgive her for breaking the rules. After all, Rachel was going to follow her instinct, and she was doing what was best for the child.

RACHEL'S STOMACH ROLLED AS HER DRIVER'S VAN STEERED up the long rock driveway to the Lantz farm. She climbed from the car and buttoned her sweater as she walked up the front steps to the door. She took a deep breath and then knocked. A few moments later, the door opened, revealing Mike's cousin Marie.

"Rachel," Marie said, pushing the door open. "What a surprise. How are you?"

"I'm fine, *danki*." Rachel gripped John's journal in her hands.

"John is in the barn doing chores," Marie said. "I'll go get him."

"Oh no, that's fine," Rachel said, shifting her weight on her feet. "I was actually wondering if Mike was home. I'd like to speak with him."

"No, he's not." Marie shook her head. "He's still at work at Bird-in-Hand Builders. This is their busy season, so some nights he doesn't get home until almost seven."

"Who's at the door?" a gravelly masculine voice called from behind Marie.

"It's Rachel, John's teacher, *Onkel* Raymond." Marie motioned for Rachel to step into the foyer. "She came to talk to Mike."

Rachel walked inside and saw an older man with salt-and-pepper hair and a matching beard sitting in a wheelchair in the center of a large family room. Sympathy overcame her as she studied him. His blue eyes were tired, and his skin seemed to have a yellowish tone. His long face was gaunt, and his body was thin. He looked sickly. He gave her a halfhearted smile and a small wave.

"Hi," Rachel said. "My cousin Malinda and I are John's teachers. I was hoping to speak to Mike for a moment."

"Is there a problem with John?" Raymond asked, his thin face crumbling with concern.

"Oh no." Rachel shook her head and mentally kicked herself for telling a fib. Yet she couldn't bring herself to upset this frail man. "I just wanted to talk to him about the note he wrote in the journal last night." She held up the journal. "I have some ideas for things we can do at home to help John."

"That's *wunderbaar*." Marie smiled. "I could pass along the message if you'd like."

"Oh no, *danki*." Rachel shook her head. "It's not a problem. I'll speak to him another time. Have a nice evening." She waved at Raymond, quickly left the house, and walked back to the van.

"Is everything all right?" Charlotte Campbell, her driver, asked as Rachel climbed into the front passenger seat.

"*Ya*, everything is fine." Rachel tried to ignore her growing disappointment as she rested the journal on her lap.

The image of John's ill father flashed through her mind as Charlotte steered the van down the long driveway toward the road. John's behavior suddenly made sense. The little boy was crying out for the attention he wasn't getting from his father, and she had to help him. She couldn't stand to see him struggling with his schoolwork or bullying the other children.

"Charlotte," Rachel began, "do you know where Bird-in-Hand Builders is?"

"Of course I do." Charlotte gave her a sideways glance as she merged onto the paved road. "It's right up on Old Philadelphia Pike, across from the farmer's market. I bought a few planters and a wishing well there. They make good quality items, and the prices aren't bad at all."

"Oh." Rachel ran her finger over the plastic cover of the journal. "Could we possibly stop there?"

"Now?" Charlotte asked with surprise.

"*Ya*." Rachel said. "If it's no trouble."

"Oh, it's no trouble at all." Charlotte smacked on the blinker. "My sister got this cute little windmill there, and I was thinking about getting one too. My husband says we have enough decorations in our yard, but I think it will look really cute."

While Charlotte prattled on about her yard, Rachel reflected on what she would say to Mike when she saw him. Malinda's warning echoed in her mind, but she couldn't stop herself from giving in to her desire to speak to Mike in person. Receiving his terse note wasn't good enough, and her stubborn spirit won.

Charlotte parked in the lot outside the store and Rachel climbed from the van. As she walked toward the front door, she passed beautifully crafted wishing wells, planters, swings, lighthouses, and other lawn ornaments on display. Apprehension bit into her shoulders as she stepped into the showroom, where a bell announced her arrival. The showroom displayed more lawn ornaments, along with large wooden signs, stars, small ornamental signs, shelves, and other wooden decorations.

A young man who looked to be in his late twenties with light brown hair, a matching beard, and brown eyes stood behind the counter near the cash register. "Hello," he said. "May I help you?"

"Hi." Rachel gripped the journal in her hands. "I was hoping to speak to Mike Lantz. Is he here?"

"Ya." The man smiled. "He's working in the shop. I'll go get him."

"Danki." Rachel glanced toward a display of birdhouses as she tried to remember the speech she'd mentally practiced during the ride over. Malinda's warning still nipped at her, but she pushed it out of her mind. She was doing the right thing by talking to Mike. After all, she just wanted to help John.

"Excuse me," a masculine voice said behind her. "Did you want to talk to me?"

Rachel spun and found Mike Lantz looking at her with a confused expression. He somehow seemed even taller, and his hair seemed more golden blond as the overhead skylights flooded the large showroom with warm sunlight. His blue button-down shirt complemented his powder-blue eyes, which now flickered with recognition.

"Rachel?" He took a step toward her and his expression became worried. "Is something wrong with John?"

"No." Rachel shook her head and lifted the journal. "I want to talk to you about the note you wrote in the journal last night."

His gaze moved to the journal and he frowned. "Janie said you wouldn't be *froh* about it," he muttered.

"What?"

"Nothing." He crossed his arms over his wide chest. "I'm in the middle of finishing up an order for two custom wishing wells, but I have a couple of minutes. What did you want to say about it?"

"I'm concerned about John," she began, holding up the journal. "I've written you notes in the journal and also left you a voice mail."

"I know." Mike nodded and grimaced. "I've gotten your messages, but I've been busy."

"This is important," Rachel insisted with frustration. "John has been misbehaving in class and on the playground. I believe his behavior is a cry for help. I want to discuss his home life. Is he getting the attention he needs?"

Mike glanced around the showroom, where tourists were browsing the sea of wooden creations. Then he pointed toward the far end of the showroom. "Let's go talk somewhere more private."

They walked together across the showroom toward a doorway. Mike opened the door and led her into a hallway, closing the door behind her. They stood by a door with a window. When she glanced through it, she saw a large shop where a half-dozen men worked, making lawn ornaments. The hammers, saws, and nail guns blasted while voices boomed in Pennsylvania Dutch.

"Isn't it unusual for a teacher to visit a scholar's guardian?" Mike asked. "I thought only the school board chairman could request a conference."

She spun to face him and found him glaring at her. The irritation in his eyes both surprised and intimidated her. She cleared her throat and mustered all her confidence while trying to remember what she'd planned to say to him.

"*Ya*, it is unusual for a teacher to visit a guardian," she began, "but it's important to me to help John. He's really struggling, and I want to do everything I can to help him learn how to behave both inside and outside of the classroom."

"It's important to me too. I know he needs extra help. That's why I agreed to send him to your school." Mike leaned back against the wall and studied her. His unrelenting eyes made her suddenly feel self-conscious, and she hugged the journal to her chest.

"I can't help him without your support," Rachel continued. "That means you have to actually read what I write in the journal and respond. I truly believe John is desperate for attention. That's why I asked you if he's getting enough attention at home. I stopped by your *haus* on my way here, and I met your *dat*. I'm certain he needs a lot of care."

Mike blinked as if contemplating what she'd said. His stare became frostier, sending a shiver through her. "Are you insinuating I ignore John at home in order to care for my chronically ill *dat*?" His voice held an edge of indignation that rattled her to the core.

"No, not exactly." Rachel tried to pull her thoughts together. "I truly believe his behavior is an indication that he's craving some reassurance. He deliberately won't participate in class, and he's already pushed one child off a swing and another off a chair. *Kinner* who behave this way want to get in trouble so someone pays attention to them. I'm trying to work with him, but if he continues pushing and hitting other *kinner*, then he won't be able to go outside for recess. Instead, he'll have to sit at his desk with worksheets."

"You're going to let him miss recess?" Mike asked, his booming voice echoing in the small hallway. "How does that teach him to interact with other *kinner* if you're keeping him separated?"

"He'll learn bad behavior has consequences," Rachel said,

lifting her chin. "If he wants to have fun, then he will have to do what he's supposed to do."

"How long have you been teaching?" Mike asked, his glance unmoving and his eyes flashing with fury.

She blinked. Why was he attacking her ability to teach? "This is my first week at the school."

"This is your first week?" His voice rose. "You haven't been in a classroom for a full month, and you're diagnosing my *bruder's* issues? Malinda told me she's been teaching for two years. Have you even discussed this with her?"

"*Ya.*" Rachel blinked as her confidence dissolved. "I have."

"And what did she say?" Mike asked.

"You need to write in the journal and work with me," Rachel continued, ignoring the question. "We have to work together to help John. I believe he's a very bright *bu*, and given the right guidance, he'll be a *wunderbaar* scholar, maybe even at the top of his class when it comes to his work."

"Are you avoiding my question?" Mike took a step forward, his steely glare trained on her.

Rachel tried to swallow to wet her parched throat.

"What did Malinda say about John?"

"She said to give him time," Rachel said softly. "I insisted I wanted to speak with you because I'm worried about him. I care about the *kinner* in my class."

"I'm worried about him too," Mike said. "But like Malinda said, it's going to take time. You can't expect him to be the perfect scholar when it's his first week in a new school. If the *kinner* irritate you, then maybe you need to find another job." He started toward the door. "I don't have time for this. I'd like to actually get home before seven tonight."

Mike wrenched open the shop door, and the sounds of hammers banging and saw blades whirling filled the hallway. The heaviness of sawdust, the pungent odor of stain, and the sweet aroma of wood washed over her.

"Wait!" Rachel called. "We need to discuss how to help John."

Mike let the door shut with a loud bang. When he faced her, his face twisted with a grimace. "I really don't have time for a lecture, Rachel. I've already told you. I'm busy."

He stepped over to her and stood so close that she could smell his scent—soap mixed with sawdust. He seemed larger than life as he glared down at her, and she suddenly felt like a small child gazing up at an angry parent.

"You seem to think I've been deliberately ignoring your notes and voice mail messages because I don't care about my *bruder* or his bad behavior," Mike began, pointing at her. "The truth is, I'm working myself to death, trying to support my *dat* and my *bruder*. I work long hours here, building wishing wells and lighthouses for *English* customers. I'm doing my best to keep the business *mei dat* and his *bruder* built running and thriving along with my cousin. I'm thankful two of my cousins help take care of the *haus* and cook the meals while I'm at work. When I get home, my cousins leave, and I take care of my *dat*, who can't even walk to the bathroom alone because he's so ill and frail. He has fallen so many times that I have taken to sleeping on the sofa so I can be close-by if he needs me. And when I say I sleep on the sofa, I mean I toss and turn all night long and wake up with back pain.

"When I'm not caring for my *dat*, I'm trying to be a *mamm* and a *dat* to *mei bruder*. I read stories to him at night and try to come up with answers when he asks me why he doesn't have a *dat* who can walk or why his *mamm* died."

Rachel gasped as tears pricked her eyes. "Mike, I—"

"Wait." Mike held up his hand to quiet her. "I'm not done. You want to know if John gets enough attention at home?" He nearly spat the bitter words at her. "Well, maybe he doesn't get enough attention. Maybe I should spend more time with him, asking him how he feels about not having a *mamm* and living with a *dat* who can't play games outside and help us with our chores. All I can tell you is I do the best I can. I try to show him I love him and that our *dat* loves him. Maybe I'm distracted, and maybe I'm too busy, but I am only one person trying to carry the load for three of us." He held up three fingers. "I'm under a whole lot of pressure, more than most men my age."

Rachel cleared her throat in hopes of alleviating the lump that swelled there. She longed to take back her accusations and heated words, but her shame stole her speech as she stared up at him.

"So when you ask me why I haven't responded to your notes," Mike continued, his expression impassive, "the truth is I've forgotten to because I've been busy." He snatched the journal from her hand and held it up in front of her. "The reason why my one note was so short was because I was so exhausted I couldn't think of what to say. My cousin said the note would upset you, but I was honestly too worn out to be concerned about it."

Rachel wiped away a tear with her trembling hand. "I had no idea you had so much to deal with." Her voice was soft and shaky. "I didn't realize how difficult your situation was."

"I imagine you didn't." He handed her the journal and started for the door to the shop. "I'll be sure to write you notes now. You don't need to come see me again." He stopped in front of the door. "And if I want to talk to a teacher, I'll call Malinda. Or maybe I should call the school board chairman and tell him about our little chat today."

Rachel's stomach pitched. "Mike, please don't do that," she said, but he had already disappeared through the door to the shop, and the door slammed shut in her face. She squared her shoulders and cleared her throat again before stepping into the showroom. She gave the young man at the counter a half wave and then marched out to the van. She wondered if Mike would call the school board chairman. And if he did call, would she lose her job after only one short week of teaching?

Rachel climbed into the passenger seat of the van as worry and regret weighed heavily on her shoulders. She'd made a terrible mistake.

"Is everything all right?" Charlotte asked as she looked over from the driver's seat.

"Everything is fine. *Danki*." Rachel forced a smile as she sagged into the worn, gray cloth seat and hugged her sweater over her chest. "I'm just ready to go home."

As the van motored out onto Old Philadelphia Pike, Rachel reflected on Mike's sad story about his parents. She had no right to confront him and accuse him of not properly caring for his brother. She yearned to take back her thoughtless words and tell him how sorry she was to hear he had so many burdens to overcome. She never should have allowed her stubbornness to overrule her good judgment. Now she'd managed to hurt Mike Lantz's feelings and possibly lose her job.

His angry words and his threat to call the school chairman echoed through her mind as she gripped the journal in her sweaty hands.

She had made a mess of things, and now she had to face the consequences.

CHAPTER 5

ANGER PUNCHED MIKE IN THE GUT AS HE MADE HIS WAY BACK to his work stall, where the two wooden lighthouses sat awaiting the final coat of clear stain. He approached a can of stain and kicked it with all his might, sending searing pain radiating through his right foot. He grumbled under his breath and hopped over to a stool, where he sat down and closed his eyes. The pain subsided to a dull throb as he pondered the thoughtless and insensitive accusations Rachel had fabricated about him and how he was raising John. How dare she judge him when she knew nothing about his situation?

"Mike?" His cousin Samuel appeared beside him. "Are you all right?"

"*Ya.*" Mike opened his eyes and nodded. "I hurt my foot."

"Oh." Sam grinned and jammed a thumb toward the front of the store. "Who was that *maedel*?"

"John's teacher." Mike frowned.

"Really? She's his teacher?" Sam rubbed his beard. "Are you seeing her?"

"Am I seeing her? Do you mean dating her?" Mike asked, and Sam nodded. "No. I've told you a million times I don't have time to date. Even if I had the time, I certainly wouldn't date her."

"Why not?" Sam looked incredulous. "She's *schee.*"

"She may be *schee*, but she's not my type at all." Mike stood and limped over to the lighthouses. "I need to get back to work."

"Are you limping?" Sam asked. "Did you get angry and kick something again? Is that why that can has a dent in it?"

"No." Mike grumbled as he picked up the can of stain and placed it on his workbench.

"What's going on?" Sam asked, raising a curious eyebrow. "Did something happen when you talked to Rachel?"

Mike sighed. Since he and Sam had grown up together, they'd always been best friends. No one knew Mike as well as Sam did. "I suppose you could say Rachel and I had an argument."

"What did you and John's teacher argue about?" Sam asked with surprise. "Did John do something and get in trouble? You've mentioned he's been having a tough time lately."

"*Ya*, that's what happened." Mike sat down on the stool across from Sam and shared the conversation while his cousin listened with his eyes wide. "I told her I'm doing the best I can, but that didn't seem to be *gut* enough for her. I really don't know what else I can do. I'm the one carrying the load for the family. I sent John to the special school hoping the teachers there could give him the extra help he needs, but they're blaming me for not giving him enough attention at home."

Fury exploded through Mike once again. "What else can I do for him? I'm already trying to be both *mamm* and *dat* to him. Isn't it the teacher's job to teach him how to read and write? Isn't it her job to teach him math? Don't we pay the teachers to do that for us?"

"All right, Mike," Sam said slowly while motioning for him to calm down. "You need to just relax. It's going to be fine."

Mike shoved his hand through his hair. "I just don't know what else to do, Sam. I'm already exhausted from sleeping on the sofa so I can be close-by if *mei dat* needs me. I don't want him to fall again."

"Your *dat* is falling now?" Sam looked concerned, and Mike nodded. "You didn't tell me that."

"I was going to." Mike scowled. "I've just been preoccupied with everything. Now I have to worry about his teacher being upset with me."

"She came here to see you about an issue with John without going through the school board chairman?" Sam asked, and Mike nodded. "Isn't that against the rules?"

"*Ya*, it is." He shook his head as he gripped both of his suspenders. "I told her I might call the school board chairman and tell him about our conversation."

"Are you going to call him?" Sam asked.

"Probably not." Mike blew out a frustrated sigh. "I just don't understand who she thinks she is to judge me. I'm doing the best I can to take care of *mei dat* and John."

"You're doing great," Sam insisted. "You're actually working too hard."

"Too hard?" Mike asked. "Why am I working too hard? I have to do my part to make sure we keep up with the orders. It's our busy season."

"But if you feel like you need to be home more, then you should go," Sam said. "If you think John needs more attention, then maybe you should go home earlier."

"No." Mike shook his head. "*Mei dat* wants me to make sure the business keeps going, so I need to be here. We don't expect you and your *dat* to take up all the slack."

Sam gave him a wry smile. "You're still as stubborn as you were when we were six years old and you refused to stop fishing in the lake until we caught at least three fish. You didn't even care we were late for supper and you'd get a whooping for staying out too long."

"What's your point?" Mike asked, crossing his arms over his chest.

"My point is, we're family, and we're here to help you. If you need Marie and Janie to stay overnight at the *haus* to help with your *dat* so you can get more sleep, then let them know. They'll be *froh* to do that. All you have to do is ask."

"That's not necessary." A yawn overtook Mike's words. He rubbed his eyes and then limped over to the awaiting lighthouses. He had to keep busy to work off his frustration. "I need to get back to work."

"All right." Sam stood and smacked Mike on the back. "You know, you could ask Marie and Janie to work with John too."

"What do you mean?" He looked back at his cousin.

"Marie and Janie could give John some extra help when he gets home from school every day. They could talk to him about how to behave in school and help him with his reading and math." Sam shrugged. "It's just an idea. They could get the teachers to stop complaining about him, and it would make things less stressful for you."

Mike shook his head. "*Danki*, but I don't think it's necessary. I believe John will adjust to school, but he needs more than a week to do it. Rachel is just being unreasonable."

"Fine." Sam shrugged. "I just thought it might be a *gut* idea." He started for the door. "I'd better get back out to the showroom. I'll see you later."

Guilt shoved away Mike's rage, and he regretted complaining to his cousin. Sam had been his rock and closest confidant since *Dat* had become ill.

"Sam," he called, and his cousin spun around. "How's Mandy doing?" Mandy was Sam's wife, who was pregnant with their first child.

"She's *gut*." Sam beamed as he always did when he spoke of his wife. "She's complained very little, even though she looks pretty worn out. It's difficult to believe the *boppli* will be here in less than four months. It's gone so quickly. Life as we know it is going to be changed forever."

"*Ya,*" Mike said, a smile stealing his frown. "But it's a *wunderbaar* kind of change."

"That's true." Sam grinned. "I can't wait to see if it's a *bu* or a *maedel*. But we'll be *froh* no matter what God chooses to bless us with."

Mike nodded. He was happy for Sam and Mandy. They had met through the youth group when they were sixteen and married when they turned twenty, and now, four years later, they were expecting their first child. They had everything Mike had always wanted—a loving marriage, a small house to call their own, and now a growing family. Mike pushed away the twinge of jealousy that teased him. He had no right to long for those things when he had his father and his brother to look after. His focus should be on them, not his own needs.

Sam's smile transformed to an expression of concern. "You do realize you have a right to be *froh* also. You're permitted to date if you meet the right person."

Mike shook his head. Sam just didn't get it sometimes.

"What?" Sam's expression challenged Mike. "You're looking at me as if to say I'm *narrisch*."

"All right." Mike slouched against the workbench behind him. "I'll answer that. Sam, I know you mean well, but you are *narrisch*. How am I supposed to date when I can't leave *mei dat* and *bruder* alone at night? How am I supposed to go visit a *maedel*, if I even meet one who would be interested in me?"

"Why wouldn't a *maedel* be interested in you?"

"I think that question has an obvious answer. I'm raising *mei bruder* and caring for my chronically ill *dat*. What *maedel* in her right mind would want to date me when she knows she'd have to help me do that?"

He lifted a paintbrush from the workbench and pointed it for emphasis as he spoke. "You know the answer as well as I do. No *maedel* would choose to have a ready-made family and responsibilities like that. All the *maed* I know want to get married and raise their own babies." He opened the can of stain, and the pungent odor stifled the air around them. "That's why I'm alone. I don't have time for any *maedel*, and there isn't anyone who'd want to be with me anyway."

"That's not true." Sam frowned. "You just haven't found the right *maedel* yet."

"She doesn't exist," Mike muttered as he pulled on his respirator.

Sam stared at him for a moment, his expression incredulous.

"Go back to work," Mike ordered, his voice muffled by the mask.

As Sam walked away, Mike shook his head. He longed to have a family of his own, but he was called to care for his father and brother. It was best this way, and any thoughts of finding a wife were wasted dreams.

MIKE STOOD IN THE DOORWAY OF JOHN'S ROOM LATER THAT evening and found him leaning against the headboard of his bed and staring at a book. Mike studied him for a moment, wondering if John could read better than he'd let on at school. When his brother didn't turn the page, he realized John most likely couldn't read at all.

"Hi, Johnny," Mike said, causing his brother to jump with a start.

"I didn't know you were standing there." John placed the book beside him. "You just got home?"

"*Ya*, I did." Mike frowned as a pang of guilt rang through him. "I didn't realize how late it was until I finished my last project. I'm sorry I missed eating supper with you."

"It's okay." John smiled. "I know you have to work."

Mike was thankful for John's understanding, but it did little to lessen the guilt he felt. "What are you reading?" He sat down on the corner of the bed.

John held up the book. "I was just looking at it."

"Do you want me to read it to you?" Mike offered.

John shook his head. "No, it's okay. You look tired."

"I'm never too tired for you." Mike touched John's little arm as he recalled his frustrating conversation with Rachel earlier in the day. "How was school today?"

John averted his eyes by studying the cover of the book. "School was *gut*."

"Is there anything you want to tell me?" Mike gently prodded.

John met his eyes with a frown. "I don't like school. I don't want to listen and follow the rules. I don't want to make *freinden* or read." His voice was thick with emotion. "I just want to stay home and help you and *Dat*. Or maybe if I came to work with you, then you wouldn't have to work so late."

So that's it. John still wants to stay home and help us instead of going to school.

Mike swallowed a sigh. Maybe what Rachel had said earlier was correct. Maybe John was acting out because he wasn't getting enough attention at home. Maybe Mike needed to do a better job of parenting him. Maybe Mike wasn't a good example for him. Should he ask Janie and Marie to stay over and serve as John's mother? But Janie and Marie had their own lives. They both were active in their youth group, and they had their own chores to do at home as well.

Confusion simmered inside Mike as he watched John fidget with the quilt on his bed. How could Mike be a good parent to John when he didn't really know what he was doing? His parents had been good to Mike when he was John's age, but the situation was different when he was little. Both of his parents were healthy.

His mother was home caring for the house while his father was building lawn ornaments. It all changed when his mother died in an accident when Mike was ten. She was hit by a speeding car as she walked to a friend's house one afternoon while Mike was in school. Mike had witnessed *Dat*'s going through the motions of life without *Mamm*. *Dat* tried to hide his sadness, but Mike sometimes found him crying in the barn.

Everything changed again five years later when *Dat* met Vera. After dating for nearly a year, they were married. Vera was kind and soft-spoken, and she treated Mike like her own son. Mike was certain their family was going to be complete, and he was thrilled when Vera was going to give him a sibling. But tragedy struck his family again when Vera died giving birth to John. *Dat* had lost his new *fraa*, and Mike had lost his new stepmother. And now, instead of only being a big brother to John, Mike also had to serve as a parent to John, and he was lost without his stepmother's guidance.

"Did you take your bath?" Mike asked.

"*Ya*." John nodded with emphasis. "I also brushed my teeth."

"Are you sure you don't want me to read to you tonight?"

"No, not tonight. I'm too tired." John yawned as he scooted under the covers. "Maybe you can read to me tomorrow night." Mike took the book from beside John and placed it on his bookshelf.

"That sounds like a *gut* idea." Mike kissed John's head. "Do you want to pray together?"

"*Ya*," John said before folding his hands and squeezing his eyes shut. "God, please bless our family and please make *Dat* feel better soon. Amen." When he opened his eyes, he yawned again. "*Gut nacht*, Mike."

"*Gut nacht*, Johnny."

As Mike descended the stairs, he reflected on his conversation with Rachel again. He couldn't stop thinking about her accusations, but he also began to reevaluate his response to her. Had he lost his temper too quickly? Had he been too outspoken? Was he out of line when he'd lectured her about all the stress in his life? What would *Dat* say if he knew how he'd spoken to Rachel? Mike grimaced. *Dat* had taught him respect, and he was supposed to be humble when he spoke to others.

Mike was aware of his short temper and his stubbornness, and both had overtaken him today. Rachel had gotten under his skin. After considering her words, he agreed she had valid points, but he didn't know how to address the issues.

As he stepped into the family room, Mike found *Dat* sitting in his recliner and perusing the *Budget*. *Dat's* hands shook slightly as he held the paper. Mike took in his gaunt face, slim frame, and bony arms and hands. He looked to be nearly half the size he'd been before he was diagnosed with kidney disease. The illness seemed to be consuming his father and leaving a shell of who he once was in his place.

All of Mike's perplexing emotions about his father's illness and his brother's school troubles bubbled to the surface, and his eyes misted over. He longed to ask *Dat's* advice, but Mike didn't want to add stress to his father's life when he was struggling so much with his health.

"You worked late again tonight," *Dat* said, breaking through Mike's tense thoughts. His voice was tired and quaky.

Mike cleared his throat to fight back his threatening tears. "*Ya*, I was trying to get caught up." He dropped into the chair beside *Dat's*. "I'm sure you remember what spring was like at the shop."

Dat smiled, and a faraway expression overtook his face. "*Ya*, I do. It was my favorite time of year. I loved being busy, and I enjoyed working with my hands." He held up his shaking hands and smiled. "They aren't much use to me now. I can't even hold a cup of *kaffi* without sloshing it all over." His smile collapsed. "*Was iss letz*, Michael?"

"Nothing's wrong." Mike rested his elbows on his knees. "I'm just tired."

"You're working too hard. You should be home in time for supper. John needs you."

Mike bit back a sardonic snort. "I know he does."

Dat studied him, and his expression softened. "I know you're running yourself ragged for our family." He blinked, and his blue eyes glistened with tears. "Michael, I'm sorry I'm not able to do more to help you take care of John."

"Don't worry about it, *Dat*." Mike touched his father's thin arm as sadness constricted his chest. "John and I are doing just fine. Marie and Janie are a tremendous help to us. I'm just worried about your health."

"I can't stand being a burden to you." *Dat* swiped at his tears with a shaky hand. "That's why I want to stop my treatments. It would be better for you and John if I—"

"Stop," Mike said, a little more harshly than he meant to, and *Dat* winced with surprise. "I'm sorry. I didn't mean to startle you." He took a deep, shuddering breath. "I will take care of everything, but I have one thing I need you to do for John and me."

"What's that?"

"I need you to be strong for us," Mike said, leaning forward and touching his father's arm again. "I need you to keep up with your treatments and take care of yourself. John and I need you." His voice trembled. "Can you do that for Johnny and me?"

"*Ya*." His *dat* nodded. "I can do that."

"*Gut*." Mike stood. "Are you ready for bed?"

"*Ya*, it's about that time." *Dat* placed the newspaper on the end table beside him and then Mike lifted him from the chair and helped him back into the wheelchair.

As Mike pushed his father to his bedroom, he hoped he understood how much he and John needed him. He couldn't cope with the notion of losing *Dat* and John becoming an orphan. He needed his father, and so did John.

CHAPTER 6

RENEWED GUILT WASHED OVER RACHEL AS SHE WROTE THE class schedule on the dry-erase board the next morning. She'd tossed and turned most of last night as she remembered the anguish in Mike's eyes when he shared all the stress he faced daily. She longed to go back and relive the events of yesterday so she could take it all back.

If only she'd listened to Malinda and not gone to visit Mike. Now she'd made her relationship with him worse. How could she and Mike possibly work together to help John when she had offended him?

When she'd arrived home yesterday, she thought about telling her mother what had happened, but she was too embarrassed. How could she admit her stubbornness and quick temper had gotten the best of her again? She'd broken the rules and jeopardized her job. But, worst of all, she'd hurt Mike Lantz, who was already carrying enough stress on his shoulders. The last thing she needed to do was add to the poor man's troubles.

"I think we should encourage the students to read on their own today and then have them summarize aloud what they read to test their comprehension. Do you think that's a *gut* idea?" Malinda lifted a stack of reading books and began to place them on the students' desks.

"*Ya*, that sounds like a great idea." Rachel fingered the marker in her hand as she watched Malinda distribute the books. It was time to tell Malinda the truth. After all, Malinda would find out what Rachel had done when the school board chairman came to visit them and fired Rachel.

"I need to tell you something," she blurted.

"What?" Malinda faced her.

"I didn't listen to your advice yesterday." Rachel placed the marker in the small tray below the board. "I did exactly what you told me not to do."

"What are you talking about?" Malinda's expression clouded with puzzlement.

"Yesterday you told me not to go talk to Mike Lantz." Rachel's stomach tightened as Malinda gaped at her. "I should've listened to you, but like you said, I'm too stubborn for my own *gut*."

"*Ach*, no." Malinda shook her head. "Tell me you're joking. You didn't really break the rules again, did you, Rachel?" When Rachel didn't respond, Malinda glowered.

Rachel swallowed. "I did, and I'm very sorry."

Malinda groaned as she sank into Luke King's chair. "What happened?"

Rachel explained how she'd gone to visit the Lantz farm and then went to Bird-in-Hand Builders. She detailed her conversation with Mike, and as Malinda listened her eyes darkened with a combination of disappointment and anger.

"I never should have done it," Rachel said, her voice trembling with both guilt and shame. "I realize now I did more harm than *gut*."

Frowning, Malinda bent her arm on the desktop and then rested her chin on her palm. "You have no idea how hard I've worked to build a *gut* relationship with the parents and the school board, and you managed to undo that in one conversation."

"I'm so sorry." Rachel dropped onto the desk chair beside Malinda.

"I know you're sorry." Malinda wiped her hand across her face.

"But that doesn't change the fact that Mike Lantz could complain to the school board chairman and get you fired."

"I know," Rachel said softly. "He said he might."

Malinda glared at Rachel. "What were you thinking?"

"I wasn't thinking clearly. You know how I get when I'm focused on something. I was completely fixated on working with Mike to help John."

"You could have done that without accusing him of neglecting John." Malinda sat up straight and wagged a finger at Rachel. "That's what the journal is for. We're supposed to write in the journal and communicate with the parents that way, not by visiting them at work or home."

"I know." Rachel studied the toes of her black shoes. "I'm going to make this right."

"How can you possibly do that?" Malinda asked, looking skeptical.

"I'll write a note of apology in the journal and tell Mike I was completely out of line," Rachel began as the ideas popped into her mind. "I'll give John extra attention, and I'll be extra patient with him. I'll do everything I can to help him with his reading, math, spelling, and classroom behavior." Excitement burst through her. "I'll take care of everything. I promise you, Malinda."

When Malinda's expression remained stoic, Rachel added, "And I'll talk to the school board chairman if you'd like. I'll apologize and tell him it's all my fault, and that you told me not to handle this on my own. I'll take full responsibility."

Malinda shook her head. "You don't need to talk to the school board chairman. Mike may not say anything to him, so we don't want to bring this to his attention." Her expression relaxed. "You just write the apology in the book and work with John as much as you can without neglecting the other students in the class."

"I'll do my best." The knot in Rachel's stomach eased slightly. "I'll be the best teacher I can be, and I'll make this up to Mike and John."

"Fine," Malinda said. "But in the future, you need to follow the rules. If you don't follow the rules, then we won't be able to teach together anymore."

"I won't let you down again," Rachel promised.

"*Gut.*" Malinda stood. "Let's get ready for the students to arrive."

Rachel worked one-on-one with John most of the morning while they concentrated on reading, spelling, and math. She was patient but also firm when he told her he didn't want to work on his math sheet. She encouraged him to try, and she managed to convince him to try three subtraction problems.

During lunch, Rachel stayed in the classroom and lifted John's journal out of his tote bag. She turned to the page where Mike had written the note and studied his handwriting. Her thoughts again wandered back to their conversation yesterday and the pain she'd found in his powder-blue eyes.

With a deep breath, she began to write.

Dear Mike,

Please accept my sincerest apology for our conversation yesterday. I was out of line, and I'm sorry for upsetting you. I have spoken with Malinda, and we are discussing a plan to work more closely with John and give him the attention he needs. I will continue to keep you updated by writing in this journal daily. Please do your best to write in the journal as often as you can. Thank you for your patience with me as I work toward becoming a better teacher.

Most sincerely,
Rachel Fisher

Rachel studied her note and then closed the journal. She hoped Mike would accept her apology and decide not to contact the school board chairman. If he did, however, she would face the consequences.

R ACHEL STOOD BY THE PASTURE FENCE AND HUGGED HER sweater to her middle on Sunday evening of the following week. She looked toward where the youth group members played volleyball in makeshift courts and pondered the previous week at school. She had worked closely with John, and she'd seen a slight improvement in both his schoolwork and his behavior. He no longer bullied the other children, but he was still socially withdrawn. He was also still struggling with his schoolwork, but she vowed not to give up on him. Rachel was growing attached to the child. She could see glimpses of a very sweet boy who just needed some encouragement and affection.

While she watched the other young people laugh, talk, and play volleyball, she reflected on Mike Lantz. Rachel continued to write notes to Mike every day in John's journal, and she'd been thankful that she'd received a response. The response, however, had come from his cousin Marie. The reply was positive, thanking Rachel for her hard work with John. But she'd hoped Mike would respond, telling her he accepted her apology. Perhaps Marie hadn't relayed her apology in the journal.

Surprisingly, the school board chairman had not contacted Malinda or Rachel, which Rachel believed was evidence that Mike hadn't reported her behavior after all. She was thankful he hadn't, but she was also surprised. She hoped that meant he'd forgiven her.

A sudden burst of giggles drew Rachel's attention to her right. She spun around, and her stomach twisted when she saw David and Sharon coming toward her. Sharon giggled as David whispered something to her.

Although Rachel had done her best to put her two-timing ex-boyfriend and former best friend out of her mind, she frequently saw them at church and now tonight at youth group. She took a deep breath and fought back the resentment bubbling up in her throat. She had to find a way to release her anger and forgive them, but it was difficult for her to heal when their happiness was constantly shoved in her face. She bit back the sour taste of jealousy as Sharon's eyes met hers.

"Rachel." Sharon's smile crumpled. "It's so *gut* to see you. How are you?"

"I'm doing fine." Rachel gripped the fence post beside her and leaned on it for strength. "How are you?"

"Fine, fine." Sharon cleared her throat and turned toward David.

David gave Rachel an awkward smile before lifting his straw hat and pushing his hand through his dark hair. David always fidgeted when he was uncomfortable. Did he feel guilty for breaking her heart?

"I heard you're teaching at the special school with Malinda," Sharon continued. "That's really great. How do you like it?"

"I like it a lot." Rachel glanced toward the crowd of young people playing volleyball and searched for her sister Emily. Where was she when Rachel needed her? "The *kinner* are *wunderbaar*. I enjoy them."

"Oh, that's nice." Sharon's smile was a little too forced. "I'm certain you're a *wunderbaar* teacher."

"*Danki.*" Rachel stared at Sharon and David as they stared back, standing close to each other.

A tense silence hung over them all, and Rachel found herself wondering why she hadn't noticed the attraction that had been growing between Sharon and David. Why had she been so blind when David and Sharon seemed to always gravitate toward each other at social gatherings? Why hadn't she realized David didn't respond when she mentioned marriage or children? Had Rachel been so immature that she hadn't seen the obvious clues that David had never loved her?

The questions roared through her mind like a tornado as anxiety and regret clamped down on her shoulders.

"Rachel!" Emily's voice sang. "I've been looking for you!"

Relief flooded Rachel as her younger sister rushed toward her. Emily always had perfect timing, and Rachel was so thankful for her intuition.

Emily smiled at Sharon and David. "Hi," she said. "It's so *gut* to see you." She took Rachel's arm. "I need to steal her for some *schweschder* time. We'll see you later."

While David and Sharon muttered something that sounded like good-bye, Emily led Rachel toward the far side of the pasture. "Why were you hiding over here?"

"I wasn't hiding," Rachel said, which wasn't exactly the truth. She couldn't stand the idea of trying to mix with the other young people when her mind was stuck on Mike, John, and her guilt. She had thought about staying home tonight, but Emily had insisted they come out and see their friends.

"*Ya*, you were." Emily gently squeezed Rachel's arm. "I know you, Rach. You used to love going to youth gatherings, but you've changed during the past weeks. Is it because of David and Sharon?"

Rachel shrugged. "I guess that's part of it."

They stopped by a small pond and sat on a bench, and Rachel folded her arms over her middle as the confusing feelings about David and Sharon swirled in her gut. Jealousy was a sin, but it still reared its evil head when they were around. But if Rachel didn't love David anymore, then was she really jealous of Sharon? Or did she simply miss having a boyfriend?

"I can't stand seeing you so unhappy. You know you can tell me anything, *ya*?" Emily asked, her voice breaking through Rachel's mental tirade.

"I know that." Rachel gave her sister a grim smile. "I'm not sure what's wrong with me. I don't really miss David, but I miss my friendship with Sharon. I suppose I miss both of their friendships."

"If they were sneaking around behind your back, then they weren't ever really your *freinden*, right?" Emily sat back on the bench and smoothed her blue dress over her legs.

The question was so simple, but the meaning unlocked something deep in Rachel's soul. Why did she allow Sharon and David to continue to hurt her when she had done nothing wrong? Her only mistake had been to trust them.

"*Ya*, that's true." Rachel kicked a small stone with the toe of her shoe as she considered her sister's words.

"David wasn't the right man for you, but you'll find the right one," Emily continued. "*Mamm* always says we'll find the one man to marry eventually. There's no set timeline."

Rachel turned toward her ever-positive younger sister. "You're right. I just have to get used to seeing David and Sharon together and so *froh*."

"I'm sure it will get easier over time," Emily insisted. She searched Rachel's face for a moment. "Is there something else bothering you?"

Rachel's thoughts moved to Mike again. "I haven't told you everything that happened my first week at school." She shared the story of John's behavior and then her confrontation with Mike. She also explained what she'd learned about John's home life, her attempt to smooth things over with an apology note, and her worry about losing her job.

"I still feel terrible for criticizing Mike even after more than a week," Rachel admitted. "I let my stubbornness and impatience get the best of me, and I should've listened to Malinda."

"You didn't know about the burden he was carrying," Emily said, rubbing Rachel's arm. "You were only trying to do your job. You apologized, so it's okay now. I'm certain he'll forgive you."

"I don't know." Rachel shook her head. "He hasn't responded to any of my notes. His cousin Marie, who helps him at the *haus*, is the one who answered. She thanked me for all the work I'm doing with John, but I haven't heard from Mike."

"He told you how much he works, right? He's probably just too busy to answer."

"*Ya*, I know. But I still feel terrible. I can't stop thinking about him and John." Rachel leaned her elbow on the arm of the bench and then rested her chin on her palm. "I just keep remembering how upset Mike was when we talked. His eyes were so sad and desperate. I feel like I really hurt him, and I want to make things right. I just don't know how."

Emily smiled. "You can do something really nice for him to show him how sorry you are."

"Like what?"

Emily shrugged. "I don't know. Maybe send a meal home with John. That would help his cousin out too. She's going to his *haus* to help him, but I'm sure she also has chores to do at home. What if you send a meal home with John with a note saying you wanted to do something nice for him as a way to apologize for your argument?"

Rachel gasped. "That's a great idea!" She hugged Emily. "You always have the best ideas. *Danki!*"

Emily chuckled. "It wasn't much of an idea, but I think it will work."

"I can't wait to get home and go through *Mamm*'s recipes," Rachel said, rubbing her hands together as excitement seized her. "Would you help me choose one?"

Emily shrugged. "Sure. We can head home now if you want, since neither of us is playing volleyball."

"Great!" Rachel hopped up. "Let's go."

CHAPTER 7

AFTER STOWING THE HORSE AND BUGGY AND HANGING UP her sweater, Rachel hurried into the family room where her parents were sitting in their favorite chairs. Her mother read a Christian novel as her father quietly snored with a copy of the *Budget* spread over his middle.

"You're home early," *Mamm* said quietly.

Rachel beckoned *Mamm* to follow her. *Mamm* placed her book on the end table and walked with her to the kitchen, where Emily was already sitting at the table.

"What's going on?" *Mamm* looked back and forth at each of them. "Why did you leave the youth gathering early?"

Rachel grinned at Emily. "Em gave me a great idea, and I couldn't wait to get started on it." She pointed to the kitchen table. "Let's sit and talk."

Rachel sat down across from her sister and mother, then shared the story she'd told Emily earlier.

Mamm gaped as she stared at Rachel. "You went to visit John's guardian?" When Rachel nodded, *Mamm* continued, "Why would you deliberately go against the school board's rules?"

Rachel nodded and frowned as shame crept up on her again. "I know now it was a bad decision."

"You realize a teacher isn't supposed to behave that way," *Mamm*

71

began, disappointment overtaking her expression. "Teachers are always supposed to discuss problems with the school board chairman, and teachers never speak to a parent directly."

"I know," Rachel said, scowling. She couldn't stand the idea that she'd let her mother down. "I'm ashamed." She cleared her throat. "I want to make it right. I've already written him a note of apology in the journal, but he hasn't responded. Emily came up with a great idea."

Emily sat up taller and smiled. "What if Rachel sends a few meals over to Mike and John? It will take the pressure off his cousins, and it will also show Mike that Rachel understands their situation and wants to help."

"Right," Rachel chimed in. "I could send a couple of meals home each week. I can take a cooler and ice to the school to keep the food fresh."

"That's a very nice idea." *Mamm* smiled. "I love it."

"*Danki.*" Rachel nodded with emphasis and hoped her mother would no longer be disappointed with her. "I just need to find something to send the meals home in."

"What about a basket?" Emily asked with a shrug. "Didn't Veronica say she saw one in the attic when she was cleaning it out last year?"

"That would be perfect!" Rachel jumped up. "I'll go look for one." She took a Coleman lantern from the mudroom and rushed up the stairs.

"Don't clean," *Mamm* called after her. "It's Sunday."

"I know," Rachel responded as she climbed the spiral staircase in the old farmhouse that had been in her father's family for four generations. She continued up the stairs, passing the second floor, where her bedroom, Emily's room, Veronica's former room, and the sewing room were. When she reached the third floor, she pulled open the old door, which creaked loudly in protest, revealing the large, open attic that spanned the top floor of the big, white, clapboard house.

The heavy scent of dust blended with stale air-filled Rachel's lungs. She held up the lantern as she surveyed the haphazard sea of boxes, old oil lamps, furniture, and toys. She wondered for a moment if she should wait until the morning to search for the basket, but she had to leave early to get to school in the morning. She either had to find one now or look tomorrow night, but she was too excited to wait until tomorrow. She wanted to start planning the meal she would send to Mike on Tuesday. She hoped this gesture would make things right between them. She didn't want to add to his stress or his pain any longer.

Rachel scanned the attic. Finding no basket, she began to cross the floor, weaving past various boxes and random items. She saw a box marked "Dolls," and then climbed past two marked "Books" before finding an empty area. She wondered if that was where her mother's hope chest used to be.

Nearly a year ago, her sister Veronica had been cleaning the attic when she discovered their mother's cedar hope chest and found a recipe for raspberry pie that had belonged to their grandmother. Veronica began making the pies, and they were so popular that she'd opened a bake stand to sell them. Rachel scanned the attic again, but she didn't see the hope chest. Where had it gone? She didn't recall *Mamm* asking *Dat* to move the chest for her, but it seemed to have disappeared. She'd have to ask *Mamm* what had happened to it.

Rachel glanced toward a shelf on the far wall behind her and saw a beautiful picnic basket that had to be the one Veronica found. When she reached the shelf, she examined the large, brown, woven-wood basket with a two-hinge lid and two handles. When she lifted the lid, the inside looked as if it were large enough to hold a Pyrex serving dish.

Rachel smiled. "It's perfect," she whispered, and her smile widened with excitement. Then she noticed something written on the inside of the lid. In neat, familiar penmanship, she read, *2 Corinthians 1:7: And our hope for you is firm, because we know that just as you share in our sufferings, so also you share in our comfort.*

A chill skittered up Rachel's spine. Not only was the basket perfect, but the verse was exactly what Mike needed. She ran her fingers over the worn, woven wood and closed her eyes. She hoped this basket would be a blessing to Mike and his family.

Rachel carefully navigated through the cluttered attic with the lantern in one hand and the basket in the other. Setting the basket down momentarily, she closed the attic door behind her. When she descended the stairs, she found *Mamm* and Emily sitting at the kitchen table and drinking tea.

Mamm's glance settled on the basket, and her eyes widened. "Where did you find that?"

"It was on a shelf at the far end of the attic." Rachel set the basket on the table. "It's perfect."

"It's so *schee*." Emily ran her fingers over it. "It just needs to be wiped off a little." She lifted the lid. "*Ya*, this is perfect."

"Look at the Scripture verse written inside the lid," Rachel said.

Emily read the verse aloud and then turned toward *Mamm*. "Is that *Dat's* handwriting?"

Mamm nodded and sniffed. Her eyes suddenly looked teary.

"Did *Dat* make this for you?" Rachel asked, sinking into the chair beside Emily.

"I don't think he made it, but he wrote the verse in it." *Mamm* cleared her throat. "He used to bring me meals in it."

"*Dat* cooked for you?" Emily chimed in, sounding equally surprised.

Mamm stood and picked up a dish towel. "Your *dat* is a very *gut* cook." She went to the sink to wet the towel, wrung it out, and then returned to the table. "He brought me meals." She began to gently wipe off the basket. "I had forgotten about this basket. It brings back memories."

Rachel and Emily shared curious expressions.

"*Dat* used to bring you meals?" Rachel asked again. "That's unusual."

Mamm kept her focus on the basket as she cleaned it.

Emily got up and took a notepad and pencil from the counter. "So what do you want to send over to Mike first, Rachel?"

"I was thinking about making a tuna casserole for them." Rachel tapped her chin with her finger. "I suppose I should find out what they like first."

"That's a *gut* idea. You can ask John." *Mamm* opened the basket and wiped the inside.

Rachel studied the Scripture verse. "Why did *Dat* choose that verse for your basket?"

Mamm stopped wiping and stared at the verse. "It always had a special place in my heart."

Rachel took in her mother's blue eyes, longing for her to elaborate on the basket's story, but she didn't. Her mother gently touched the basket, and it was obvious it was special to her. There seemed to be a significant story behind the basket, and Rachel longed to know what it was. But perhaps her mother wasn't ready to share it.

"*Mamm*," Rachel began, "are you sure it's all right if I use this basket to send meals to the Lantz family?"

Mamm met Rachel's concerned expression. "Of course it is. Why wouldn't it be?"

"The basket seems to be very important to you." Rachel touched the handle. "If you'd rather I put it back in the attic, I will."

"I'd be *froh* if you used it." *Mamm* smiled. "It's not doing anyone any *gut* by sitting in that dusty old attic."

"*Danki.*" Rachel ran her fingers over the basket and smiled.

Emily wrote on the notepad. "I'll buy all the ingredients for the tuna casserole tomorrow when I go to the grocery store. What else do you think you might want to make this week?"

As Rachel thought through the shopping list, at the same time she hoped this gesture would help Mike forgive her.

MONDAY AFTERNOON RACHEL STOOD AT THE DOOR AND waved good-bye to the children as they filed out of the trailer. When John started out, Rachel placed her hand on his shoulder.

"John," she said. "I want to ask you a question."

He placed his straw hat on his head as he looked up at her. "*Ya,* Teacher Rachel?"

She bent down and smiled at him. "What do you like to eat for supper?"

"I don't know." He shrugged. "I like anything, really."

"Do you like tuna casserole?"

John tilted his head with curiosity sparkling in his pretty blue eyes. "I don't know if I've ever had it, but I think I like tuna. My cousin Marie has made me tuna fish before and put it on one of her homemade rolls."

"If you like tuna fish, then I imagine you'd like tuna casserole. Do you know if your *dat* and *bruder* like tuna?" she asked, excited.

"*Ya.*" John lifted his lunch pail and tote bag to get a better grip. "I think they do."

"*Gut.*" Rachel removed her hand from his shoulder. "You have a nice evening. I'll see you tomorrow."

As John trotted down the rock pathway toward his waiting van, a smile spread on Rachel's lips. She couldn't wait to get home to make the tuna casserole. She only hoped Mike would be grateful to receive her gift.

MIKE STEPPED INTO THE MUDROOM AND YAWNED. HE WAS thankful he'd survived another long and arduous day at the store. After finishing the two gliders he was building, he stayed late to work on the accounting books, but he was thankful to still be home early enough to spend some time with his brother and father. He pulled off his work boots, placed them under the bench, and hung his straw hat and jacket on the peg on the wall before stepping into the kitchen.

The aroma of tuna drifted over him as he crossed the kitchen to where Marie stood at the sink, scrubbing a pan.

"Hi. Another long day?" She glanced over her shoulder and gave him a bleak smile.

"*Ya*." He leaned a hip against the counter as he surveyed a half-empty serving dish with tuna casserole. He bent down and inhaled the scent of tuna. "It smells *appeditlich*. I haven't had tuna casserole since my stepmother died."

"It's very *gut*." She wiped her hands on a dish towel and then scooped a large chunk of casserole onto a plate.

"How was *Dat*'s dialysis treatment today?" he asked.

Marie shrugged. "I suppose it went better than most. He's been worn out since he got home. It takes so much out of him."

"I know." Mike sat at the table. "I worry about him. I find myself waiting for the phone to ring with bad news."

"You need to expect good news instead of bad news, Mike. Have faith." She turned toward the sink and began washing a handful of utensils.

"I know. I do." After a silent prayer, he forked a large bite of the casserole into his mouth and closed his eyes as the delicious food began to satisfy the hunger that had been gnawing at him all evening. He never seemed to plan for his late evenings at the shop, and he was always famished when he arrived home. "This is fantastic, Marie."

"I'm glad you like it." She turned toward him. "Your *dat* ate a little bit of it. He wasn't very hungry after his dialysis treatment. John enjoyed it too. In fact, I had to tell him to slow down because he was eating it so quickly."

"*Danki* for making it." He forked another bite.

"As I said, I'm glad you like it, but I didn't make it," Marie said simply as she placed the utensils in the drain rack.

"You didn't make it?" He looked up at her as he wiped his mouth with a paper napkin. "Did Janie make it?"

"Nope." Marie pointed toward a large, woven-wood basket sitting at the end of the counter. "John's teacher sent it home with him. She left a note in the basket for you." She dried her hands on a towel and brought the basket to him.

Mike stared at it. "Malinda sent home a meal for us?"

"It wasn't Malinda." Marie returned to the dishes.

"Rachel sent this?" he asked, dumbfounded. The teacher who had accused him of neglecting his brother had sent a meal. He scowled. Did she send food because she thought John was too skinny and wasn't eating right? The delicious tuna casserole suddenly tasted like sawdust in his mouth.

Mike studied the basket and silently debated whether he should read the note from Rachel.

"Mike?" Marie faced him. "Is everything all right?"

"What does her note say?"

"It's really sweet. She says she's been thinking of you and your family and thought she could help lend a hand. She sounds like a really nice *maedel*."

He lifted a suspicious eyebrow. "Is that so?"

"Just read it." She opened the lid on the basket and handed him a note written on plain white paper. "I know you always say you don't need any help, but she's reaching out to you. She seems very kind and thoughtful."

Mike took the note and unfolded it.

Dear Mike,

I hope this note finds you well. I've been thinking of you and John since we talked that day at your shop. I wanted to do something to help you both, so I thought I could send you a meal a couple of times a week to help lighten your load.

I've been working one-on-one with John, and he's improving both with his behavior and his classroom work. I've written about it in his journal, but I'm not sure if you've seen my notes since your cousins have been responding to them.

I know you are very busy, so I understand if you can't respond to the journal. I just wanted you to know John is making progress every day.

I hope you enjoy the casserole.

Most sincerely,

Rachel Fisher

Mike rubbed his chin. This note didn't sound like it came from the irate teacher who had berated him in his shop a couple of weeks ago. What had caused her change of heart?

"Isn't that nice?" Marie asked. "And I love the basket. Look at the Scripture verse written inside the lid." She pointed toward words written in nice penmanship. They were a bit faded, but could still be clearly read.

When Mike read the verse, he felt a pang in his chest. It was as if the Lord were speaking directly to him. He let the words roll through his mind, and they warmed his soul.

"She sounds very sweet," Marie said, interrupting his thoughts. "I assume she's single, *ya*?"

"Please don't start." Mike shook his head and frowned. "You sound like your *bruder*."

"Really?" Marie sat on the chair across from him, and her eyes sparkled with curiosity. "What did Sam say?"

Mike speared more casserole. "Sam asked me if I was dating

Rachel the day she came to the shop and complained to me about John's behavior."

Marie looked confused. "She came to the shop?"

"I figured Janie had told you what happened." When Marie shook her head, he ate more casserole and wiped his mouth before sharing the story. Her expression became more and more bewildered as he spoke.

"I'm surprised Janie didn't tell me. Maybe she mentioned it to *Mamm* and *Mamm* forgot to tell me. Anyway, I had no idea Rachel complained about John and criticized you. That doesn't sound like the teacher who has been writing in the journal." She fished the journal out of John's tote bag and then handed it to him. "Read what she's written since then."

Mike chewed on more casserole while he flipped through the journal. He read her apology twice before finding page after page of positive comments about John, detailing his improved behavior and attitude in the classroom and on the playground. He shook his head with amazement. Why had Rachel's attitude changed? Was she still afraid he would call the school board chairman and report her, which would cause her to lose her job?

"*Was iss letz?*" Marie asked.

"I don't understand it," Mike said, still studying one of Rachel's notes from last week. Her handwriting was perfect—neat and tidy. The notes sounded like something a teacher would write. He imagined her sitting at the desk in the classroom while writing them.

"Aren't you thankful he's doing better?" Marie prodded, looking bemused.

"I am, but this sounds like a different teacher wrote them. Rachel had nothing nice to say about John when we spoke at the shop." He closed the journal and pushed it over to her.

Marie shrugged. "She's changed her opinion of him. I think

that's a *gut* thing." She stood and put the journal in the tote bag before returning to the sink.

John appeared in the doorway. "You're home, Mike." He crossed the kitchen and sat down across from his brother. "Did you like the food Teacher Rachel sent home?"

Mike nodded while chewing another bite. "It's very *gut*."

"She asked me yesterday if we all liked tuna. I told her we did." He rested his chin on his palm. "She said she's going to send something else home later this week if it's okay with you. I'm going to tell her it's fine."

Mike blinked. He hadn't heard his brother sound so enthusiastic about anything in a long time. His smile warmed Mike's soul.

"Teacher Rachel is so nice," John continued. "She's been helping me with my spelling, reading, and math. Every day we work together while the rest of the class reads out loud. She says I'll be reading out loud soon too."

Marie gave Mike a knowing smile. "She sounds like a very *gut* teacher."

"She is. I really like her. She's much nicer than Teacher Sadie was." John pointed to the basket. "We have to send the basket back if we want more food. I'll put it by my tote bag."

"I need to wash the casserole dish," Marie said, scraping the remaining bits of the casserole onto a plate. "You should write a thank-you note, Mike. I think she'd appreciate hearing from you."

John popped up from the chair, got a pen and notepad from the counter, and placed it next to Mike's dish. "Here you go. I'm going to take my bath." He disappeared into the hallway.

Mike examined the notepad. What should he say? He was never good at writing notes or letters.

"Just say thank you for the food," Marie said as if reading his thoughts.

He took a deep breath, poised the pen, and then started writing.

Rachel,

    Danki for the delicious casserole. John, *mei dat*, Marie, and I enjoyed it. I'm glad to hear John is doing better in class and on the playground. Thank you for the extra help you're giving him.

Sincerely,

Mike Lantz

"Well, that was short and to the point." Marie peered over his shoulder and snickered.

Mike craned his neck and furrowed his brow. "I think it's sufficient. What would you write in the note?"

Marie shrugged. "You always were a man of few words." She stepped over to the counter and began drying the dishes stacked in the drain board.

Mike folded the note in half and dropped it into the basket as he reflected on Rachel's actions. She seemed to have transformed from an impatient, thoughtless *maedel* into a patient, giving teacher nearly overnight.

"Janie said she'll come tomorrow," Marie said, breaking through his thoughts. "I'm going to help *mei mamm* with the grocery shopping. Let me know if I can pick something up for you."

"Okay. *Danki.*" Mike nodded while scooping up the last of the casserole. It was the best tuna casserole he'd ever eaten. Rachel certainly was a fantastic cook. He was thankful for her generous gesture, but he couldn't shake the notion that she had a hidden agenda. Was she concerned about losing her job? Did she hope sending meals to Mike and John would stop Mike from visiting the school board chairman?

Once his plate was clean, Mike stood and carried it to the counter. "*Danki* for taking care of things tonight. I had to stay late to finish the books, but I'm hoping to get home earlier the rest of the week."

Marie dropped the plate into the water and began to wash it. "You know I don't mind helping you, and Janie doesn't mind either." She gave him a wary expression. "Still, we're worried about you."

"Why are you worried about me?" To avoid her serious expression he busied himself placing the clean dishes in the cabinet.

"I'm perfectly capable of putting those away, Mike."

"I don't mind helping you."

"As I was saying, Janie and I were discussing you last night, and we are both concerned you're working too much." Marie placed the dish rag on the counter and faced him. "For example, you really didn't need to stay late tonight. You could've worked on the books tomorrow morning. I imagine Sam would've been *froh* to help you with the books or handle your projects while you finished the books."

Mike sighed. "Marie, I appreciate your concern, but you don't know how busy we are right now." He turned to putting the utensils in the drawer.

"*Ya*, I do," Marie insisted with an empathetic nod. "I've worked in the store before. I know how busy it gets, but you have plenty of help. *Mei dat* and Sam are always willing to help you. You don't have to do everything, Mike. We're all willing to help you." She had finished drying the casserole dish and stowed it in the bottom of the basket, placing the note inside of it. "Stop acting like you're all alone. Everyone wants to help you, even John's teacher."

"*Danki*." Mike put the glasses in the cabinet above the counter. "I appreciate it."

Marie looked out the window above the sink. "Oh, my driver is here. I'll see you Thursday." Marie lifted her tote bag. "Call me if you think of anything you need from the market."

"I will."

"*Gut nacht*," she said before going out through the mudroom.

Mike extinguished the lanterns and started to leave the kitchen.

But as he stepped into the doorway, he looked back toward the basket. Were Rachel's intentions pure when she sent over the meal? The question haunted him as he turned and walked to his father's bedroom.

CHAPTER 8

RACHEL ENTERED THE KITCHEN AFTER WORK AND GASPED WHEN she saw her older sister sitting at the kitchen table with Emily and their mother.

"Veronica!" Rachel set her bag and the picnic basket on the floor before hugging her sister. "It's so *gut* to see you! How are you? How's Jason?" She always loved when Veronica visited so the three sisters could be together again. Rachel's favorite times were when she shared a cup of tea with her mother and her sisters.

"We're doing great." Veronica's smile was wide. "I brought two lemon meringue and two chocolate pies for you all. I thought I would try a couple of *Mammi*'s other recipes, and I think they turned out pretty well." She pointed toward the counter, where four pies sat covered in aluminum foil. "Jason is going to build me a bake stand when the weather warms up, so I'm practicing my baking to get ready. Let me know how you like these pies."

"Oh, *wunderbaar*." Rachel rubbed her hands together. "We love your pies."

Emily popped up from her chair. "I'll get you a cup of tea, Rachel. Sit down with us."

"*Danki*." Rachel sat down across from *Mamm* and Veronica. "I would love a cup of tea."

"So, Rach, how was your day?" Veronica asked, slipping a strand of blonde hair back beneath her *kapp*.

"It was *gut*," Rachel said. Emily placed a cup of hot tea in front of her. "*Danki*."

"How do you like teaching?" Veronica asked before sipping her tea.

"I love it," Rachel admitted. "I was *naerfich* at first, but I'm learning more and enjoying it more every day. I'm working closely with one of the students, and I love seeing him improve. It's such a blessing to watch a *kind* learn. The expression on their faces is so special when their eyes light up with excitement because they understand something they've been struggling with."

"Is the student John Lantz?" Veronica asked. "*Mamm* told me about the conversation you had with his *bruder*."

"*Ya*, it's John." Rachel nodded. "He's starting to read by himself now. He's doing great."

"That's *wunderbaar*. I bet you're a fantastic teacher," Veronica said. "You've always been so organized, and you're a *gut* leader."

Emily refilled Veronica and *Mamm*'s cups and then sat down on the chair beside Rachel. "Did you hear back from Mike about the casserole?"

"*Ya*, I did." Rachel retrieved the note from her pocket and handed it to Emily. "John told me they really enjoyed it."

Emily grinned. "I'm so glad."

Mamm held out her hand. "May I see the note?"

"*Ya*, of course." Emily handed it to her.

"So what are you going to make tonight?" Veronica asked.

"I don't know." Rachel chuckled as she remembered the conversation with John this morning. "John asked me if I'd make pizza."

"He asked for pizza?" *Mamm* laughed. "What did you tell him?"

Rachel shook her head. "I told him I didn't have a recipe for it."

"We could have it delivered to his *haus*," Emily suggested with a grin.

Veronica snickered. "We also could try to find a recipe for it."

"That's what I told John I would do, but I don't know if it would taste that great warmed up." Rachel sipped her tea. "I asked him if he liked macaroni and cheese, and he said he did. So I thought I'd make that tonight."

"I'll help," Emily offered.

"*Danki*," Rachel said.

"Why don't you send one of my pies too?" Veronica offered. "They might enjoy it for dessert."

"That's a great idea." Rachel sipped her tea.

"I think Mike appreciates your help," *Mamm* said. "I'm sure the cooking is a lot on him, as well as his cousins who are helping to care for his *dat* and *bruder*." She handed the note back to Rachel.

"*Ya*, I wonder about that all the time." Rachel studied the note, taking in his neat script handwriting.

"Did he respond to your notes in the journal too?" Emily asked.

"No, this is the first note I've received from him since we spoke." Rachel frowned. "I think this means he forgives me. I still feel terrible for being so rude to him."

"Of course he forgives you," *Mamm* insisted. "That's our way. We forgive, just like the Bible tells us to."

Rachel cradled the warm cup in her hands. "I know that. Some people forgive but don't forget. He may forgive me, but he could still resent what I said."

Veronica shook her head. "Rach, we all make mistakes. We all say things without thinking it through. You're no guiltier than a customer who may have been unhappy with one of his lawn creations."

Rachel furrowed her brow. "Is that supposed to make me feel better?"

Emily laughed. "Don't be so serious all the time, Rach. Veronica is just saying it's okay. You've apologized, so you don't need to worry about it anymore."

Rachel shook her head. "No, I do need to feel bad about it. I need to be mindful of the things I say and do."

"We all do," *Mamm* said. "We've all made mistakes. You need to forgive yourself."

Rachel nodded, but guilt still coiled in her stomach. She had to do better.

Veronica glanced at the clock on the wall. "I'd better get going. Jason will be home soon and I need to warm up supper." She hugged *Mamm*, Emily, and Rachel, and then walked toward the door. "I'll see you soon."

"So we'll make the macaroni and cheese after we eat?" Emily asked after Veronica left.

"*Ya*," Rachel said. "I'd love that."

"Great! I'm making ham loaf for supper." Emily started for the counter and began pulling together the ingredients.

While *Mamm* and Emily talked about what else they'd have for their meal, Rachel's thoughts moved to the note she held in her hand. She hoped Mike had forgiven her and would someday call her a friend.

MIKE STEPPED OUT OF THE BARN THURSDAY AFTERNOON just as John's van pulled up in the driveway. He thanked John's driver and then opened the back door. When he saw the picnic basket beside John, Mike's eyes widened with surprise.

"What have you got there?" Mike pointed toward the basket.

"Teacher Rachel sent supper and a dessert today," John said with a wide grin as he handed the basket to Mike.

"She sent another meal to us already?" Then he remembered Rachel mentioned sending meals a couple of times a week in her note. But Mike had just returned the basket yesterday with his thank-you note and he hadn't given more meals from her any thought. "That's so generous."

"I know!" John nodded with emphasis. "I can't wait to try the pie. It smells so *appeditlich*. Can we have it now as our snack?"

Mike grinned. "I don't know if Marie will let us have dessert first, but it's a *gut* idea."

John climbed from the van, and they both waved as the driver steered down the rock driveway toward the main road.

"Mike!" Marie appeared on the porch. "You're home early."

"*Ya*, I am." He walked beside John as they ambled up the rock path toward the back porch. "I imagine you and Janie had something to do with that."

"What do you mean?" Marie gave him an innocent look.

"Sam gave me a lecture today about working too hard," Mike said as he and John climbed the steps. "He said I had to go home early or he would give my orders to someone else."

Marie's small smile gave away her guilt. Mike had suspected the two sisters prompted that discussion with Sam. When Mike had arrived for work that morning, Sam was waiting for him in the office. He lectured Mike about getting more sleep and spending more time at home with John. The speech reminded him of the conversation he'd had with Marie Tuesday evening.

He appreciated that his cousins were worried about him, but Mike was coping just fine. He didn't need any help or lectures, but he acquiesced to Sam's suggestion to keep the peace.

"So you and Janie told Sam to lecture me, huh?" Mike shook his head when she nodded. "I'm grateful for your concern, but I'm doing okay."

"You may think you're okay, but you're exhausted, and you know it," Marie said, her eyes filling with worry. "You need to be home and get some rest before you wind up ill like your *dat*."

"Marie is right, and I'm *froh* you're home early," John said, looking up at Mike. "You can help me with my chores."

"Oh *ya?*" Mike grinned and touched John's straw hat with his free hand. "I'm glad I'm home early too. And I will help you with your chores."

"*Danki!*" John said.

Marie peered at the basket as Mike stepped past her, following John into the mudroom where he hung up his and John's jackets on hooks. "Did Rachel send a meal home again tonight?"

"*Ya,*" John said. "Teacher Rachel sent home macaroni and cheese for supper and a pie for dessert. I think we should try the pie now."

Marie gaped. "I can't believe she really sent you a meal twice in one week. I suppose I don't need to worry about cooking tonight."

John placed his tote bag on a kitchen chair and turned toward Mike, who set the basket on the table. "So can we have the pie now?" he asked with a hint of a whine in his voice. "I promise I'll do my chores after we have a piece of pie. Maybe just a small piece?"

Mike turned toward Marie, who shrugged. "*Ya,* you can have a small piece and then you have to do your chores."

"Great!" When John lifted the pie plate wrapped in aluminum foil from the basket, a folded piece of paper fluttered to the floor. He placed the plate on the table and removed the foil. The aroma of chocolate stole over Mike, causing his stomach to gurgle in response.

"Look at that pie," Marie gasped as she examined it. "It's *schee.*"

Mike picked up the paper, opened it, and found a note.

Dear Mike,

I'm so glad you and your family enjoyed the casserole. John told me he likes macaroni and cheese, so I'm sending my favorite recipe for your supper. *Mei schweschder* Veronica is known for her pies, and she brought four over this evening to share. I thought you, John, and your *dat* might like to try one. If you like the pie, then I will send another one soon.

I hope your *dat* is doing better. I'm keeping him in my prayers.

John is continuing to improve with his schoolwork and behavior. Let me know if there's anything else I can do for him while he's at school. Feel free to write in the journal. Please return the basket, and I'll prepare something for you next week.

Sincerely,

Rachel Fisher

Mike pored over the note, allowing her kind words to filter into his mind. Like her last, this note did not sound as if it was written by the *maedel* who had criticized him only a couple of weeks ago. Not only was Rachel sending another special meal for Mike and his family, but she was also praying for his father. A part of him was beginning to believe her intentions were pure, but an inkling of doubt remained at the back of his mind. But when his focus moved to the Scripture verse written on the basket lid, warmth seeped into his tired soul.

"This pie is amazing," Marie said, interrupting his thoughts. "Mike, you have to try a piece."

Mike looked up. His cousin and brother were already sitting at the table, inhaling the pie. He placed the note next to the basket.

"*Ya*, it's *gut*," John agreed.

"Let me cut you a piece," Marie insisted. She sliced a piece, set it on a plate, and handed it to Mike. "You are going to love it."

Mike forked a piece into his mouth and the sweetness of the chocolate overwhelmed his taste buds. It was delicious, and the gesture was so thoughtful. He tried to imagine Rachel filling the basket with the food and writing the note. Had he mistaken Malinda for Rachel? Could it really be Malinda who was sending these notes and meals on Rachel's behalf?

What a stupid notion. He shook his head.

"Don't you like the pie?" John asked, watching Mike from across the table.

"*Ya*, I do." Mike nodded. "It's fantastic."

"Then why do you look so *bedauerlich*?" John tilted his head in question.

"I'm not sad. I was just thinking about something." Mike forced a smile and then took another bite. "So . . . you like Teacher Rachel."

"Oh, *ya*." John set his fork down next to his plate now dotted with crumbs. "She smiles all the time, and Teacher Sadie never smiled at me."

"Really?" Marie blinked, looking astonished. "That's so *bedauerlich*. Teachers should always smile at the *kinner*."

John fingered his fork. "And Teacher Rachel told me I'm really *schmaert*." He met Mike's gaze. "Teacher Sadie said I'd probably never read because I'm lazy, but now I'm reading whole pages."

John beamed, and Mike felt his pulse in his throat. He was speechless for a moment at the thought of what John must have gone through with a teacher who did not seem to care about him as much as Rachel seemed to. John got up from the table.

"Are you going to come and help me feed the chickens?" John jammed his thumb toward the mudroom.

"You can get started, and I'll be there in a few minutes." Mike dug his fork into the pie. "I want to finish my snack. Don't forget your jacket. It's still cool out."

"All right." John rushed out through the mudroom, and the back door clicked shut behind him.

Marie stacked John's empty plate on top of hers. "Rachel sounds like a blessing. I'm so *froh* you had John moved to that school. In the beginning, I was concerned that the special school was too far away since it's not in our church district, but it makes sense to send John there so he can get the extra help he needs."

Mike nodded slowly as he chewed his last bite of pie. Doubts floated through his mind.

"What's bothering you?" Marie rested her elbows on the table. "Are you angry with Janie and me for talking to Sam about you? You know it's because we care. You've always been like our second *bruder*."

"No, I'm not angry with you." He handed Marie the note. "I can't figure out who Rachel really is. Read this."

Marie read the note and then gave him an incredulous expression. "This is a very sweet note. What don't you understand?"

Mike set his jaw as he gathered his thoughts. "This is the same *maedel* who showed up at my work and berated me about how I'm raising John. Why is she sending me thoughtful notes and *appeditlich* meals?"

Marie chewed her bottom lip as she studied him for a moment. "I think it's obvious. She's concerned about John and wants to help. Why else would she be so thoughtful and generous to him?"

"Maybe she's worried about losing her job." Mike shook his head as Marie frowned with confusion. "Think about it, Marie. She went against the rules by confronting me. Instead, she should've gotten the school board chairman involved. If I call him, she'll be fired. Maybe that's her motivation for all this." He pointed toward the basket.

"I don't think so." Marie handed him the note. "She sent a note of apology in the journal. This is going above and beyond an apology."

"But I didn't respond to the note," Mike continued. "She didn't get a note from me until after she sent the first meal."

"That's right, but she still sent another meal. She didn't have to ask John what he likes to eat and then send another meal. I think she truly cares about John, and I think you should be grateful." Marie carried the plates to the sink and turned on the faucet.

"I *am* grateful. I just don't understand it."

"Your problem is that you don't want to accept anyone's help," Marie said as she watched the sink fill with water. "You think you should take care of John by yourself, but no one expects you to do that."

"That's not true," he grumbled. "I'm going to check on *Dat* and then head outside to help John." Mike got up from the table and left.

He stood in the doorway leading to the family room, where his father was asleep in his favorite chair. While *Dat's* snores rumbled throughout the room, Mike recalled how, when he was John's age, *Dat* would take him fishing in a nearby lake on warm Saturday afternoons after their chores were done. Now *Dat* was too ill to walk to the lakeside.

Mike leaned on the doorframe as sadness clogged his throat. He would have to take John fishing and tell him about his favorite memories of *Dat*. He'd do his best to be the father figure John deserved.

Mike headed back through the kitchen. "I'll be outside with John."

"Have fun." Marie waved, sending foamy bubbles up into the air like confetti.

After pulling on his jacket, Mike stepped outside, and the crisp late-March air tickled his nose as he strolled toward the chicken coop. He found John tossing the feed grain in the air as the chickens pecked around the ground.

"You're doing a *gut* job," Mike said, leaning against the enclosed fence. "You don't need me."

"You just don't want to work," John teased with a grin. "You want me to do everything."

Mike leaned his head back and gave a deep belly laugh. Where had John's sudden sense of humor come from? He hadn't heard his brother crack a joke like that in months—not since their father had taken a turn for the worse.

John tossed the remainder of the chicken feed into the air and then exited the fenced-in area where the chickens ate. "Could we invite Teacher Rachel over for lunch sometime?" John rubbed his hands together. "Maybe we could invite her to visit and see the farm."

Mike raised his eyebrows. "Why do you want to invite Rachel over?"

"I like her, and I think it would be a nice way to thank her for the meals." John grinned. "Maybe she'll give us another yummy pie if she comes to visit."

Mike considered this, crossing his arms over his chest. "I don't know if it's a *gut* idea to have company. *Dat* hasn't been feeling well, and I don't know if he'll want people around."

John's smile faded and his enthusiasm dissipated. "All right."

When John started walking toward the house, Mike's chest squeezed. He couldn't stand to see his little brother disappointed after just witnessing the joy that had suddenly blossomed inside of him.

"Johnny, wait," Mike called, hustling after him. "Let's talk about this."

John stopped and faced him. "It's okay." His little voice quaked. "You already said no." His bottom lip quivered, and his blue eyes glistened with tears.

"Just tell me," Mike began, holding his hands up to calm his brother, "why is it so important to you to have Rachel over?"

John sniffed. "I remember we used to have *freinden* over before *Dat* got so sick. It was fun."

"Okay." Mike nodded. "If that will make you *froh*, then I will invite Rachel over sometime soon."

John beamed. *"Danki!"*

"Now, she might not be able to come," Mike said, cautioning him. "If she says no, then you can't be upset with me. And don't say anything to her at school until I have a chance to call her, okay?"

John nodded. "Okay."

Mike smiled. "Now, you head into the *haus* and see if *Dat* needs anything. I have something I need to take care of."

"All right." John trotted off toward the house as Mike stepped into the barn to the phone. He found Rachel's first message on his voice mail and jotted her number on the notepad sitting on the small workbench. Then he dialed and cleared his throat.

After several rings, a voice mail picked up and a sweet young feminine voice said, "Hello. You have reached the Fisher family. Please leave us a message and we'll call you back soon. Thank you."

"Um, hello," Mike stammered. "This is Mike Lantz. This message is for Rachel. John and I want to thank you for the meal you sent home with him today. The pie was amazing, and we're looking forward to having the macaroni and cheese too." He cupped his forehead with his hand, feeling silly. When was the last time he'd called a *maedel*? He grimaced. Six years. He hadn't called a *maedel* since he was eighteen. He had no idea what to say.

"Well, uh . . ." He wound the telephone cord around his finger like a fidgeting child. "John asked me to call you and invite you over to visit. Are you available the day after tomorrow, Saturday? Maybe you can come for lunch. John would really like to see you." He paused and exhaled out a nervous breath. "But I'm not going to tell him I've already called in case you can't make it Saturday. I don't want him to be disappointed. So thank you again. Good-bye."

Mike placed the receiver back on the phone and rolled his eyes. He'd sounded like a complete moron. What on earth would she think of him when she received the message? He glanced out the window toward the house and thought of John. He'd called Rachel for him. Now he just had to hope Rachel would come. Would she break his little brother's heart and decline his invitation to visit on Saturday . . . or ever?

On the other hand, if she did come, what on earth would Mike discuss with her during the visit? They couldn't possibly have anything in common, other than a vested interest in John.

He shoved his anxiety aside as he stepped into the late-afternoon sunlight. Mike had to have faith that Marie was right about Rachel. That she did care about John. It seemed as if something positive was happening with John, and he owed it to the teacher. Perhaps Rachel was just what John needed.

CHAPTER 9

RACHEL WALKED UP THE BACK PORCH STEPS OF THE HOUSE and exhaled a deep sigh. She was exhausted after the long week at school, but a feeling of satisfaction had settled inside of her earlier in the day. John had made wonderful strides with reading, spelling, and math. She was making progress, and seeing him smile while he read warmed her soul. She reached the top step and pulled open the screen door.

"Rachel!"

Rachel turned and found Emily waving her hands wildly. She was walking from their father's store toward the phone shanty.

"*Kumm!*" Emily hollered. "There's a message for you on the phone!"

"There is?" Rachel set her tote bag and lunch pail on the steps and rushed to the phone shanty.

Emily's smile was wide. "I didn't check the messages until this morning, and I've been waiting all day for you to come home. I think you're going to be *froh* when you hear who it is."

"Oh?" Rachel raised her eyebrows as she held the receiver to her ear. She pushed the pass code and then hit the button to replay the messages. When she heard Mike's voice, she gasped. He'd finally called her back! She took in his every word as she listened. He actually sounded self-conscious as he stammered his way through the message. Why would he be nervous?

Emily grinned and bumped Rachel's arm with her elbow as Rachel listened to Mike's final words.

Rachel shook her head and stared down at the receiver in her hand. "I can't believe he called me." She met her sister's wide smile. "He went from not responding to my notes to calling me. You were right, Em. Sending over supper was the best way to show him that I truly care about John's well-being. And this might be why John had an extra gleam in his eye whenever I caught him looking at me today."

"I think it's funny that they ate the pie before supper." Emily chuckled.

"I can't believe Mike invited me to come to his house for a visit." Rachel looked down at the receiver again as questions ricocheted through her mind. "What should I do?"

"I think you should go over to their *haus* for lunch and take a pizza," Emily said simply. "I think it's *wunderbaar* that he wants you to go over there. That means they want to get to know you better."

Rachel nodded. "I guess this means he's forgiven me."

Emily laughed and looped her arm around Rachel's shoulders. "Why are you still worrying about that? Of course he forgave you. Now go to his *haus*. You might have a nice time, and apparently it will mean a lot to John."

Rachel pondered this as she placed the receiver on the cradle. "I'm so honored they invited me."

"I agree that it's an honor, and you should definitely take lunch." She led Rachel toward the house, and their shoes crunched on the rock path. "You can have a driver stop at the pizza place on the way to their *haus* tomorrow. Now we just have to figure out dessert. Do we have a brownie mix?"

"Brownies sound like a *gut* idea." Rachel smiled as an idea took shape in her mind. "I could take a couple of books with me and give John a little extra help with his math and reading. We can even work on some spelling."

Emily retrieved Rachel's bag and lunch pail from the steps. "That's a great idea. Not only will you give John some help, but Mike will be able to see the progress you've been making with him firsthand."

Rachel followed her younger sister into the house. "On second thought, I don't know if it's a *gut* idea for me to go." She sat down on the bench in the mudroom and thought about going to the Lantzes' house. "I should probably stay here tomorrow and help you with chores. You and *Mamm* handle them all week when I'm teaching, so it's not right for me to go off on a Saturday." She pointed to her sister. "Why don't you come with me?"

"Don't be *gegisch*." Emily waved off the suggestion. "You know I don't mind the chores."

Rachel shook her head. "No, it doesn't feel right to me."

"You have to go, Rach." Emily dropped onto the bench beside her. "John's going through a difficult time with his family right now, and you're one of the few constants in his life. He'll be so thrilled to see you at his *haus*!"

"*Ya*, that's true." Rachel nodded as Emily's wise words rolled around in her mind. She had to go, no matter how awkward it might be with Mike. "You're right. I need to go for John."

"Go and have a *gut* time." Emily stood, and after hanging up her sweater, she walked into the kitchen. "I'll take care of your chores. What would you like for supper tonight? I've been thinking about pork chops all day. Does that sound *gut* to you?"

"*Ya*, it does." Rachel placed her sweater on a hook and followed her younger sister into the kitchen.

RACHEL'S HANDS SHOOK AS SHE WALKED UP THE BACK PORCH at Mike's house the next day. She balanced a pepperoni pizza in her hands, along with a tote bag containing a math book, a reading book, and a pan of brownies she'd baked that morning. She hoped Mike would approve of the food she'd brought, but doubt had crept into her mind during the ride to the Lantz farm. Maybe she shouldn't have brought the pizza. Emily was always so idealistic and expected the best in people, but it could've been a mistake. Apprehension squeezed at her gut.

She climbed the steps and took a deep breath.

"Rachel?"

She spun and saw Mike walking toward her from the large barn. She smiled and her foot slipped off the step. She righted herself, and the pizza teetered in her hand. As she took hold of the pizza box, she dropped her tote bag, sending the books and pan of brownies crashing to the ground. Her cheeks burned with embarrassment as she tried to figure out how to bend to retrieve the bag and items sprawled on the rock path without dropping the pizza.

Mike rushed toward her. "I got it." He picked up the bag, dropped the books into it, and balanced the pan of brownies in his other hand, all while giving her a nervous smile. "I didn't expect you to bring lunch. If you came, I was going to make sandwiches for us."

"I wanted to bring John a pizza. He told me he likes it." Her cheeks continued to blaze, and she hoped they wouldn't explode. "Oh, is it okay if he has pizza? I suppose I should've asked your permission first."

"*Ya*, it's okay." Mike looked down at the box. "I think he's only had it once before when he was small. I'm surprised he even remembers it." His shy smile was back.

Rachel hadn't noticed until that moment just how handsome Mike Lantz was. He had a strong jawline and facial features that looked as if they had been chiseled from a fine stone. His face was clean-shaven, and for a split second she wondered why he wasn't married. She surmised he was in his mid-twenties, and he most likely had a girlfriend. After all, the eager young women snatched up the handsome young men in her youth group as soon as they were baptized and permitted to start dating.

When he raised his eyebrows in question, she realized she'd been staring at him. "Would you like to come inside?" he asked.

"Oh, *ya. Danki*." She cleared her throat and lifted the pizza box a little higher. "I hope John likes pepperoni."

"I think John will just be thrilled that you're here. He talks about you nonstop." Mike climbed the steps and held the door open for her.

"Really?" Rachel was surprised to hear this. "He's doing really well in school. I brought a couple of books if he wants to get some extra practice with his reading and math. I don't mind helping him." She moved past him and breathed in his scent—soap blended with earth. He towered over her by at least six inches, and she had to look up to see his sad blue eyes. She pulled off her sweater and hung it on a peg by the door.

"Oh." Mike nodded. "I appreciate that you came over. I know it's not the norm for a teacher to visit a student on a weekend, but John was insistent about wanting to have you over."

"I don't mind at all. I want to help him." She squared her shoulders. Now was the perfect time to apologize to him for being so rude to him the first time they talked. "I'm really sorry—"

"Teacher Rachel!" John bounded into the kitchen. "You came to see me!" He grabbed her arm and tugged. "What's that good smell?"

"It's pizza." Rachel smiled down at him. "I hope you like pepperoni."

John gasped. "It's my favorite!"

Rachel breathed a sigh of relief as she followed John into the kitchen. She placed the pizza in the center of the table. "I also brought a pan of fudge brownies for dessert."

John clapped his hands together. "*Wunderbaar! Danki!*"

"*Gern gschehne.*" Rachel pointed toward the cabinets. "Would you like me to get the dishes?"

"No, *danki.*" Mike placed her bag on the table and then shucked his jacket. "I can do that. I just need to hang up my jacket."

He disappeared into the mudroom for a moment. Returning to the kitchen, he put the pan of brownies on the counter and then brought dishes to the table. Rachel glanced at the brownies and was thankful that the pan had a lid on it. Otherwise, it could've been disastrous when she dropped it.

John opened the box, and the warm aroma of the pizza filled the kitchen. "I can't wait to have a piece."

"May I get the drinks?" Rachel offered while fingering the hem on her apron.

"No, we'll get it." Mike turned to John. "Get the pitcher of water out of the refrigerator, please."

John fetched the pitcher and placed it on the table. "Do you think *Dat* might want some pizza too?"

Mike shook his head. "He can't have it because he's supposed to avoid cheese. He has to watch his calcium intake."

"Oh." Rachel grimaced. Pizza was a bad idea. "I'm so sorry. I should've brought something he could eat. I didn't realize pizza wasn't *gut* for your *dat.*" She'd managed to mess up this visit already. At least she'd decided to bring brownies instead of ice cream.

"Please don't worry about it," Mike said, his expression kind. He placed three glasses on the table. "*Mei dat* is resting right now. He doesn't eat much lately. His dialysis treatments take a lot out of him."

"Oh." She frowned while worrying about Mike's father. "Maybe he can join us for dessert."

Mike gave a noncommittal shrug. "Maybe. I'll check on him after we finish the pizza."

"All right," she said. "I hope he feels better soon."

"*Danki*." Mike gave her a quick nod before pointing toward the chairs. "Let's have lunch."

Rachel sat across from Mike and John, and after a silent prayer, they each took a slice of pizza.

John took a bite and grinned. "It's so *appeditlich. Danki*, Teacher Rachel."

"I'm so *froh* you like it. And you can call me Rachel outside the school if it's okay with Mike." She felt Mike watching her. When she met his expression, her cheeks heated again. Why did he make her feel so self-conscious?

"*Ya*, it's okay with me if he calls you Rachel. And I agree the pizza is *appeditlich*," Mike agreed. "It's been years since I've had pizza."

"Did Rachel tell you how *gut* I'm doing in school?" John asked between bites of pizza.

Mike nodded. "She told me you've been doing great."

"I brought a couple of books if you want to work on your math and reading today," Rachel said. "You can even show Mike how well you're doing." She took a bite of pizza, savoring the delicious flavor.

John shrugged. "Okay. I finished my chores already, so we can do some schoolwork."

Rachel saw her basket on the counter, and Mike noticed.

"I'm sorry we didn't return the basket yesterday. I just forgot to put it in the van with John. I didn't mean to be rude."

"Oh, that's okay. I can take it with me when I go home today."

They ate in silence for a few moments, and Rachel tried to think of something else to say. She wanted to know more about Mike's life, but she didn't want to pry.

"Do you have any brothers or sisters?" John asked before reaching for a second slice.

Rachel pushed the box of pizza toward John, and he chose the largest slice, which made her smile. He certainly was enjoying this special lunch.

She wiped a napkin across her mouth and then cleaned her greasy fingers with it. "I have two *schweschdere. Mei schweschder* Veronica is a year older than I am, and Emily is three years younger than I am." She took a sip of water.

John bit into the large slice. "Are you married?" he asked while chewing.

"John," Mike warned through gritted teeth. "That's rude. You shouldn't pry into other people's lives—or talk with your mouth full."

"I don't mind answering," Rachel said with a smile. "No, John, I'm not married."

"Do you have a boyfriend?"

"John," Mike said, warning him with another growl.

"It's all right." Rachel averted her eyes by glancing down at her half-eaten piece of pizza. "No, I don't."

"Do you live alone?" John asked between bites of pizza.

"I live with my parents and *mei schweschder* Emily. *Mei* older *schweschder*, Veronica, got married in February, and she lives in a *haus* her husband built on his parents' farm. She made the chocolate pie I sent over Thursday. Her husband is going to build her a bake stand where she'll sell those pies."

"Really?" John's eyes widened as he turned toward Mike. "Maybe you can get us more pies from your *schweschder*."

Rachel chuckled. "I can get you more pies." She turned toward Mike. "That's as long as it's okay with you."

Mike nodded. "I enjoyed the pie also. I'll have to give you some money for them."

"No, no." Rachel shook her head. "Veronica frequently brings us several pies, and I'm *froh* to share them with you."

Mike nodded slowly and looked at her as if she were an intricate math problem. "*Danki.*"

They ate in silence again for a few minutes, and John grabbed a third slice of pizza.

"I think you should slow down," Mike said, placing his hand on John's arm. "You might get a stomachache if you eat too much."

John placed the piece back in the box. "Could we have the brownies now?"

Rachel bit the inside of her lip to stop her threatening smile. She glanced at Mike, and a smile slowly spread across his lips. She was surprised by how his handsome face lit up. She hoped to see that more. She smiled at him, and something special passed between them. She hoped it was friendship.

Mike pushed back his chair. "I'll get the brownies."

"No, I will." Rachel popped up and retrieved the pan, then located a knife from the block on the kitchen counter. She sliced a small rectangular brownie and placed it on John's plate.

"Could we have ice cream too?" John asked.

"Michael!" a weak, gravelly voice called. "Michael!"

Mike jumped up. "Excuse me. I'll be right back." He disappeared through the doorway.

"That's *mei dat*," John said. "He's sick. He has to have dialysis three times a week. It makes him really tired, and he can't eat much." He pointed toward the refrigerator. "Do you think we can add ice cream to the brownies? My cousin Janie brought some vanilla over last week."

"Oh." Rachel paused. "I don't know if Mike would approve."

John nodded with emphasis. "Oh, he will. Mike likes ice cream."

Rachel bit the side of her lip to stop another smile. Should she allow John to have ice cream? What if Mike disapproved and he asked her to leave? It seemed as if they were finally becoming friends. She looked at John, and he gave her puppy-dog eyes.

"Please, Rachel?" He tilted his head. "I promise Mike won't be upset with you. He lets me have ice cream on weekends."

"All right." Rachel located a carton of vanilla ice cream in the freezer and brought it to the table, along with three bowls and spoons.

As John dropped his brownie into a bowl and smothered it in vanilla ice cream, Rachel grinned. He'd apparently made a brownie sundae before.

"Are you going to make one?" he asked with a mouthful of brownie and ice cream.

"*Ya*, I will." She cut a small brownie, put it into one of the bowls, and dropped a few small scoops of ice cream on top of it. She savored the sweet taste as she chewed the first bite, then swallowed. "It's fantastic."

"I told you." He grinned. "So what is your favorite dessert?"

Rachel thought about the question while enjoying another bite. "I suppose it's ice cream."

"*Ya*, that's mine too." John shoveled in more of the vanilla treat. "Do you eat dessert every night?"

"I try not to," Rachel admitted. "But it's difficult since *mei dat* likes dessert. I usually give in to the temptation."

"Do you live on a farm?" John asked.

"We have a small farm, but *mei dat* owns a harness shop. It's called the Bird-in-Hand Harness Shop, and it's on our property."

"Oh." John was thoughtful for a moment as he stared at his half-eaten sundae. "*Mei dat* and *onkel* own Bird-in-Hand Builders, but *mei dat* can't work there anymore. Mike works there."

"I know," Rachel said. "Do you think you'll want to work there someday?"

"Oh *ya*." John nodded. "I love working with wood. *Mei dat* was starting to show me how to make a wishing well, but then he got really sick. Hopefully he can help me finish it someday soon when he's better. The dialysis makes him feel horrible, but he needs to have it to live." He suddenly smiled. "But someday he's going to be better, and he's going to work with me in the woodshop out in the barn. Mike is going to work with us too, and we'll all finish the wishing well."

Rachel's heart squeezed, and she fought back the tears threatening her eyes. She silently prayed his father would get well so they could finish the wishing well together. "I'm certain you will," she said softly.

The sound of wheels moving across the floor drew their eyes to the doorway, where Mike was pushing their father in a wheelchair.

"*Dat!*" John leaped from the chair and rushed over to the wheelchair. "Rachel came to visit and brought pizza and brownies. Would you like a brownie?"

"*Ya,*" Raymond said, his voice thin and shaky. "I would like one."

John rushed over to the table and pushed away the chair next to his. "You can sit by me, *Dat!*"

Mike pushed the wheelchair over to the table, and Rachel nodded at the older man.

"How are you?" she asked as she cut a brownie for him.

"Tired." Raymond smiled, and for a moment Rachel felt as if she were looking into Mike's face. The Lantz boys had inherited their father's kind features and smile.

"It's *gut* to see you," Rachel said as she pushed the brownie over to Raymond. "I'm sorry you can't eat the pizza I brought, but I'm thankful that you can enjoy the brownies." She felt someone staring at her, and she looked up to find Mike watching her with a curious expression.

"*Danki* for the *wunderbaar* meals you sent over this week," Raymond said. "We've enjoyed them."

"*Gern gschehne.*" She smiled and then looked at Mike again. "Do you want a brownie sundae?"

"That sounds *gut.*" Mike took a seat beside his father.

As Mike seemed to be watching his father's every move, Rachel made his sundae and passed it across the table to him.

"*Danki.*" Mike pushed his spoon through the dessert and took a bite. "This is *wunderbaar.*"

"I'm glad you like it," Rachel said.

As they all continued to eat, John entertained them with stories about the animals on the farm. Rachel found herself smiling and laughing, and she frequently noticed Mike looking at her. She wondered what he thought of her. Had he forgiven her for arguing with him or did he still resent her? She longed to know if he considered her a friend.

When their bowls were empty, Rachel stood, gathered up the dishes, and went to the sink.

"You don't need to do the dishes," Mike said, carrying the pizza box to the counter. "I'll do them later."

"Oh, I don't mind." She began to fill the sink with hot water.

"It's really not necessary," Mike insisted. He sidled up to her and gestured toward his brother, who was talking to their *dat*. "I'm certain you have to go home soon. Why don't you read with John? I need to get *mei dat* settled."

"Oh. That's a *gut* idea." So he wanted her to leave soon. She couldn't help but feel a little disappointed, but she understood. This visit was John's idea, and Mike was most likely eager for her to leave so they could spend the rest of their Saturday as a family. "I'll get started on the schoolwork now."

As Mike wheeled his father out of the kitchen, Rachel went to the table, retrieved the reading and math books from her tote bag, and then sat next to John. "What would you like to work on first?" she asked him.

John tapped his lips with his finger and then pointed at the math book. "How about math?"

"Sounds *gut*." Rachel opened the book to the most recent lesson. As she began asking John about the math problem, Rachel hoped Mike would be happy with her work with John and would realize how sorry she was for the horrible things she'd said to him.

CHAPTER 10

"Michael," Dat began, "would you please push me into the *schtupp*? I'd like to read for a while."

"*Ya*, of course." Mike pushed *Dat* into the family room, lifted him from the wheelchair into his favorite recliner, and handed him the latest copy of the *Budget*.

Once his father was settled, he moved back to the doorway leading to the kitchen. He leaned against the doorframe for a moment and watched Rachel work with his brother. Sitting beside John, she spoke softly while encouraging him to solve a math problem. When John said the correct answer, she cheered and clapped her hands. Then she leaned in close to him and squeezed his shoulder while he worked on another math problem.

The tenderness in Rachel's expression caused Mike's heart to feel as though it were turning over in his chest. He was still surprised to see her so eager to help John and so focused on him after the way she'd behaved that day at his work. He stood quietly and watched them for a moment, silently marveling at her expertise and tenderness.

When Mike finally stepped into the kitchen, one of the floorboards squeaked under his weight, and Rachel lifted her eyes to meet his. She sat up straight and gave him a nervous smile as her porcelain cheeks flushed, nearly matching her rose-colored dress. Her eyes were a deep brown, matching the dark hair peeking out from under her prayer covering. She was pretty. Very pretty.

Whoa.

Mike mentally pushed away the thought. Rachel was John's teacher, and he didn't have time to even consider liking a *maedel*, let alone dating one. His focus was on his father and his brother. He couldn't afford the distraction of a *maedel* right now.

"Mike," she said quickly. "I didn't see you standing there."

"I didn't mean to startle you." Mike crossed the kitchen. "I'll be outside finishing my chores."

"Can Rachel stay for supper?" John asked, throwing an eager expression over his shoulder at Mike.

Mike was speechless for a moment as he pondered his brother's admiration for Rachel. He didn't want to disappoint John, but he also didn't want to lead Rachel on by inviting her for supper too. He had to draw the line somewhere with his brother's attachment to her, but how could he say no without hurting John's feelings or offending Rachel?

"Oh, *danki*, John, but I can't stay tonight," Rachel began while looking embarrassed. "I appreciate the offer, but I have to get home in a little bit. *Mei schweschder* Emily is doing all my chores today, and I need to get home to help her. I promised her I'd be home in time to make supper."

"Oh." John's smile crumbled for a moment, but then his expression brightened again. "Maybe you can stay another time." He turned toward Mike for his approval.

"Sure," Mike said as relief coursed through him. He was thankful Rachel said no and didn't make him look mean in his brother's eyes.

"That would be nice," Rachel said to him and then gave his brother an adoring expression.

Admiration spread through Mike once again. The warmth that passed between Rachel and John astounded him. Rachel instructed John to look at the next math problem, and Mike quickly exited the kitchen and went out the back door, pulling on his jacket as he walked down the back steps.

He ambled up the rock pathway toward the large barn. When he entered the barn, the aroma of animals wafted over him. He passed the stalls and went to the small shop in the back of the barn. During the past several months, the shop had become his escape from the stress of his father's illness. It was the one place where he could be alone with his thoughts and prayers.

It was also his solace after a long day of working at Bird-in-Hand Builders and then coming home to fulfill the role of his father's caregiver and his brother's guardian. Sometimes he snuck out to the shop to tinker for a few minutes after John and *Dat* were both tucked into their beds for the night. Working with wood, especially when it wasn't to fulfill customer orders, always relaxed Mike and helped him release some of the worry and stress that burdened him daily.

The smell of wood dust was overpowering as he stepped into the small shop. He flipped on the Coleman lanterns, splashing the soft yellow light into the room. An array of tools cluttered his long workbench. A pile of wood sat in the corner, beckoning him to transform it into something useful.

Mike sat down on the stool in front of the workbench and examined the three-tiered shelf he'd been working on for the past week. He wasn't certain what he would do with the shelf when it was complete, but creating it had been cathartic.

He took a piece of sandpaper from the drawer under the bench and began to sand the shelf as he reflected on Rachel. He was overwhelmed by the way John had taken to her. He'd gone from hating school to inviting his teacher over to visit, and he owed the transformation entirely to Rachel. What had caused her to change her mind about John? Was her change of heart genuine or just a means of survival?

As he sanded the shelf for the next hour, his thoughts turned again and again to John and how much he'd improved in his schoolwork. It was a miracle, a blessing for certain.

A knock drew his attention to the doorway. Rachel gave him a little wave, and her expression was tentative, possibly even a little nervous.

"I was wondering if I could use your phone," she finally said, hugging her black sweater to her middle. "I need to call my driver and see if he can pick me up soon. John and I were working on his reading, and then I happened to look at the clock in your kitchen and saw how late it's getting."

"Oh, of course." Mike dropped the sandpaper onto the desk beside the shelf. "The phone is by the entrance to the barn."

"*Danki*. What are you making?" She stepped over to the bench and examined the shelf. "That's lovely." She smiled at him, and he could smell the hint of her flowery shampoo. "Are you going to hang it in the *schtupp*?"

He shrugged. "I'm not really sure what I'm going to do with it yet."

"You could put books on it," Rachel suggested, running a thin finger over the dusty wood. "Or maybe even candles and special little trinkets." She looked embarrassed. "I'm sorry. I didn't mean to tell you what to do with your shelf."

He nodded slowly. "I think it's a *gut* idea."

Rachel started for the door, then stopped in the doorway and faced him. "John is reading a chapter in the book I brought, so I thought I'd call my driver and then finish up with him. He's done really well today. I see a big improvement in his reading skills."

"*Danki*," he said. "You've been a great help to him. I appreciate it."

Her face clouded. "I want to apologize again. I was out of line that day I came to your shop and complained about him." She wrung her hands as she spoke. "John is a *gut bu*, and I enjoy working with him. I never should've confronted you, and Malinda had warned me not to do it. Both Emily and Malinda told me my stubbornness got the best of me, and they were right."

Rachel's pink lips quivered, and Mike held his breath, hoping she wouldn't cry. He couldn't stand to see women cry. It made him uncomfortable, and he never knew what to say.

"I'm just too outspoken for my own good," she continued. "I'm really sorry for everything I said. I hope you can forgive me."

"It's forgiven," he said, wiping his hands on his trousers, brushing away the wood dust. "It's our way to forgive, so you shouldn't have worried about it at all."

She sniffed and swiped her fingers over her eyes. Tension hung in the air between them. He gritted his teeth. *Please don't cry.*

"I know it's our way to forgive," Rachel continued with another sniff, "but people don't always forget. I was just frustrated, but then I realized *I* was the real problem." She pointed to her chest. "I needed to be a better teacher instead of blaming John for the problems he was having. I decided to just do my best and encourage him instead of blaming you for the problems." She paused as if contemplating her thoughts. "I've been concerned that every time you look at me, you'll think about the awful things I said to you. I didn't mean them."

"You should stop worrying about it," he said. "It's not important. John is doing better, and that's what matters."

As she wiped away a tear, he sighed. He needed to apologize too, and now was as good a time as any.

"I owe you an apology also." Mike leaned against the workbench. "I shouldn't have lost my temper with you."

Rachel shook her head and sniffed. "No, I deserved it."

"No, you didn't." Mike grimaced. "*Mei dat* wouldn't have been *froh* with me if he'd heard me yell at a *maedel* the way I did. So I'm sorry too."

She nodded and then gave him a shy smile. "I suppose I should call my driver now."

He nodded. "All right."

"*Danki.*" She hesitated for a moment. "Would it be all right with you if I come back to tutor John again next Saturday? I think the one-on-one without the distractions of the rest of the class is really helpful for him. He can concentrate better when it's just him and me."

"*Ya,*" he said. "That would be fine. I'll pay you to tutor him."

"That's not necessary." She jammed a thumb toward the front of the barn. "I'm going to go call my ride."

"All right."

She padded across the hay toward the front of the barn. As she disappeared from view, an awkward feeling settled over Mike. Was it rude for him to stay in his workshop? Should he have led her to the front of the barn and showed her where to find the phone, or would it have been ruder for him to hover over her?

He ran his hand down his face, then returned to sanding.

Why was he so uncomfortable around *maed*? Was it because he hadn't had a girlfriend since he was a teenager? But Rachel wasn't his girlfriend; she was John's teacher. All the same, Rachel was a guest in his home, and Mike needed to be friendly and make her feel comfortable. Why did he feel as self-conscious as a teenager when he attempted to make conversation with her? He didn't have any hesitation when he spoke to his cousins.

But they were family. Rachel was a stranger.

"My driver will be here in about fifteen minutes," she said, suddenly appearing in the doorway again. She stepped over to him and studied the shelf again. "Who taught you how to work with wood?"

"*Mei dat.*" He dropped the sandpaper on the bench and cleaned his hands with a rag. "He learned from his *dat.*"

"And your *dat* owns Bird-in-Hand Builders, right?" she asked, perching on the stool across from him. It was the stool where his *dat* used to sit when they worked on projects together before his kidney disease progressed.

"*Ya*," Mike said, studying the shelf while he spoke. "He and his *bruder*, Timothy, started the business about thirty years ago. *Mei onkel*, my cousin Sam, and I still work there, along with a few *freinden*. *Mei dat* worked there until he was too ill."

He ran his finger over the shelf. "I've always loved to work with wood. I work with it all day, and I sometimes come out here to relax by working on my own projects. When my days get too stressful, it helps me. I even come out here late at night when I can't sleep. Tossing and turning in my bed doesn't help me, but coming out here does. It's like my private therapy, I suppose." The revelation surprised him. He'd never opened up to a *maedel* this way. He glanced up and found her watching him, her bottomless brown eyes full of sympathy.

"When did your *dat* become ill?" she asked, folding her hands on her lap.

"He was diagnosed with kidney disease three years ago," Mike said. "It came as a surprise since it's not hereditary. They think it was environmental, that he came in contact with a chemical that caused it. The disease progressed quickly, and he went on dialysis about six months ago."

"I'm sorry to hear that." She shook her head. "How often does he have to do dialysis?"

"He has treatments at the dialysis center three mornings a week. My cousin Marie usually goes with him so I can work." Mike's fingers sought the edge of the workbench as he reflected on how the dialysis affected his father. "The treatments purify his blood and clear the toxins out of his body, but they wear him out. Some days he comes home and just sleeps. It saps the life right out of him. It's difficult for me to see him so frail, but I know he needs the treatments to live."

"Can he get a kidney transplant?" Rachel's expression was full of hope, and it sent warmth coursing through his soul.

"Unfortunately, no." He shook his head. "I've offered to be tested as a possible donor, but *mei dat* isn't strong enough to endure the surgery. His heart is too weak. The doctors have said *Dat* will live longer if he stays on dialysis."

"*Ach,* that's so *bedauerlich,*" she said softly. She was silent for a moment, as if she were mulling over the information about his father. "It must be a challenge for you to have to take care of your *dat* and your *bruder.* You're carrying an enormous load for your family."

"My cousins help." He shrugged off her comment as if it weren't a big deal at all. "You've met Marie. She and her *schweschder* take turns coming over. They've been helping me for years. Their *mamm* also helps if they aren't available. *Mei mammi* lived with us after John was born. She raised him until she passed away a couple of years ago. My cousins took over after she was gone."

"I'm sorry you lost your *mammi* and your *mamm.*" Rachel's expression became hesitant. "May I ask you a question?"

"*Ya.*" He nodded.

"What happened to your *mamm?*"

Mike drew in air through his nose as he thought about his mother.

Rachel's eyes widened with panic. "You don't have to tell me," she said quickly, holding out her hands as if to stop him from speaking. "It's none of my business. I say things without really thinking them through sometimes, and I don't mean it."

"It's okay." He brushed dust off his trousers again to avoid her eyes. "*Mei mamm* died when I was ten."

Rachel's brow furrowed. "She died when you were ten? I don't understand."

"John and I had different mothers," Mike explained. "*Mei mamm* was Esther, and *mei dat* married Vera when I was sixteen."

"Oh." Understanding softened her features. "Was your *mamm* ill?"

"No," Mike explained. "She was in an accident. She was walking to a friend's house for a quilting circle. A car came speeding down the road, turned the corner too fast, and didn't see her. She was killed instantly when the car hit her. I was at school when it happened. A neighbor came to get me. I was devastated. I had kissed her cheek before I left for school that morning, and I never imagined that would be the last time I saw her."

"*Ach,* that had to be so difficult for you." Rachel's eyes shimmered with sympathy. "And then you lost your stepmother?"

"*Ya,* that's right, a couple of years after *Dat* married her. Vera wanted to give birth to John at home with a midwife. Something went wrong, and the midwife yelled for my father to call the rescue squad. The EMTs didn't get here in time," he said softly. "She was already gone by the time they reached the bedroom. John was perfectly fine, but we lost her." He met her eyes as she gasped, cupping a hand to her mouth.

"I'm so sorry," Rachel said, her eyes sparkling with tears in the low light. "I can't imagine how difficult that was for you and your *dat.* Your *dat* had a newborn and lost his *fraa.* That's devastating."

"*Ya,* it was. But as I said, *mei mammi* was still alive back then, and she helped a lot. *Mei aenti* did too. But it was still difficult."

Rachel's bottom lip quivered, and he gave her a bleak smile, hoping to stop her tears.

"I had no idea," she whispered, her voice shaky.

"We make do," he continued. "I try to handle as much as I can so I'm not a burden on my cousins."

"You can't possibly manage it all yourself." Rachel gestured around the shop. "You have a farm and a business to run, and your *dat* is ill. Plus John needs attention. You shouldn't feel like a burden at all."

Mike nodded as he studied her expression. He found both sympathy and understanding in her eyes.

Rachel glanced toward the corner of the shop where a few shelves and picture frames sat. "Do you sell these?"

Mike stood and picked up a shelf. "*Ya*, I usually wait until I have about a dozen and then take them to the store. They sell fairly well."

She nodded and smiled. "You're really talented."

"*Danki.*"

They stared at each other for an awkward moment, and the only sound came from birds tweeting in the trees around the barn.

Rachel suddenly popped up from the stool. "Well, I'll finish with John and pack up my things."

"I'll walk with you," he offered.

Mike followed her into the house where she sat down next to John and began to talk to him about the book he was reading. Mike washed her brownie pan and placed it on the counter beside the basket. While he finished washing the rest of the dishes, he stole several glances over his shoulder to peek at Rachel and John.

The kitchen window was open a crack, and when Mike heard the crunch of tires on the rock driveway, he turned toward Rachel. "Your driver is here."

"Oh." Rachel closed the book and then touched John's arm. "You did great today. We'll work on reading more at school next week."

John smiled and hugged her, and Mike's chest constricted. He hadn't seen John be that affectionate with anyone outside of close family members. What was it about Rachel that drew his little brother to her?

Rachel packed up her books while Mike gathered up the basket and the brownie pan.

"We'll walk you out," Mike said, motioning for John to head

toward the back door. He followed Rachel and John out to the waiting van. He nodded at the driver before placing the pan and basket in the back seat and then faced Rachel.

"*Danki* for coming over today, and *danki* for the meals. I appreciate all you're doing for John."

"*Gern gschehne,*" she said before climbing into the van.

Mike and John said good-bye and waved as the van steered toward the main road.

John trotted toward the wooden swing set and fort their uncle Timothy and other friends from Bird-in-Hand Builders had created for John when he was four.

Mike sauntered back into the house and found his father napping in his favorite chair with the newspaper draped over him like a blanket. Mike picked up the paper, and *Dat* snored in response. As Mike folded the paper and set it on the end table, his father's eyes fluttered open.

"Sorry," Mike said. "I didn't mean to wake you."

"It's all right." *Dat* cupped his hand over his mouth as he yawned. "Is Rachel still here?"

"No, she just left." Mike sat on the sofa beside *Dat*'s chair.

Dat smiled. "She's a sweet *maedel.*"

Mike nodded as he picked a piece of lint off his trousers. "*Ya,* and she's *gut* with John."

"She's also *schee.*" *Dat*'s voice held a hint of mischief.

Mike's eyes met his father's coy grin. "What are you getting at, *Dat?*"

"Is she your girlfriend?"

Mike blinked as he studied his father's expression. *Does* Dat *look hopeful?*

"No, she's not my girlfriend. I told you. She's John's teacher." Maybe his father was confused. Was he developing dementia? Could it be a side effect from the dialysis treatments? Alarm gripped him.

Dat gave him a wry look. "I know she's John's teacher, but I think she likes you."

"What?" Mike asked with surprise. *Dat is definitely befuddled.* "She doesn't like me. She's only concerned about John."

Dat chuckled. "My kidneys may not work, but my eyes do, Michael. That *maedel* likes you. You should find out which youth group she attends and go to a meeting."

Mike shook his head. "You know I don't have time to go to youth group."

"You should make time," *Dat* said, patting Mike's arm. "It's not natural for you to be cooped up with John and me at your age. You should be out meeting other young people and looking for a *fraa.*"

"I'm not worried about that." Mike rested his ankle on the opposite knee and then gripped his leg. "Besides, I can't leave you and John alone for hours just so I can go sit and talk to people. That's not right."

"You can ask Sam to come and sit with me while you go," *Dat* suggested as if it were the most logical solution to the problem. "Sam likes to talk to me, and he's great with John. It will be fine."

"I don't want to ask Sam to do my job," Mike insisted. "My obligation is here with you and John, and it's where I want to be." He pointed to the floor. "This is where I belong."

Dat's eyes gleamed with sadness. "I don't want you to put your life on hold for me. I'm not going to be here forever, and you need to live, Michael. I want you to get married and have a family. It's what you're supposed to do."

A lump expanded in Mike's throat, and he tried to clear his throat against it. He didn't want to think about losing his father. "You're going to be here a long time, *Dat*, and I'll be by your side taking care of you." He stood. "Are you hungry? Do you want a snack before supper?"

"No, *danki*. Those *appeditlich* brownies filled me up." *Dat* smiled again. "Is there any pizza left?"

Mike nodded. "*Ya*, there are a few pieces. John and I had two, and Rachel only ate one."

"Could I have a piece of pizza for supper?" The anticipation in his father's eyes made him look like a little boy, possibly even a boy John's age.

"You're not supposed to have that much cheese, *Dat*. You know the doctor told you that." Mike suddenly felt like a parent lecturing a child.

"Just one piece?" *Dat* asked. "I haven't had pizza since I was a *kind*."

Mike smiled, but shook his head. "No, *Dat*. We need to watch your diet so your lab tests improve. How about I make you a sandwich?"

"Fine, fine. *Danki*." *Dat* looked toward the windows. "Could I sit outside and watch John play?"

"It's chilly out," Mike warned. "The sun is warm, but the breeze is a little cold."

"I don't mind. I'll take a blanket." *Dat* gestured toward the window. "I want to spend some time with John."

Mike picked up an old quilt his grandmother had made and then pushed the wheelchair out to the porch. He placed the quilt on *Dat*'s legs and started back inside.

"Wait," *Dat* called. "Sit with me for a moment, Michael."

Mike nodded and sat down on the swing beside his father. A smile turned up the corners of his father's lips as John pumped his legs and swung higher and higher toward the bright blue sky.

As a chilly breeze soaked through Mike, he silently thanked God for his father and brother. He was certain this was where he belonged.

But if that were true, why did his father's words about looking for a wife echo deep in his soul?

CHAPTER 11

WHEN SHE ARRIVED HOME, RACHEL FOUND HER MOTHER AND Emily working on a king-size Lone Star quilt in the sewing room.

Mamm looked up from her pinning as Rachel stepped into the room. "How did it go with John and Mike?"

"It went fine." Rachel sat down on a chair across from the sewing table.

Emily smiled. "Did John like the pizza?"

"He loved it. Mike had to stop him from eating the entire pie himself," Rachel said while absently running her fingers over the smooth arms of the wooden chair. "I also worked with John a little on his reading and math. He's doing much better. I feel like he's almost ready to read aloud in class."

Rachel recalled the grief in Mike's powder-blue eyes as he shared the stories of his mother's and stepmother's deaths, and shame tightened her chest. How could she have been so rude to him the first time she met him? She had no right to criticize him when she hadn't known his story. She hugged her arms to her middle.

"*Was iss letz?*" Emily asked while still pinning. "I thought you said the visit went well."

"It did go well." Rachel slumped back in the chair. "It went really well, but I feel so guilty."

"Why do you feel guilty, *mei liewe?*" *Mamm* asked, placing the corner of the quilt in her lap and focusing her attention on Rachel.

"Well, I told you I was rude to Mike when I first met him,"

124

Rachel began as her fingers sought the seam of her rose-colored dress. "He told me how he lost his *mamm* today." She explained how she'd sat in his woodshop with Mike while he talked about how his mother and John's mother had died.

"I just feel terrible." Rachel's voice quaked. "I accused him of neglecting John when Mike is only trying his best to take care of his *dat* and *bruder*. I'm a terrible person."

"No, you're not a terrible person," Emily insisted. "You have a wonderful heart, Rach."

"Emily's right. You didn't know the whole story." *Mamm* reached over and touched Rachel's leg. "Don't punish yourself. You were only looking out for John's best interests."

"But I always say the wrong thing." Rachel sniffed. "I'm always so impulsive, and I jump to the wrong conclusion. I'm certain he thinks I'm terrible, and he's right to think that about me."

Mamm handed Rachel a tissue from the box on the sewing table. "Now, just calm down, Rachel. If he thought you were terrible, he never would've invited you over."

"He invited me because John wanted me to come over." Rachel wiped her nose.

"I think he likes you," Emily countered.

Rachel studied her sister. "Why would you say that?"

"It's obvious." Emily shrugged. "Why would he share a personal story like that about his mother with someone he didn't consider a *freind*?"

"Because I was nosy enough to ask him what happened to her." Rachel blew her nose. "I'm just too outspoken for my own good."

"Stop saying that." *Mamm*'s face creased with a frown. "You sent meals to his *haus* and then you took lunch and dessert over to him. You also helped John with his schoolwork. You've shown him how sorry you are for what you said to him. You need to forgive yourself."

"That's right," Emily agreed. "Did you bring the basket home?"

"*Ya.* I left it on the counter downstairs." Rachel set her elbow on the arm of the chair and rested her chin in her hand.

"Why don't we start planning to send two more meals over this next week, like you originally said you would?" Emily suggested. "Maybe that will make you feel better."

Mamm picked up the quilt and began to stitch again. "I agree. We'll have to think about what we can send."

"His *dat* even thanked me for the meals," Rachel said. "He said he'd really enjoyed them."

"It's settled then." Emily beamed. "We'll come up with a menu, and I'll pick up supplies at the market on Monday."

Rachel snapped her fingers. "Why don't I make something today to send on Monday?"

"That sounds like a great idea," Emily agreed.

"I'm going to get started." Rachel stood and moved toward the door. "I'll call you when supper is ready."

As Rachel hurried down the stairs, excitement shoved away her shame and guilt. Maybe if she continued to help the Lantz family, she could forgive herself for the horrible things she'd said to Mike when they first met.

"Teacher Rachel?"

Rachel glanced up after slipping journals into the students' tote bags to find John smiling at her. "Hi, John." She stood up straight. "Are you ready to head home?"

"Uh-huh." He nodded, and his straw hat shifted on his blond head.

"You've worked hard this week." She touched his shoulder. "I wrote in the journal that you've been an outstanding student. I didn't have to tell you to behave at all." She handed him his tote bag. "Here you go."

"*Danki*." He fingered the handles. "Mike and *mei dat* want me to make sure I thank you for the meals this week. Mike liked the meat loaf the best, and *Dat* liked the chicken casserole."

"Oh *gut*." Rachel smiled. "What was your favorite?"

John grinned. "I like everything you send, especially the chocolate chip *kichlin*."

Rachel laughed. "So the way to your heart is with dessert, huh?"

He nodded. "Are you coming over tomorrow to work with me some more? Mike said you can tutor me again this weekend like you did last Saturday."

"*Ya*, I will." She sat on the chair beside him. "What time does your *bruder* want me to come over?"

John shrugged. "He said you'd probably come around lunch time again."

"Okay." Rachel touched his hat. "I'll see you tomorrow then."

John hustled toward the door, and the other students followed him. Rachel and Malinda stood out on the porch and said goodbye to the students as they hurried off, then stepped back inside to finish up their work.

"Did I hear John say he wants you to go tutor again?" Malinda asked as she crossed to the front of the classroom.

"*Ya*, he did." Rachel gathered up a pile of math papers and then sat down at a desk to grade them.

"You tutored him at his *haus*?" Malinda stood by the desk at the front of the room.

Rachel nodded. "*Ya*, I went over to his *haus* last Saturday and worked with him. It went really well. I see a big improvement with his math."

Malinda shook her head. "You know that's not necessary. You're not going to get a larger salary by tutoring."

"I know." Rachel looked down at her task.

"So then why are you going to spend your Saturday over at the Lantz family's *haus?*" Malinda asked. "You're already giving John plenty of one-on-one time here."

"I don't mind helping him," Rachel said as she corrected a paper with a red pen. "Mike has a lot of pressure on him because his *dat* is very ill, and John needs extra help. I feel like I'm making a difference when I go over there and help him."

"Is that why you've been sending the meals home with John?"

"*Ya.*" Rachel looked up and found Malinda studying her. "I still feel guilty for what I said to Mike that day. It makes me feel better when I'm helping him. I know I need to forgive myself, but I'm still ashamed."

"Oh." Malinda didn't look convinced. "But don't get too tied up with his family."

"What do you mean?" Rachel asked with bemusement.

"I just don't want to see you get hurt," Malinda said with a shrug. "You tend to get attached, and then you love with all your might and wind up with a broken heart."

Rachel frowned as the anguish David had caused came back to her in full force. She'd tried to put it behind her, but Malinda had brought it all back with just that simple statement. The pain stabbed at Rachel's chest.

"I don't want to date Mike, if that's what you're getting at," Rachel snapped, more rudely than she'd intended. "I'm not looking for a boyfriend, and I'm certainly not using one of the *kinner* in my class to find one."

"That's not what I meant," Malinda said, holding her hands up as if to calm Rachel. "I'm not accusing you of using John to get to Mike at all. I'm just worried about you. You've always been so impulsive, and I know how badly you want to get married."

"Don't we all want to get married?" Rachel asked with exasperation. "Isn't it supposed to be our dream to get married and raise several *kinner* on a farm?" She frowned again. "I'm not anxious about finding a boyfriend or even getting married. Right now I just want to be a *gut* teacher, and giving a special student some extra help makes me feel like I'm doing a *gut* job. Is that so bad?"

"No, no." Malinda shook her head. "I'm sorry for criticizing you. I'm just worried about you. That's one reason I asked you to teach with me. I knew you needed something to occupy your time after David and Sharon hurt you so badly."

"I appreciate that," Rachel said before pointing to the math papers. "I'm going to finish these so I can head home soon. I'm tired. It's been a long week."

"*Ya*, it has."

Malinda sat down at the desk and began rearranging papers while Rachel continued grading. An uncomfortable silence overtook the room.

"You know, Rachel," Malinda suddenly began, breaking through the silence. "You're a very *gut* teacher. Don't ever doubt that."

Rachel looked up. Malinda was smiling at her. "*Danki*. I enjoy teaching. I'm grateful you asked me to join you."

Malinda's words marinated in Rachel's mind as she finished grading the math papers. At first she had been offended that her cousin would accuse her of using John to try to get a date with Mike, but she was certain Malinda hadn't meant that. She was only warning Rachel to be careful with her heart, which was good advice.

But Rachel didn't want a boyfriend. She just wanted to be a good teacher and find a way to help the Lantz family through their difficult time.

"This is the best chicken potpie I've ever tasted," Raymond said the following afternoon as he sat across from Rachel.

"*Danki*." Rachel's cheeks heated as Mike and Raymond smiled at her from across the table. "I used my *grossmammi*'s recipe. *Mei schweschder* Veronica found a box of our *grossmammi*'s recipe cards in the attic last year, and we've been trying them. That's where she found a raspberry pie recipe that led to her opening a bake stand last year."

Why was she prattling on and on about recipe cards when men rarely cared about that sort of thing? She always babbled when she was nervous. She gnawed at her lower lip.

Why was Mike sitting there studying her? He was the reason she was nervous. He was so handsome, and he was looking at her with interest. Malinda's words echoed in her mind, and she pushed them away. She was here to help John, not pursue a relationship with Mike. She forked her potpie and ignored the anxiety that had taken hold of her the moment she'd stepped into the Lantz family's house.

"What does your *dat* do for a living?" Raymond asked.

"He owns the Bird-in-Hand Harness Shop," Rachel said after she dabbed her mouth with a paper napkin. "It's located on our property. He owns the shop with our neighbor. They've had it since they were young men."

"I've been in there before," Raymond said. "It's a very nice shop. Your *dat* does great leatherwork. He's a *gut* man."

"*Danki*. I'm certain he's disappointed he didn't have a *bu* to take over the business." Rachel took a small bite.

"Maybe he'll have a son-in-law who wants to do it," Raymond said.

"Maybe he will," Rachel said. She started to move the chicken potpie around on her plate rather than eating it. Veronica's husband, Jason, built sheds for a living, but maybe Emily would find a husband to run the harness shop with *Dat*.

"I always enjoyed working with wood," Raymond said. His voice was just as weak and gravelly as it had been the week before, but his smile was wide. "I admire men who can work with leather. It's not easy."

"He really enjoys it," Rachel said. She was glad Raymond was proving to be a better conversationalist than she was today.

She saw Mike glance at his father before he looked over at her, then gave her a shy smile. She tried to understand what his expression meant, and then it clicked. Perhaps Raymond didn't normally talk this much. Was Mike happy to see his *dat* so talkative? Did her presence help the Lantz family more than she'd expected?

"Did you bring another chocolate pie today?" John asked.

He was sitting beside Rachel, and she smiled down at him. "*Ya*, I did."

"Great!" John clapped.

"You need to finish your potpie before you can have any chocolate pie," Mike reminded him.

"I know." John spoke through a mouthful of potpie. "It's *gut*." Then he looked sheepishly at Mike, who had asked him again during this meal not to talk with his mouth full.

"I'm glad you like it," Rachel said, deciding not to look at Mike's face. "After dessert we'll work on your math again, all right?"

John nodded.

They made small talk about the weather and a few mutual friends while they finished the chicken potpie and then ate dessert. Once their plates were empty, Rachel helped Mike and John carry them to the counter.

"I'll take care of the dishes later," Mike said. "I need to fix the sink."

"You're going to finally fix the leak?" Raymond asked.

"*Ya, Dat*. I know I've been talking about it for six months," Mike said, his tone holding an edge of self-deprecation.

"Well, we don't want to rush into these things." Raymond had a twinkle in his eye, and Rachel chuckled.

Mike gave her a feigned looked of annoyance. "Don't encourage him."

"I'll try not to." Rachel touched her lips while suppressing another smile.

"I think I'm ready to read in the *schtupp*." Raymond tapped the armrests on his wheelchair.

Rachel gripped the handles on the back of the wheelchair. "I'll push you in there."

"*Danki*, but I'll take him." Mike stepped over to her. "He'll need—"

"No, no." Raymond shook his head. "You get started on the sink, and Rachel can take me into the *schtupp*."

Mike looked back and forth between Rachel and his father. "But she can't lift you into the chair, *Dat*."

"It's fine." Raymond smiled up at Rachel. "She can hold the wheelchair steady while I move myself into the recliner. That's how I do it when the *maed* are here taking care of me."

Mike hesitated, but then turned toward Rachel. "Call me if you need help."

"You worry too much, Mike." Raymond pointed toward the doorway leading to the family room. "Let's go."

Rachel looked at Mike, who still seemed surprised. "I'll be right back." She glanced at John. "You can get my tote bag and pull out the books. We'll get started on your work as soon as I get back."

She pushed the wheelchair into the family room and stopped in front of the recliner. She locked the wheels and then held Raymond's arm as he shakily shifted his body into the chair. She parked the wheelchair in the corner and then handed him the newspaper.

"*Danki*." Raymond smiled at her and took her hand. "You're a *wunderbaar maedel*. I can see the difference you're making in both Mike and John. I'm so *froh* the Lord sent you to us."

Rachel blinked as tears threatened her eyes. "I enjoy helping John."

"You're helping Mike too." Raymond released her hand.

"I am?" The question leapt from her lips before she could stop it.

"*Ya*, you are." A knowing smile slipped across the older man's lips. "He seems to relax a bit when you're around. He's been uptight ever since I was diagnosed with this horrible disease. I'm glad you started coming by. You're definitely a *gut* influence on my two sons. And I appreciate the *appeditlich* meals too." He opened the paper on his lap.

"I'm so glad you enjoy the meals. Call if you need anything," she said.

He nodded and then began to read the paper. She turned toward the doorway as Raymond's words echoed in her mind. She'd been helpful to both Mike and John? How could she have possibly helped Mike by coming over? He didn't seem very relaxed when she observed him. Perhaps Raymond saw something she didn't.

Rachel found John sitting at the kitchen table studying the math worksheets he'd retrieved from her bag. Mike had disappeared.

"Okay," Rachel said as she sat down beside him. "Which math problem would you like to start with?"

John pointed to one in the middle of the page. They began talking through it, and soon Mike reappeared with a small toolbox and started to work on the sink. She found herself sneaking glances at him while he worked, and a couple of times he was looking at her at the same time. Her cheeks warmed when their eyes locked, and she quickly looked down at the math paper.

After all ten problems were completed, Rachel asked John to read aloud from the book she'd brought. He read slowly, sounding out words. She rubbed his back and quietly encouraged him. When he finished the chapter, she clapped.

"You did a *gut* job, John," Mike said, beaming like a proud father. "Your reading is *wunderbaar*."

John puffed up like a proud rooster. "Do you want to hear me read some more?"

"*Ya*, I do." Mike leaned a hip against the counter. He raised his eyebrows and touched his chin as John began to read again, stopping occasionally to sound out a word.

Rachel smiled at Mike and then leaned over to see where John was on the page.

After he finished two pages, John leaned back in the chair. "I'm tired. I think I need to rest."

Rachel chuckled. "You did great." She glanced at the clock on the wall. It was almost two thirty. "This is the perfect place to stop. My driver will be here in a few minutes." She gathered up the worksheets and books and slipped them into her bag. "You're going to be the top student in the class with the way you're improving."

"Really?" John's eyes widened as he gasped.

"*Ya*, I mean that." Rachel retrieved her basket and serving dishes from the counter. "I'll see you on Monday, John. *Danki* for inviting me to come over."

"I'll walk you out." Mike looked at John. "I'll be right back."

"I'll go check on *Dat* and see if he needs anything." John said good-bye to Rachel before walking into the family room.

"Let me help you." Mike took the basket from her. "*Danki* for another great meal. You're really spoiling us." His smile was genuine and also seemed a little shy. Did he feel as self-conscious around her as she did around him?

"*Gern gschehne.*" She pulled on her sweater and adjusted the strap of her tote bag on her shoulder. "I'm sure your cousins cook nice meals for you too."

He nodded. "They do."

They stood together by the driveway. She glanced toward the road, looking for the van.

"You're doing an incredible job with John," Mike said. "I'm

astounded by how well he reads. He refused to read aloud when he was at the other school, and his teacher had no patience with him. You're a very talented teacher. I'm so grateful you're working with him. I can't thank you enough." The genuine admiration in his eyes surprised her. "Did you mean it when you said he'll be the best in the class?"

"Of course I did," she said. "I would never lie to him."

"*Danki*." Mike looked relieved. "John needs someone he can count on." He glanced over his shoulder at the house as if checking to make sure they were still alone. "The situation with *mei dat* is scary, and John needs to know he can depend on you," he said softly. "You're one of the most important adults in his life."

"He can always depend on me." Rachel said the words slowly to emphasize her commitment to them.

"*Gut*."

Mike's expression grew more serious, and Rachel suddenly felt something in the air shift between them. Was he attracted to her? Was that what his father had alluded to in the family room? Alarm bells blared in her mind. She couldn't risk her heart again. Besides, he was the guardian of one of her students; therefore, a relationship with him would be inappropriate. She took a step back as if putting more space between them would snuff out the attraction she felt electrifying the air around them.

"You seem to have an amazing effect on *mei dat* too," Mike continued, seemingly oblivious to the attraction she felt growing between them. "It's been months since I've heard him chat and joke like he did during lunch today. He really likes you."

"I enjoy talking with him," Rachel said, hefting her tote bag higher on her shoulder. His father's words echoed in her mind, and she was thankful she could help his family.

The rumble of an engine drew Rachel's attention to the end of the driveway as her driver approached.

"That's my ride," she said, even though it was obvious.

"Thanks again for coming over," he said. "Maybe you can come again next Saturday?"

"*Ya*," she replied, at the same time wondering why he wanted her to come again. Was it only for John? Or was it so she could spend time with Mike and Raymond too?

Mike set the basket on the back floor of the van and then said hello to Rachel's driver. Rachel hopped into the front passenger seat and smiled at him. "Enjoy the rest of your weekend."

"You do the same." Mike waved as the van rumbled down the driveway.

Rachel sucked in a breath and then smiled. She finally felt as if she were becoming friends with Mike, and she was grateful.

But she definitely did not want their friendship to become anything more.

CHAPTER 12

MIKE STOOD IN THE DRIVEWAY AS THE VAN STEERED TOWARD the road. Rachel had the most beautiful smile he'd ever seen. In fact, she was the prettiest girl he'd ever met with her dark hair and chocolate eyes.

He groaned, covering his face with his hands. Was he falling for her?

No, no, no!

He couldn't allow himself to think that way about her. After all, she was John's teacher, and Mike's life was already too complicated with all his obligations. Besides, why would Rachel want to have a relationship with someone who was responsible for his father and younger brother?

Not that Mike even wanted to get married. Why would he even consider marriage at this point in his life? He had to worry about his father, not try to figure out how to be a good husband.

Mike shook off the thoughts of Rachel and marriage as he made his way back into the house. He found his father and brother talking in the family room.

"And I read the whole chapter," John was saying. "She said I did a *wunderbaar* job. In fact, she said I'm going to be the top student in the class."

Dat patted John's arm. "You're such a *gut bu.*"

Tender tears sparkled in his tired blue eyes, and Mike's chest seized.

"I'm going outside," John announced as he started toward the door. "I'm going to feed the chickens and then play on the swing set." He disappeared through the kitchen.

"Don't forget your jacket, John! It's still cool out there." Mike leaned on the doorframe and looked at his father. "Do you need anything?"

"No, I'm fine."

Dat smiled.

"You know, Michael, Rachel is a *wunderbaar maedel.*"

Mike nodded, and a vision of her beautiful eyes filled his mind. He tried to ignore the memory, but it continued to haunt him.

"You should find out if she has a boyfriend," *Dat* prodded.

"*Dat*," Mike began with exasperation, "you know I don't have time to date." John had already confirmed Rachel didn't have a boyfriend, but that didn't matter. Mike had enough obligations to juggle.

"You shouldn't be alone." *Dat*'s smile crumpled with a look of concern.

"I'm not alone. How can I be alone with you and John here?" Mike tried to joke, but *Dat* didn't smile again. "I'm fine, *Dat*. We need to be concerned with your health, not my social life. May I get you a glass of water?"

Dat cleared his throat. "*Ya*, that would be *gut.*"

Mike left to get the water and then returned.

"*Danki.*" *Dat* took a long drink and then placed the glass on the end table beside him. "I'm going to nap."

Mike felt sadness swell inside of him. He remembered the days when *Dat* worked late in the evenings at the store. Some days *Onkel* Tim would have to insist *Dat* go home for supper. Perhaps Mike had gotten his stubbornness and workaholic tendencies from his father.

Mike missed the days when *Dat* was active and stubborn. Instead, he napped in his chair all afternoon from the exhausting combination of his kidney disease and dialysis.

"I'm going to clean up the kitchen," Mike finally said. "Call if you need anything."

As he stepped away, Mike again thought of Rachel. He would be honored to date a feisty, smart, and beautiful *maedel* like her, but he knew he wasn't worthy of someone as special as she was. He was better off alone. This was where he belonged, and he was thankful for his *dat* and *bruder*.

"NOW I WANT TO HEAR YOU READ THIS CHAPTER ALOUD ALL BY YOURSELF," Rachel said, pointing to the books. "I know you can do it."

Mike stood by the fence and rested a hammer on the slat beside him. He'd been determined to fix the fence today, but he couldn't stop his eyes from moving to the porch where Rachel worked with his brother. When John had shared that Rachel was going to come over to help him with his math and reading today, Mike actually smiled. He found himself thinking about her all week and hoping she would come over again this Saturday.

Why was he torturing himself with thoughts of her? She was only here to help John, not to get to know him.

John read the chapter aloud, clearly saying each word and only looking at Rachel for guidance once or twice. Whenever his young brother glanced up at Rachel, she gave him an encouraging smile and told him to try to sound out the word.

Mike tore his glance away from Rachel and John and began repairing the fence. He forced himself to put any thoughts of Rachel out of his head as he hammered in the posts.

After a while, he wiped his brow with his hand and glanced up at the sky. Dark clouds had been gathering all day, and the faint scent of rain drifted through the air.

After Mike finished repairing the fence, he stowed his tools in the barn and walked toward the porch, where John was working on a math worksheet. His tongue stuck out of his mouth and his brow was crinkled with concentration. Rachel looked up at Mike and smiled. He returned the expression as he tried to ignore the warmth rushing over him. He couldn't allow himself to like her, but the feeling was overwhelming.

"I think I got it." John pointed the pencil at the paper. "Is that right?"

"*Ya!*" Rachel clapped and then hugged his shoulders. "You got it, John. You're doing fantastic." She glanced up at Mike. "I need to see what time it is. I asked my driver to pick me up at three today."

"Cancel your ride," Mike said without thinking it through. She raised an eyebrow with surprise. "Stay for supper."

"*Ya!*" John jumped up from the rocking chair. "Mike and I will cook for you since you've cooked so much for us."

Rachel looked back and forth between them as if debating her response.

"Please stay," John asked, his eyes pleading with her.

"All right," she said. "I'll stay. I'll just need to cancel my ride and let my family know I'm going to eat here." She started toward the phone in the barn, then spun to face Mike, her black sweater fluttering around her slim body. "What time should I ask my driver to come by?"

"I'll take you home." The words slipped from Mike's mouth before his brain had engaged. What would he discuss with her while they were alone in his buggy? Not only was it several miles, but it had been years since he'd taken a *maedel* home alone, and he was actually nervous. He felt as if he were eighteen again.

Rachel studied him with a hesitant expression before she nodded slowly. "Okay."

"What are we making for supper?" John asked after Rachel disappeared into the barn.

"Pot roast." Mike touched John's straw hat. "Do you want to help me cut up the vegetables?"

John shrugged. "Sure."

Mike walked into the kitchen with John in tow. Mike washed his hands and then pulled out the ingredients for the pot roast. He was grateful Marie had picked up all the supplies he needed when she did the grocery shopping on Friday while *Dat* was at the dialysis center.

"You can start peeling the potatoes if you'd like," Mike said, placing potatoes on the counter. He fetched the peeler from a nearby drawer.

John pushed a chair over to the counter and stood on it. After washing his hands, he began trying to peel the potatoes. The peeler slid across the potato, and he narrowly missed slicing his fingers.

"Hang on a minute, buddy," Mike called from the other side of the kitchen. "I'm trying to find the big pot. Janie said she put it in the pantry."

John dropped the peeler on the counter and groaned. "I can't do it." He stomped his foot on the chair.

"May I help?" Rachel appeared behind John. "What are you trying to do?"

"Peel these potatoes, and it's not working," John whined. "The peeler is broken."

Rachel looked as if she were trying to suppress a smile. She was adorable. "I don't think the peeler is broken. Would you let me try?"

"*Ya.*" John handed her the peeler.

"Let's try it this way." Rachel leaned in close to John while she demonstrated how to use the peeler. "See? Now you try."

Mike located the pot and lifted it from the bottom of the pantry. He brought it over to the sink and consulted the recipe in his mother's favorite cookbook.

"What are we making?" Rachel asked.

"It's *mei mamm's* favorite pot roast recipe." Mike pointed to the cookbook.

"I love pot roast." She looked down at John. "Do you like pot roast?"

John's head bobbed up and down. "*Ya*. Mike does a *gut* job when he makes it. It's almost as *gut* as Marie's pot roast."

Mike shook his head, and Rachel laughed. He enjoyed the sound of her laugh, and the way her face lit up with her mirth.

Then she clamped a hand over her mouth. "I'm sorry."

"It's fine. Feel free to laugh at my expense." Mike chuckled.

"You should laugh more," she said. "You have a great smile."

"*Danki*." He admired her pretty face before she turned back to the potatoes.

They worked side by side as they discussed their favorite meals and desserts. Mike sliced the carrots and celery while Rachel and John finished the potatoes. Then Rachel quartered a large onion. Once the roast was cooking, Rachel helped Mike clean the counters.

"Could we have the rest of your chocolate pie for dessert?" John asked, sweeping the floor.

"Of course we can." Rachel said, wiping the counter clean. "If I had known you wanted me to stay, I would've brought something else to share."

"We don't expect you to feed us all the time," Mike said. "We're just thankful you came to visit again."

A crash sounded outside the window, and they all jumped.

Mike looked out the window just as lightning flashed. "Looks like we're going to get our first spring storm. If *Dat's* still asleep, I hope it doesn't wake him up."

Rain pounded on the windowpane as another clap of thunder sounded.

"Let's play a game," John suggested. "Hey, should I get Scrabble from the closet in the *schtupp*? We have the one they make for kids, Rachel! I think my reading is good enough now for me to play it."

Mike glanced at Rachel and she nodded.

"That sounds like fun, and you'll be practicing your spelling," Rachel said. "We haven't gotten to your spelling yet today."

Mike grinned. She truly was a great teacher. "John, you grab the game, and I'll check on *Dat*. I want to make sure he's okay."

Mike left the kitchen. When he peeked into *Dat's* bedroom, he found him snoring.

For the next hour, the three of them laughed and joked as they played Scrabble. Mike silently marveled at how Rachel went out of her way to talk to John and help him. She almost seemed like his guardian angel.

When John grew tired of Scrabble, they moved to card games and continued to play as the thunder rumbled, the lightning sparked, and the rain beat against the windows. When the room grew dark, Mike gathered two Coleman lanterns and set them on the table. The aroma of the pot roast filled the kitchen as the afternoon wore on. Mike slipped a tray of dinner rolls into the oven and then put a pot of carrots on a burner beside the roast. He set the timer and then returned to their card game.

When the timer rang signaling that the rolls were ready, Mike stood. "I'm going to make a salad. Johnny, you put the game and cards away."

"I'll set the table," Rachel offered, pushing her chair back. She located the dishes and utensils and began her task.

Mike set the roast on a serving platter and then gathered the ingredients for a salad.

"Let me help," Rachel said, coming up beside him. "I can make the salad if you need to go help your *dat* get ready for supper."

"Are you sure?" he asked.

"Of course I am. I'm an expert salad maker." She chuckled, and he enjoyed the sound of her sweet laughter.

"*Danki*." Mike padded into his father's room and found him sitting in a chair beside the bed. "When did you get up?"

"A few minutes ago. The pot roast smells heavenly. My stomach was actually growling." *Dat* pointed toward the wheelchair. "I thought I'd try to walk out to the kitchen, but my legs wouldn't agree to it. I've been sitting here thinking about how to get over to the wheelchair."

"Why didn't you call me?" Mike asked, pushing the wheelchair over to his father. He stopped the chair and locked the wheels.

"I wanted to do it myself." *Dat* looked determined. "I need to try to walk, don't I? The doctor said I should do things for myself sometimes so I don't lose all my strength."

"That's true, but I don't want you to fall." Mike took his father's arm and lifted him. "I just don't want you to get hurt."

As Mike pushed the wheelchair toward the kitchen, they could hear John's and Rachel's voices.

"John, would you please put glasses and the pitcher of water on the table?"

Dat grinned up at Mike. "Is Rachel still here?"

Mike nodded. "*Ya*, I asked her to stay for supper."

"Did you ask her to be your girlfriend yet?" *Dat*'s voice was hopeful, and Mike felt a twinge of annoyance.

"Shh. No, I haven't asked her, and I'm not going to," Mike whispered with a frustrated sigh. "She's only my *freind*, and she's John's teacher."

"Your *mamm* and I started out as *freinden*, and Vera and I were also *freinden* first." *Dat*'s grin was back, but at least he lowered his voice. "That's the best way to get to know each other before you get married."

"No one is getting married. Right now we're having supper."

Mike steered the chair toward the doorway. "Please stop talking about it, all right? Let's just enjoy our supper."

"Fine, but you'll marry her someday," *Dat* said. "You heard it from me first."

Mike swallowed his annoyance. *Dat* wanted the best for him and John, but marriage had to be the furthest thing from Mike's mind right now.

"Raymond!" Rachel exclaimed as Mike pushed the chair into the kitchen. She placed the large salad bowl on the center of the table.

"It's good to see you still here, Rachel." *Dat* smiled at Rachel and then craned his neck to look up at Mike. Mike suppressed the urge to frown. He hoped Rachel didn't read more into his father's greeting than just a friendly hello.

"How are you feeling after your nap?" Rachel asked as she approached his wheelchair.

"Well, I was hoping to walk into the kitchen, but my weary old legs had other plans." *Dat* shook her outstretched hand. "I'm *froh* you stayed for supper."

Mike held his breath, hoping *Dat* wouldn't ask her when the wedding was.

"Thank you for having me." She gestured toward the table. "John and I have everything ready. I can't wait to try that pot roast."

Rachel sat down beside John and across from Mike as Raymond took his spot at the head of the table. After a silent prayer, they began filling their plates. They ate in silence for several minutes, and Mike wondered what he could say to start a conversation with Rachel.

"What is the most popular item you make at the store?" Rachel asked as she buttered a roll.

"Wishing wells," Mike said, relieved she had saved him. "I make at least three every week during the spring and summer months."

"Would you butter a roll for me?" John asked Rachel.

"Here you go." She handed him her roll, which she had already buttered. "You can eat that one." She smiled at him, and Mike found genuine love in Rachel's eyes when she looked at his brother. The realization sent affection flowing through him and stole his ability to speak.

"So wishing wells are the most popular item at your store?" Rachel swiped another roll from the basket in the center of the table.

"That's right," Mike said when he found his voice again. "The large planters that look like baskets are always popular."

"Has it always been that way, Raymond?" Rachel asked while buttering her roll.

Dat nodded. "*Ya*, I think so. The tourists love anything that's made by the Amish, but their favorites were always the wishing wells and the planters."

"What are the easiest things you make?" Rachel asked.

Mike spent the rest of supper talking about the items he made at the shop. Soon their plates were empty, and Rachel insisted on helping to clear the table of the dishes. As she worked, she continued peppering him with questions about his work and what he enjoyed about it the most. Then she brought the chocolate pie to the table and put on the percolator to make coffee.

As they lingered over dessert, their conversation moved to the weather. Everyone in the community was concerned about how well the crops would do this year with some threat of drought. When they were finished, Rachel immediately began cleaning up.

"I didn't even realize the storm was over," she said, peeking out the small kitchen window above the sink. "It's just a light rain now."

Mike sidled up beside her and breathed in the scent of her flowery shampoo. "You're right."

She looked up at him. "I guess we should get on the road soon. I don't want you to be driving back in the dark when it's raining."

Mike nodded. "That's a *gut* point." He turned toward the table where *Dat* sat talking with John. "I'm going to take Rachel home in the buggy."

He realized then that he didn't know what he'd been thinking when he'd offered to take Rachel home. He wasn't entirely comfortable with the idea of leaving his father and John home alone for that length of time. "*Dat*, let's get you settled in the recliner before I leave." He looked at John. "Do you remember how to use the phone in the barn to call nine-one-one if you need help in an emergency?"

"*Ya*." John nodded. "I remember how, and I can do it. I'll also run over to the neighbors for help after I call. I'll help you get *Dat* into his favorite chair and bring him the paper."

"*Gut bu*." Mike patted John's shoulder.

"I hope to see you again soon, Raymond," Rachel told his father as she gathered up her basket and serving dishes from lunch.

"I'm certain we'll see each other again very soon." *Dat* smiled and ignored the warning look Mike gave him.

Mike and John moved *Dat* into the family room and made certain he was comfortable in his recliner. Then Mike escorted Rachel outside, and she put her belongings inside the buggy while he hitched his horse.

He couldn't remember when he had last felt this happy and nervous all at the same time.

CHAPTER 13

"I HAD A REALLY NICE TIME TODAY," RACHEL TOLD MIKE AS he guided the horse down the main road toward Bird-in-Hand. The light rain sprinkled the windshield as the horse and buggy splashed through the puddles. "*Danki* for inviting me to stay for supper."

"I'm *froh* you could stay." He flashed a smile before glancing back toward the road ahead.

A smile found Rachel's lips as she recalled the day they'd spent together. She had enjoyed every moment with Mike and his family, and she was disappointed when it was time to go home. But at least she and Mike had a fairly long buggy ride to continue talking.

"Your *dat* seemed to be in *gut* spirits tonight," she said.

"*Ya*, he was," Mike agreed, but his expression collapsed with a frown.

"*Was iss letz?*"

His scowl deepened. "I can't help worrying about him. He used to have so much energy. It's difficult for me to see him so weak."

"I'm sorry." She fought the urge to touch his arm and comfort him. Touching him would be wrong, but she felt close to him. It was as if their friendship had deepened after spending so much time together today.

"Thanks." Mike gave her a bleak smile. "*Mei dat* really enjoys talking to you. I think your visits help him a lot."

Rachel's cheeks warmed. "I appreciate that. I enjoy spending time with him and John, and you too."

They were silent for a moment, and Rachel wondered if she'd made Mike feel uncomfortable by saying she liked being with him. She hoped she didn't give him the wrong idea.

"Since you asked me all about my job," he began with a sideways glance, "it's my turn to ask you about your work now."

"All right." Rachel settled her hands in her lap.

"How do you like teaching?" he asked.

"I enjoy it," Rachel said, watching raindrops pepper the windshield. "I actually like it better than I thought I would."

Mike slowed the horse to a stop at a red light. "You didn't always want to be a teacher?"

Rachel shook her head. "No, I really didn't. I honestly never considered being a teacher until this year."

Mike studied her with surprise. "I thought you always wanted to be a teacher. You're a natural with John."

"*Danki*, but teaching was never my goal. I honestly thought I'd be married by now." She glanced out the side window. "*Mei schweschder* was married in February, and I was sure I'd be next. I thought I'd be planning my wedding for this fall."

"Really?" Mike raised an eyebrow.

"Malinda asked me to be her co-teacher after my plans fell apart." Rachel forced a smile, despite a twinge of disappointment that threatened her happy mood. "It all worked out, and I'm really thankful Malinda asked me to help her. I learned a really important lesson."

The light turned green, and Mike guided the horse through the intersection.

"What lesson was that?" he asked, keeping his eyes focused on the road.

"I learned that sometimes God's plan is different from the one you have for yourself," Rachel said. "We have to accept that he has the perfect plan for us, and we'll find out what it is when the time is right."

Mike nodded without meeting her glance. "*Ya*, that is definitely true."

Rachel was grateful Mike didn't ask her for details about what happened to her hopes for marriage.

The rest of the trip was spent in an easy silence or talking about the everyday challenges of their jobs—just the kind of quality time Rachel thought two good friends should share.

The sign advertising her father's store came into view, and Rachel pointed out the driveway leading to her house. Mike guided the horse up the rock driveway and stopped near the back porch.

Rachel reached for the picnic basket at her feet, and Mike grasped the handle at the same time. When their fingers brushed, she felt a spark and swallowed a gasp.

"I'll carry it for you," he offered.

"Thanks." She hefted her tote bag onto her shoulder, climbed out of the buggy, and met him by the porch steps. The rain had stopped, and the aroma of wet grass and spring permeated the air. "You don't have to walk me up to the *haus*."

Rachel's heartbeat stuttered in her chest, and confusing feelings overtook her as she looked into his eyes. She was falling for Mike, but she didn't want to surrender her emotions to another man so quickly after David had broken her heart. She needed to concentrate on being a good teacher and not think about falling in love. Why were her emotions betraying her now?

"I don't mind." Mike smiled down at her, and she wondered if he felt the invisible force that seemed to pull them toward each other.

The screen door banged shut, and Rachel jumped with a start.

"Rach!" Emily appeared on the porch. "How did it go—" She stopped and smiled when she saw Mike. "Hi. I'm Emily." She descended the stairs and stood by Rachel.

"Hi." Mike shook Emily's hand. "I'm Mike Lantz."

Emily raised her eyebrows at Rachel, causing Rachel's cheeks to flare with embarrassment. She hoped Mike hadn't seen Emily's expression.

"Well, I'd better get back on the road. The sun will be setting soon." Mike handed the basket to Rachel. "Thanks again for coming over today."

"Have a safe trip home," Rachel said.

Mike waved and then climbed into the buggy. As the horse clip-clopped down the driveway, Emily wrapped her arm around Rachel's shoulders.

"Why didn't you tell me Mike is so handsome?" Emily asked as they walked up the steps toward the back door.

Rachel shrugged. "We're just *freinden*, so it doesn't matter."

"I think he likes you." Emily squeezed Rachel's arm.

"No, he doesn't." Rachel stepped into the kitchen and found her mother sitting at the table with a cup of tea. "Hi, *Mamm*." She placed her tote bag and basket on the counter and draped her sweater over the back of a chair.

"How was your day?" *Mamm* asked.

"It was *gut*." Rachel slipped into a chair across from *Mamm*, and Emily sat down beside her. Rachel told them how she spent her day at the Lantz farm.

Excitement twinkled in Emily's blue eyes. "Mike must really like you if he invited you to stay for supper and then brought you home." She turned to *Mamm*. "Don't you agree?"

"*Ya*, it looks like it to me too." *Mamm* nodded. "He sounds like a nice young man."

"He is nice, but I don't think he likes me," Rachel insisted.

"We both care about John." She stood and started for the stairs. "I'm tired, so I'm going to get ready for bed. It's been a long day."

"Are you all right?" Emily placed her hand on Rachel's arm. "You look worried."

Rachel sighed as she sat down on the chair. "Mike is a *wunderbaar* man, but I'm not ready for a relationship. I'm not interested in dating anyone right now." She shook her head. "Besides, if I get married, then I can't teach anymore. Right now I just want to concentrate on teaching."

"You're afraid he'll break your heart," *Mamm* said as understanding flickered across her face. "It's okay to be cautious. Breakups have a lingering pain that can be very difficult to overcome. Don't feel pressured to fall in love again or to have a relationship. Give yourself time to heal, but don't give up on love altogether."

She reached across the table and gently squeezed Rachel's hands. "Promise me you'll give someone special a chance when the time is right, okay?"

Rachel found deep understanding in her mother's expression. "I promise I will."

Emily's lips frowned into a thin line. "I didn't mean to pressure you."

"It's okay." Rachel had always secretly envied her younger sister's positive outlook on life. Emily was rarely sad or disappointed, and she always believed the best in people. If only she had her sister's happy-go-lucky spirit. "I'm really tired. I'm going to shower and then go to bed. Tell *Dat* good night for me."

Rachel climbed the stairs to the second floor. As she pulled out her nightgown, she wondered if Mike had felt the same strong attraction she'd felt today. Did he care about her too? Was he as nervous about giving away his heart?

As Rachel padded down the hallway to the bathroom, she wondered if she had completely misread Mike's feelings for her.

Maybe he only wanted to be friends, and she was wasting her time thinking about him.

Yet somewhere deep in her soul, she knew Mike liked her as much as she liked him, and a tingle of excitement teased her. She put thoughts of him aside and climbed into the shower. She'd keep her promise to her mother and not give up on love—even though the notion of getting hurt again scared her to death.

MIKE SAT ON THE EDGE OF JOHN'S BED AND TUCKED THE covers in around him. "Did you have fun today?"

"I had the best day ever." John gave him a toothy grin. "I love playing Scrabble! I had so much fun spelling words, and Rachel was so funny when she said you didn't know how to spell as well as I do."

Mike chuckled while recalling Rachel's sweet laugh. "She was funny. I enjoyed our time together too."

John's smile dissolved as a pensive expression overtook his small face. "Do you like Rachel?"

"Of course I like her." Mike pushed a lock of John's hair back from his face. "She's our *freind*, right?"

"*Ya*, but you do really like her?" John prodded. "Are you going to ask her to be your girlfriend?"

Mike grimaced. John sounded like *Dat*. Why was his family pushing him to date Rachel? "I don't think so. She's my *freind*."

"But you and Rachel get along really well." He tilted his head in question. "Did *Dat* and your *mamm* get along well?"

Mike nodded. "*Ya*, they got along really well." He smiled as he remembered his father and mother teasing each other. One afternoon *Mamm* chased *Dat* around the kitchen, scolding him after he had swiped a finger full of icing from a chocolate cake she'd made for his birthday. His father laughed so hard tears had streamed down his face.

"*Mei mamm* and *Dat* loved each other very much, and your *mamm* and *Dat* loved each other a lot too." He touched John's nose. "Your *mamm* loved you very much too. She'd be so proud of you if she heard you read aloud like you did today."

John fingered the hem of the sheet. "Do you think you'll ever get married?"

Mike shrugged. "I don't know. I might get married someday, but it won't be any time soon."

"Is it because of me?" John looked up at him.

"Why would you ask that?" Mike searched John's eyes.

"I heard you talking to *Dat* the other night, and you said you can't date because you have to take care of me. Am I the reason why you don't have a girlfriend?"

"No, no." Mike shook his head. "That's not why I don't date." He paused, gathering his thoughts. He had to tell his brother the truth, but he didn't want to hurt his feelings. "I choose to stay home with you and *Dat* and not go to youth group because I want to be here with you. But that doesn't mean you're the reason why I don't date. Right now the focus of my life is taking care of both *Dat* and you. Maybe someday I'll meet a special *maedel* and fall in love, and we'll get married. And if I do get married, you'll be with us. We'll all be a family. You belong here with me and *Dat* because we love you, and we're family."

John's toothy grin was back in full force. "Maybe you can marry Rachel."

Mike chuckled. "You sound like *Dat*. I don't think I'll marry Rachel."

"Why not? You said she's your *freind* and you have fun together."

Mike stood. "It's late. You need to get some sleep. We have church in the morning."

"*Gut nacht*," John said, rolling to his side.

Mike walked out to the hallway and quietly closed John's door behind him. He walked down the stairs and checked on *Dat*, who was snoring peacefully in his room. Once he was certain *Dat* was okay, Mike ambled out to his woodshop, where he flipped on the lanterns, opened the window above the workbench, and then perched on a stool to begin working on the shelf he'd started a few weeks ago.

He pulled on a mask, and while he stained the shelf, he thought about his brother's comments about Rachel. Both *Dat* and John liked Rachel and wanted Mike to date her. He liked Rachel too, but his strong feelings against dating hadn't changed during the course of the day. He still wasn't interested, and he longed for John and *Dat* to drop the subject completely.

Mike swept the brush over the wood and recalled his conversation with Rachel during their ride to her house. He was intrigued when she talked about how God's plans weren't always the plans they had for themselves. He certainly could relate to that after losing his stepmother and becoming his father's caregiver.

He found himself stuck on what Rachel had said about teaching on the way home in the buggy. She had never considered becoming a teacher until her cousin asked her to help with the special school, and that was after a man had broken her heart. She thought she was going to be married instead.

Mike had thought about asking her more about that, but he didn't want to pry into her life. The question, however, continued to taunt him while he worked. Why would a man break up with Rachel, when she was a smart, beautiful, loyal woman? Rachel had an intriguing stubborn streak that kept Mike guessing. She would make a wonderful wife.

Mike closed his eyes and groaned. He was falling into the trap *Dat* had laid for him. He had to stop thinking about Rachel and concentrate on the important tasks he had in his home.

So then why did Rachel keep sneaking back into his thoughts?

He finished staining the shelf and then set it on newspaper on the workbench before closing up the shop for the night. As he walked toward the house, he stopped and studied the rocking chair on the porch where Rachel had sat beside John earlier today. He remembered how she'd smiled and clapped as she encouraged him to read.

Rachel truly was a blessing to their family. Mike just had to keep reminding himself that she was a friend, and that was all she could ever be to him.

"I CAN'T BELIEVE HOW QUICKLY THIS WEEK FLEW BY," RACHEL said as she sat at the teacher's desk. She was writing in the students' journals. "It seems like it was just Monday, and now we're cleaning up to go home for the weekend."

"I know." Malinda erased the schedule from the board and then faced the class. "Okay, scholars. If you are done with your worksheet, please bring it up to the front of the room. It's time to pack up and get ready to go home."

Rachel lifted the next journal in the pile and smiled when she realized it was John's. She opened to a clean page and prepared to write the note for Friday.

"How are you doing on the journals?" Malinda asked, sidling up beside her.

"I'm on the last one." Rachel lowered her voice. "I just have John's left."

"Oh." Malinda smiled. "I've seen a huge improvement this week. It must be due to your tutoring sessions on the weekends. What are you going to write?"

"I'll let Mike know how well John is doing," Rachel said.

Malinda whispered, leaning in close, "I don't think you need to do the tutoring on the weekends anymore though. He's reading at a higher level than most of the other students now, and his math worksheet from yesterday was perfect."

"I agree." Rachel nodded and bit back a frown. She was thrilled John was doing so well, but she would miss their Saturday visits. At the same time, however, she knew she was needed at home to help with chores. It wasn't fair for her to expect Emily to keep doing all Rachel's chores along with helping her father in his harness shop.

Rachel poised her pen and then began to write.

Mike,

I'm thrilled to report that John's behavior and schoolwork have improved even more this week. He is excelling in his reading, spelling, and math beyond most of the other students in the class. His math worksheet from yesterday was perfect, and he read aloud without any hesitation earlier today. He also spelled all but two of the words correctly on his spelling exam this afternoon. John has been polite and respectful to both the teachers and his classmates.

Since he is doing so well, I won't need to continue working with him on Saturdays. Malinda and I are happy with John's work, and we hope you are too. Have a nice weekend.

Sincerely,
Rachel Fisher

Rachel studied the note and longed to write something more personal. She wanted to tell Mike she would miss the weekend visits and she hoped to see him soon, but that would be unprofessional. She was John's teacher and nothing more.

As Rachel slipped the journal into John's bag, she closed her eyes for a quick moment and silently prayed, asking God to somehow bring Mike back into her life. She didn't want their friendship to end.

"WHAT DID RACHEL WRITE IN MY JOURNAL TODAY?" JOHN stood beside Mike at the kitchen counter later that evening.

"You're going to like what she said." Marie smiled over from the sink, where she was drying the supper dishes. "I read it earlier while you were doing your chores."

"Let me see." Mike found the journal inside John's bag and opened to the note. His eyes scanned Rachel's perfect cursive handwriting and then he read the note aloud. "You are doing great!" He hugged John. "*Danki* for working so hard in school."

"*Gern gschehne.*" John studied the toes of his socks. "Rachel isn't going to come over on Saturdays anymore?"

Mike felt a pang of disappointment in his chest. "No, she doesn't need to come now because you're such a *gut* student."

John's expression suddenly brightened. "What if we went to see *her* tomorrow? We could take her one of the planters you make as a thank-you gift."

Mike opened his mouth to protest and then closed it. He turned toward Marie and raised his eyebrows to ask for her opinion.

Marie shrugged. "Sounds like a *gut* idea to me. *Mei mamm* and I can come by and stay with your *dat* while you're gone."

"I don't feel right asking you to come again tomorrow," Mike said. "You've been here three days already this week."

"Don't be *gegisch*." She waved off his comment and then began drying a pot. "*Mei mamm* has been asking about your *dat* and said she wanted to see him. Besides, John has been talking nonstop about Rachel and how much fun he had last Saturday. I think it would be nice if you took her a thank-you gift."

Mike studied his brother's wide smile. "All right, we'll go see her, but we don't have to take her a gift."

"*Ya*, we should give her a gift. We can give her something from the store. That way she'll know how much we appreciate her."

John beamed. "I can't wait. We're going to have so much fun." He took Mike's hand. "Do you have a planter in your woodshop?"

As Mike led John out to the shop, he smiled. He was just as excited as John was to see Rachel again. He just hoped she would be happy to see them too.

CHAPTER 14

RACHEL SWIPED THE BACK OF HER HAND ACROSS HER BROW as the late-morning April sun warmed her face. She leaned down and pulled another weed from her mother's garden and dropped it into the bucket beside her. She'd been working in the garden all morning and was finally starting to see some progress. In fact, the flowers and vegetables outnumbered the weeds.

"Rachel!" *Mamm* called from the driveway. "You have visitors."

After wiping her hands on her black apron, Rachel came around the side of the house and gaped when she found Mike and John talking with her mother beside Mike's buggy. John held up a small planter shaped like a basket with pink Gerber daisies peeking out. Rachel approached them and looked back and forth between Mike and John.

"Hi," she said. "I'm surprised to see you here today." Mike gave her a sweet smile, and a thrill raced through her.

"John insisted that we come to see you today," Mike said. "He was disappointed you aren't going to tutor him on Saturdays anymore."

"I wanted to see you, and I wanted to thank you for tutoring me." John shoved the small planter toward Rachel. "This is for you. Mike made it, and I picked out the flowers at the garden shop."

Rachel studied the planter and smelled the flowers. "This is so *schee*, but it's too much." She held it back out toward John. "You don't need to give me gifts."

"*Ya*, I do." John gave Mike an expression that asked for his help. "Right, Mike?"

"John insisted we give you something." Mike's eyes pleaded with her to accept the gift.

"Well, *danki*, John. And I truly enjoyed tutoring you." She set the planter on the bottom porch step. "I love it." She smiled at Mike.

Mike nodded and pushed his hands into his trouser pockets.

"Why don't you come in for lunch?" *Mamm* announced. "I was just putting out lunch meat and my homemade *brot*."

Mike held up his hand in protest. "*Danki*, Mattie, but I don't want to impose. We just wanted to stop by, say hello, and thank Rachel again for her hard work with John."

"Please stay," Rachel said. "I insist. My family will enjoy meeting you."

"But we didn't bring anything for dessert," John said. "Marie always says we should take something when we go to someone's *haus* to eat."

"It's fine," Rachel said with a chuckle. "We have ice cream and some *kichlin*."

"I love *kichlin*." John looked up at Mike. "Can we please stay for lunch?" he whined. "*Aenti* Sylvia and Marie are with *Dat*, so he'll be fine."

Mike smiled. "All right. We'll stay."

John clapped his hands, and Rachel laughed again.

AFTER HE TOOK CARE OF HIS HORSE, MIKE FOLLOWED RACHEL, her mother, and John into the house, where they found Emily setting out the food for lunch.

"Hello," Emily called. "I didn't realize we had company." She bent and shook John's hand. "You must be John. I'm Emily." She smiled at Mike. "It's nice to see you again."

"*Wie geht's?*" Mike said with a nod.

"You can sit," Rachel told him, gesturing toward the table. "I'll help Emily finish getting out the fixings for lunch."

"I'm going to take some food out to *Dat* at the shop and eat with him," Emily said. "It's been busy today. He said he wanted to come home for lunch, but he didn't want to leave Hank alone in case they had another rush of customers. The tourists are out in full force. They want to see a real Amish harness shop. He wasn't complaining because they were buying souvenirs. He's almost out of key chains and dog collars."

"That's *gut* to hear," Mattie said as she brought drinking glasses to the table.

Emily filled a tray with lunch meat, bread, sliced tomatoes, and condiments. John wandered over to her and stood on his tiptoes as he surveyed her work.

"Do you need some help?" John offered. "I can carry the tray to your *dat*, and you can bring the drinks. Maybe I can even eat out there with you."

Emily looked at Mike, raising her eyebrows as if asking for permission.

"It's fine with me if he won't be in your way," Mike said as he sat down at the table.

"I would love the assistance." Emily handed John three bottles of water. "Let's go see my *dat*, and I can give you a tour of the store."

Emily and John walked out the back door and talked as if they were old friends. Mike silently wondered if all the Fisher daughters had been equally blessed with the ability to relate well to children. Surely they all would be wonderful mothers someday.

Rachel sat down across from Mike with her mother to her right. After a silent prayer, they began to build their sandwiches on the homemade bread. Rachel handed Mike a bowl of potato salad.

"I made this last night. I hope you like it." She smiled, and his own smile widened. He had grown to enjoy seeing her pretty smile light up her whole face.

"*Danki*." He shoveled a small mountain of the salad onto his plate. "I really appreciate you inviting John and me to stay for lunch. We were only planning to stop by and drop off the planter. He was so disappointed when he found out you didn't need to tutor him anymore."

"*Danki* for the gift, but you really didn't need to give me anything. I was only doing my job." Rachel cut her turkey sandwich in half.

"The planter is *schee*," Mattie said as she piled ham onto her bread. "You do incredible work."

"*Danki*. I really enjoy it."

"Your family owns Bird-in-Hand Builders?" Mattie asked, and Mike nodded. "That's very nice. I imagine it stays busy."

"It does. This is the beginning of our busy season." He picked up the mustard to add to the mayonnaise on his sandwich. "When is the busy season at the harness shop?"

"I think it stays busy, right, Rachel?" Mattie said.

Rachel nodded while chewing, then swallowed. "*Ya*, it's busier in the spring and summer, but *Dat* and Hank have customers all year round."

They fell into an easy conversation, and as Mike enjoyed getting to know Rachel's mother, he noticed that Rachel frequently glanced down at her plate. Was she shy or was she nervous?

After they finished homemade chocolate chip cookies for dessert, Rachel and Mattie began to clean up. Mike put the condiments in the refrigerator.

Rachel filled one side of the sink with hot, soapy water and set the dishes in it.

"I'll wash the dishes," Mattie said, touching Rachel's arm. "Why don't you take Mike to the harness shop?"

"Are you sure? I don't want to leave you with the mess."

"Go and spend time with your guest." Mattie gave Rachel a knowing look.

"*Danki.*" Rachel turned to Mike and gestured toward the door. "Let's go find John."

Mike nodded. "*Danki* for lunch, Mattie."

Mattie smiled at him. "*Gern gschehne.* I'm so *froh* you and John came by. I've heard a lot about you."

Rachel shook her head, and the tips of her ears turned pink. Was she embarrassed? She looked adorable. Mike bit the inside of his lip to prevent a chuckle from escaping his mouth.

Mike followed Rachel through the mudroom and out to the porch. "How long has your *dat* owned the harness shop?"

"Almost twenty-six years," Rachel explained as they walked side by side toward the store. "*Mei dat* and our neighbor, Hank Ebersol, built the shop when they were in their twenties. They run it together. Emily helps out with the books every week, and sometimes she'll run the front counter and answer the shop phone. Mostly it's just *Dat* and Hank, though."

Mike's stomach knotted as they walked toward the one-story, white clapboard building. Why was he nervous about meeting Rachel's father? It wasn't as if they were dating. They were only friends. He pushed away his anxiety as he noticed a prominent sign boasting the Bird-in-Hand Harness Shop. A hitching post by the front door welcomed horses and buggies, and a car was parked in one of the three parking spaces.

"It looks like they're still busy," Rachel remarked.

Mike pulled the door open, and Rachel stepped inside as a bell over the door announced their arrival. As Mike followed her, the aroma of leather permeated his sense of smell.

The one-room store was filled with displays of harnesses, leashes for pets, pet collars, saddles, saddle blankets, doorknob hangers with bells, rope, pouches, bags, and various other horse accessories. The sales counter sat in the center of the packed showroom with a small, round display peppered with leather key chains in shapes varying from cats to horses.

Emily stood at the sales counter and spoke to an *English* customer as she rang up the man's items.

Beyond the showroom was an open area where two middle-aged men worked. John stood by one of them and nodded with enthusiasm. The man seemed to be showing him how to work on a leather strap. Rachel walked that way and Mike followed her.

"Hi, *Dat*," Rachel said. "Hi, Hank. Mike is here to visit."

"Mike." A tall man with graying, light-brown hair and a matching beard stood up from the chair beside John. He looked down at John and said, "Is this the older *bruder* you were telling me about?"

"*Ya.*" John smiled and pointed at Mike. "This is *mei bruder*, Mike. He's the best carpenter you'll ever meet."

Mike shook his head and chuckled. "You're being generous, John." He held out his hand as the man stepped away from the workbench. "*Wie geht's?*"

"I'm doing well." He shook Mike's hand with a confident, strong grip. "I'm Leroy. I've enjoyed meeting John. He's a *gut* worker. He's helping me make a dog leash. I may have to hire him to help out here."

"I'd love to work here," John said as he came to stand by Leroy. Then he frowned. "But Mike needs my help at home."

"*Ya*, I do." Mike touched John's straw hat.

Leroy smiled down at the boy. "You'll have to come by and visit me then."

Mike heard the customer thank Emily, and turned in time to see him wave as he exited the store. Then he glanced around, taking in all the items for sale, before gesturing around the showroom. "You have a *schee* store here. You do fantastic work."

"Oh no." Her *dat* pointed toward the other man sitting at the workbench. "Hank does the *gut* work. I'm still learning."

"That's right," Hank chimed in. "I taught him everything he knows, and he's still trying to catch up with me."

Leroy gave a loud, boisterous laugh, and Mike smiled. Leroy reminded him of his own father. He grinned as he recalled how much his father used to enjoy joking and laughing. Before he became ill.

John joined Emily at the counter, and she began showing him how the cash register worked. Rachel touched Mike's arm and he turned toward her. "I'm going to go help my *mamm* in the kitchen. I'll leave you out here to talk with the guys."

"Hey, I'm still here," Emily teased as John swiveled on the stool beside her.

"I'm sorry, Em." Rachel rolled her eyes, then turned back to Mike. "I'll leave you out here with the guys and *Emily*. Come back up to the *haus* when you're done, and we can sit on the porch and talk for a while."

"All right," Mike said, and his chest felt light. Rachel wanted to spend time with him, and the thought overwhelmed him.

Rachel waved to John, picked up the lunch tray he and Emily had brought out, and left the store, the bell on the door ringing as she disappeared.

"I'm going to run home and get some lunch," Hank said, walking toward the door. "I think you all can handle the store while I'm gone." He waved good-bye and sauntered out.

Leroy motioned for Mike to follow him over to the workbench. "So, you're a carpenter?"

"That's right," Mike said. "*Mei dat* and *onkel* own Bird-in-Hand Builders."

"Do they?" Leroy's eyes flashed with recognition. "I've been in there. That's a nice store."

"*Danki.*" Mike glanced over his shoulder. John and Emily seemed to be discussing how to ring up a leather belt. "I think *mei bruder* really does want to get a job here. He seems even more excited about the cash register than about woodworking."

Leroy chuckled and handed Mike a bottle of water. "Have a seat." He pointed toward a stool beside the bench. "Rachel has been *froh* to work with John. She's shared her progress with him. She's thrilled he's doing so well in school."

Mike took a sip from the bottle and then swiped the back of his hand across his mouth. "Rachel's a *wunderbaar* teacher." He glanced over at John. "She has a real gift with her students. I was surprised when she told me she hadn't planned on teaching."

"*Ya*, I never expected her to become a teacher. I was shocked when she told me she was going to help Malinda with the special school."

"How so?" Mike furrowed his brow.

Leroy fingered his beard. "Rachel didn't tell you what happened with David?"

Mike shook his head and gripped the bottle of water, which crackled in protest in his hand.

"I don't know if I should be telling you this, but I suppose she'll tell you eventually," Leroy began with a resigned sigh. "Rachel had been dating David for quite a while, and she thought he was going to propose soon. He broke up with her for someone else."

Mike grimaced. So that was what she was referring to that day he took her home in his buggy, when she mentioned she had thought she'd be marrying in the fall but the plans fell apart. How could this David break up with her for someone else? Didn't he see how special Rachel was?

Leroy wagged a finger at him. "Now, you didn't hear this from me."

Mike held up his hand. "I won't let on that I know anything."

"*Danki*. Let her tell you when she's ready." Leroy sipped some water. "Rachel was devastated, as you can imagine, and she jumped at the chance to be a teacher when Malinda asked her. I think it was a true blessing that she started teaching. Not only is it giving her a chance to start a new life, but she also has a gift to share with students."

"That's true. She's been a *wunderbaar* help to John."

"She loves teaching, and I'm *froh* she found it after the way David broke her heart." Leroy shook his head. "It was terrible. I'm so thankful she's doing better now."

Mike tried to imagine how anyone could hurt Rachel that way. It didn't make sense. He didn't want to pry, but he wondered how much better she was really doing. Had she gotten over her heartache? Would she ever trust another man?

"Have you ever done any leatherwork?" Leroy asked.

"No, I haven't." Mike examined the leash coiled on Leroy's desk. "How did you learn the trade?"

Mike enjoyed listening to Leroy talk about his work. Leroy was a friendly, confident man, and, again, he reminded Mike of how his father used to be before the kidney disease strangled most of the life out of him. Leroy was in the middle of showing Mike how to finish the leash when John appeared beside him.

"Can I help make the leash?" John asked, craning his neck to watch Leroy work.

Leroy grinned down at John. "It's fine with me if it's okay with your *bruder*."

"That's a great idea, John." Mike stood and patted the stool. "Here. You sit with Leroy, and I'm going to go see what Rachel is doing."

"Okay." John began grabbing tools. "What do we do next, Leroy?"

"Let's see." Leroy winked at Mike before turning his attention to John and their project.

"I'll leave you two to your work." Mike started for the door.

"Mike," Emily said, coming around from behind the cash register. "Wait one minute." She motioned for him to step outside with her, and he followed. "I'm *froh* you and John came by today. I'm so glad Rachel met you. Your friendship means a lot to her."

"*Danki*," Mike said with surprise. "I'm thankful for her friendship too."

"*Gut*." Emily gave him a little wave and then returned to the store.

As Mike walked toward the house, he did a mental headshake. Rachel and her family seemed too good to be true. They were so welcoming and encouraging, and their friendship warmed his soul. He hadn't realized how lonely he'd been until he'd met them.

Mike felt as if he might wake up and realize this whole visit had been a dream. For too long he'd been caring for his family with only the help of his cousins, and now he'd found some wonderful friends. He hoped he could cultivate his friendship with Rachel and the whole Fisher family.

"Mike!" Rachel waved from the porch. "I was just going to come and get you." She held up two glass mugs. "Do you like root beer?"

"*Ya*," he said, picking up the pace as he approached the steps. "I love root beer." He took the steps two at a time and then sat down in a rocking chair.

She handed him a mug and sat down in a rocking chair beside him. "*Mei dat* makes the best root beer."

Mike took a long draw from the mug and nodded. "It's the best I've had."

"I told you." She took a sip. "Did you enjoy spending time in the harness shop?"

"I did." Mike pointed toward the store. "John stayed for a leatherworking lesson."

169

"I bet *mei dat* is enjoying giving lessons." She pushed her feet on the porch, and the chair moved back and forth. Her gaze moved to the edge of the porch where the planter sat. "I love the planter and the daisies."

Mike smiled. "John wanted to give you something special since you're his favorite teacher."

Rachel shook her head. "I don't deserve that honor, but *danki*." She took another sip of root beer.

"You've really gone above and beyond your expected duties by helping John on Saturdays." He studied her brown eyes. "It's difficult to believe you didn't always want to be a teacher."

She shrugged and studied the mug of root beer. "It's like I said last week, it's funny how sometimes God has other plans for us."

"I can definitely relate to that." He sipped more root beer, savoring the cool carbonation on his throat. He enjoyed their comfortable silence and wondered if Rachel would ever trust him enough to share that painful story about David with him.

Would she ever consider Mike a close friend?

The silent question caught Mike off guard, and he shifted in the rocking chair. He hadn't allowed any young woman to awaken feelings in him for years, but now he found himself yearning to get to know Rachel better. But why? How had she managed to get under his skin and break down the barriers he'd kept secured around his soul, especially since his father had become ill?

"How's your dad doing?" she asked, jolting him from his deep thoughts.

Mike rested the root beer mug on the arm of the chair and blew out a sigh as the image of his ill father appeared in his mind. "The treatments have been tough this week. He's been more exhausted than usual."

"*Ach,* no." Rachel's eyes widened, and the concern in her expression squeezed at his chest. "Do you need to get home to him soon?"

"No." Mike shook his head. "As John said when you invited us to lunch, *mei aenti* and Marie are with him. They wanted to visit him. John and I can stay for a while longer."

"*Gut.*" She ran her finger over the condensation on her mug.

While Mike took in her beautiful face, he felt the wall he'd kept around his heart begin to crumble. A mixture of fear and happiness settled over him. He didn't want to care about her, but his feelings for her were deepening as the day wore on. He was falling for her, and it shook him to his core. He couldn't allow himself to be hurt when she rejected him because of his obligations to his father and brother.

"Do you like to go fishing?" Rachel asked, crossing her ankles.

Mike shrugged. "I do, but I don't get to go as often as I'd like to."

"Did your *dat* like to fish before he became ill?"

"Oh *ya*. Some of my best memories with my *dat* are when we went fishing." He angled his body toward her. "We used to go to this pond behind the farm. One time I caught a fish that was this big." He held up his hands to illustrate the size of the fish and told her the story of how he fell out of his uncle's boat.

Rachel laughed along with the story, and soon they were sharing their favorite childhood memories. Before Mike realized it, a couple of hours had slipped by.

"Mike," Mattie said, appearing on the porch. "Will you and John stay for supper? I'm going to make stew and cornbread."

Rachel's eyes lit up with excitement. "Oh, you and John have to stay." She reached out to touch his arm, but then suddenly looked embarrassed and stopped. "*Mamm* makes the best stew."

"*Danki*, but we have to get home. My *aenti* and cousin have stayed with *Dat* long enough, I think." Mike stood. "I should get John and head out."

"All right." Mattie shook his hand. "I'm so *froh* you could come by today."

"I'll walk you to your buggy," Rachel said, standing. "*Mamm*, I'll come in and help you cook after I see Mike and John off."

Mike and Rachel walked to the harness shop together where they found John and Leroy working on a belt.

"It's time to go, John," Mike said, rubbing his brother's straw-colored hair.

John's face fell into a frown. "But we're still working on this belt. I need to help Leroy finish it."

Mike and Leroy shared a grin.

"Why don't you come back again soon, and we'll finish this belt together?" Leroy asked with a warm smile.

"*Ya*, that's a *gut* idea." John nodded with emphasis.

"Great." Leroy shook John's hand and then shook Mike's. "It was nice meeting you both. Hope to see you again soon."

Mike and John said good-bye to Leroy and Emily and then followed Rachel out of the harness shop to Mike's horse, where he hitched up his buggy.

"*Danki* for coming over," Rachel said.

John wrapped his arms around her waist. "I had fun. I'm going to come back and help your *dat* with his store."

Rachel smiled down at him. "I hope you come back soon."

John hopped in the buggy and leaned out the window.

Mike stepped over to Rachel, and he fought the urge to tell her that he and John would like to stay for supper after all. He couldn't stand the idea of leaving her when he didn't know when he'd see her again. "*Danki* for letting us visit you."

"You can visit anytime you'd like." Rachel pushed one of the ties for her prayer covering over her shoulder. "Maybe you can stay for supper next time."

"That would be great." He shook her hand, enjoying the warm feel of her skin. The air around them felt charged, and he didn't want to release her. They stared at each other a long moment. He wanted more time with her, and he longed to pull her back up to the porch to sit and talk for a few more hours.

She suddenly broke the trance, released her hand from his grasp, and glanced back toward the house. "I'd better go help *mei mamm*."

"I'll see you Monday, Teacher Rachel," John said from the buggy. Mike spun and faced his younger brother. For a moment, Mike had forgotten John was there.

"*Ya*, you will." Rachel waved at him.

"Good-bye," Mike said before climbing into the buggy.

He waved at Rachel as he guided the horse down the driveway toward the road.

"I had a lot of fun today," John said as he gazed out the window.

"I did too."

"We need to do this more often. I like spending time with Rachel and her family."

A feeling of dread pooled in Mike's stomach. John was developing a deep attachment to Rachel, and Mike was too. But Mike couldn't allow himself to risk his emotions right now. He had to find a way to push those feelings aside and concentrate on only being Rachel's friend.

But then he recalled how much he had wanted to stay and how John hugged Rachel before they left. How could he not fall in love with Rachel, when she seemed to be just what he and John both needed?

CHAPTER 15

RACHEL WAVED AS THE HORSE AND BUGGY STEERED DOWN the driveway. Then she rubbed her hands together, climbed the back porch steps, and went through the mudroom and into the kitchen. She couldn't stop thinking about how Mike had held her hand before he left. And why had his expression seemed so intense?

It was almost as if he'd wanted to stay, even though she knew he felt an obligation to get back to his father.

"Did you have a nice visit with Mike and John?" *Mamm* asked as she chopped carrots.

"*Ya*, I did." Rachel pulled out a bag of potatoes and began to peel one, and she remembered how she'd taught John how to peel potatoes last week. She smiled while recalling John's determination. With his tongue sticking out of his little mouth, he pinched his eyebrows together and worked diligently with the little peeler. She had quickly grown to love that little boy, and she would do anything for him and his family.

She'd been so disappointed when Mike said they couldn't stay for supper. She didn't want them to leave. How had she permitted herself to get so attached to John and Mike? Rachel closed her eyes and shook her head. She couldn't allow herself to walk into another disappointment after the way David had hurt her.

"Mike seems like a nice young man, *ya*?" *Mamm* shot Rachel a knowing expression over her shoulder.

Rachel shrugged and ignored her mother's smile. *"Ya,* he's very nice."

Mamm stopped chopping and faced Rachel. "Didn't you enjoy talking with him on the porch?"

"Of course I did." Rachel shrugged again, as if it weren't a big deal that she'd spent most of the afternoon getting to know Mike Lantz.

"You two seemed to be engrossed in a conversation when I walked outside earlier to take some root beer down to the shop." *Mamm* continued to smile, making Rachel feel more and more uncomfortable.

"We were. He's very easy to talk to." *And he's handsome, sweet, kind, a gut bruder to John . . .* Rachel swallowed a groan. She had to stop thinking about Mike as more than just her student's brother. "He's a *gut freind."*

Mamm placed her knife on the counter. "Is something wrong, Rachel? You look upset."

"Everything is fine." Rachel concentrated on peeling the potato in her hand.

"I thought you'd be excited Mike brought John over to see you. You were so worried Mike didn't like you. It's obvious he likes you quite a bit."

"I am *froh* they came over. But Mike and I are only *freinden.* We really have nothing in common except we both care about John. I want to be the best teacher I can for John, and Mike appreciates that."

"You and Mike have nothing in common?" Mamm gave Rachel a withering look. "You don't really believe that, do you?"

"It's the truth," Rachel insisted. "We talk about John quite a bit. Did you know John had a nice time in the shop with *Dat?* John wanted to stay and learn more about how to make belts and leashes.

I hope they come back again soon because *Dat* said he'd let John help him finish the belt they were working on together."

Mamm walked to the table and placed her hand on Rachel's arm. She continued to look unconvinced. "Did Mike say something to upset you?"

"No." Rachel shook her head. "Why would you think that?"

"You just seemed so *froh* while he was here, and now you're upset. Did something happen before he left?"

"No, it's not that at all. He was very cordial when he left."

"Are you upset he didn't stay for supper?" *Mamm* pressed on, and Rachel shook her head again.

"Of course not. He had to get back to his *dat*. He said his *dat* has had a difficult week with his dialysis treatments. I understand he's needed at home." Rachel frowned. Why would Mike even consider wanting to date Rachel when he had so many more pressing things to think about, such as caring for his ill father?

"Rachel," *Mamm* said. "You know you can talk to me."

"I know that." Rachel wiped her hands on a paper towel. She longed to tell *Mamm* she didn't want to have such strong feelings for Mike, that she couldn't figure out how to push these feelings away. But how could she admit she was interested in someone else so quickly after losing David? What would her mother think of her? Would *Mamm* say she was immature?

"Did Mike say something to hurt your feelings?" *Mamm* asked, oblivious to Rachel's inner turmoil.

"No, no. It's nothing like that." Rachel rolled the paper towel up as if it were a softball and took a deep breath. "It's just that . . . I really like him, *Mamm*. I didn't think I would like someone so quickly after David broke up with me. It's overwhelming."

"*Ach, mei liewe.*" *Mamm*'s smile returned. "Love can be both unexpected and overwhelming."

"Love? I'm not ready for love. I don't want to get hurt again.

It's too soon." Rachel sniffed as tears threatened her eyes. "I see David and Sharon at church and at youth gatherings, and it's too painful." Her voice hitched and she cleared her throat. Why was she getting so emotional? She should be past the pain already.

"You need to forgive David and Sharon and let your heart heal." *Mamm* wiped away an errant tear trickling down Rachel's cheek. "You shouldn't be afraid to move on. You're going to meet the right man. Don't be afraid to give Mike a chance. I can tell he loves his *bruder*, and I think he really cares about you too."

"I can't risk having Mike break my heart and then having to bear seeing John at school," Rachel said, folding her arms over her apron. "I'm too connected to John and his family. It would be difficult to have to see Mike at school functions, like the picnic and the Christmas program. Besides, Malinda says I shouldn't get too involved with the scholars and their families. I could tell she didn't approve of my weekend tutoring sessions, but I felt like I owed it to Mike after the way I treated him." She wiped away another tear and focused on her peeling.

"I can understand taking your time and letting yourself heal, but don't push Mike away so quickly." *Mamm* rested her hand on Rachel's shoulder.

"I'm not pushing him away. I'm just being cautious with my emotions. I'm trying to stay realistic. I was too eager to get married, and I've learned I can't force marriage. I will meet the right person, fall in love, and get married when God decides it's my time. Right now I need to focus on being the best teacher I can. Marriage will come when the time is right."

"That's true," *Mamm* agreed as she returned to the carrots. "It will happen for you when it's the right time, but you need to keep your mind open and don't close yourself off to everyone."

Rachel enjoyed working in silence as a bird sang outside the open window and the warm breeze drifted throughout the kitchen with the aroma of earth and rebirth. After the vegetables were chopped, they dropped them into a large pot, along with stew beef, broth, and spices. Once the stew was cooking, *Mamm* pulled out the ingredients for the cornbread and Rachel considered what chore she needed to do next.

"I have gone through my own heartache," *Mamm* suddenly said as she combined the ingredients. "I was sure I'd never fall in love again, and I pushed your *dat* away at first."

Rachel raised her eyebrows. "You pushed *Dat* away?"

Mamm nodded as she kept her eyes trained on the large mixing bowl. "*Ya*, I did. I told you he used to bring me meals in that basket you've been using to send meals to Mike and his family. That basket served as a kind of mediator between your father and me. It's sort of a symbol of how we worked things out." A faraway expression overtook *Mamm*'s face as if she were recalling those early memories with *Dat*. "I'm thankful he didn't give up on me. If he had, then I wouldn't have had my three *wunderbaar dochdern*."

"I thought you and *Dat* grew up together."

"We did," *Mamm* said. "But we had a rocky start to our relationship when we became more than just friends. Sometimes things are more complicated than you expect."

Rachel studied *Mamm* as questions rushed through her mind. What difficulties did her parents have to face when they were first together? "I had no idea, *Mamm*."

"You don't need to worry about that. We worked things out, and it was for the better in the end." *Mamm* looked up at Rachel and smiled. "Don't fight God's plan for you. It will work out the way it's supposed to."

"I know." Rachel held the pan as her mother poured the batter into it. *Mamm*'s words tumbled through her mind. She knew God had the right plan for her, but she couldn't stop the anxiety that gripped her whenever she thought about Mike. She enjoyed talking to him and getting to know him, but the fear of another broken heart caused her to restrain the feelings threatening to take over her heart.

MIKE GUIDED THE HORSE UP THE ROCK DRIVEWAY TOWARD the large barn behind the Lantz farmhouse. He brought the horse to a stop, and John leaped from the buggy.

"I can't wait to tell *Dat* I made a leash!" John rushed toward the back porch.

Mike grinned as he climbed out and began to unhitch his horse.

Sam appeared beside him.

"I wasn't expecting to see you today," Mike said, but then noticed Sam's buggy next to his *onkel's*.

"*Mei mamm* mentioned she and Marie were coming over today. *Dat* came too. Since Mandy and I were in the area visiting one of her *freinden*, we thought we'd stop by and see your *dat* as well." Sam nodded toward the house and began helping Mike with his horse.

"How has he been today?" Mike asked.

When Sam frowned, Mike's stomach clenched.

"*Mamm* said all he's done is sleep. I've never seen him this worn out." Sam shook his head. "Marie and Janie told Mandy and me he was getting worse, but we had no idea he was getting this bad."

Mike nodded. "The dialysis has been taking a lot out of him lately."

"What are the doctors saying about his condition?" Sam asked as he helped Mike stow the buggy in the barn.

"He's just very weak, and his heart is getting weaker. There isn't anything they can do." Mike stepped out of the barn and led his horse to the pasture. "We just have to keep praying for him."

"I definitely keep your *dat* in my prayers." Sam leaned on the fence. "*Mei mamm* said you went to visit a *freind*. Who did you go to see?"

"John wanted to visit his teacher." Mike leaned on the fence across from him. "He wanted to thank her for tutoring him. She spent the last few Saturdays here giving him extra help. She says he'll soon be the top student in the class."

Sam lifted his eyebrows. "Did you go see that *schee* teacher who came to visit you at the shop awhile back?"

Mike nodded. "*Ya*, Rachel Fisher."

"So you like her?" A smile twitched at the corners of Sam's mouth.

"No, I didn't say I liked her," Mike said a little too quickly. "John wanted to visit her."

Who was he trying to kid? He never was a good liar. He was always the student caught when the boys tried to pull a prank in school. In fact, Mike was the only one who had to stay after and clean the schoolhouse when the boys put frogs in a couple of the girls' desks. It was Mike's expression that gave him away when the teacher asked who had brought the frogs in from the pond behind the schoolhouse.

Sam chuckled. "You are as transparent as the blue sky above us, Mike. You like her."

Mike rested his elbow on the fence. "Sure, I like her. She's a great teacher, and she's done wonders with John. You should hear him read aloud. He's more confident, and he's doing well with all his schoolwork. He's even behaving in class and on the playground, which wasn't the case when he first started there. He's like a new *kind*. I'm so thankful for all her hard work with him."

Sam continued to grin. "And she's *schee*. Isn't she the one who was sending meals home with John?"

"How'd you know about that?" Mike asked.

"*Mei schweschdere* keep *mei mamm* informed, and she shares everything with *mei dat* and Mandy. It always finds its way back to me." Sam lifted his straw hat and ran his hand through his light brown hair. "It sounds like Rachel cares a lot about you and John."

"*Ya,* she does care a lot about John, and I appreciate it." Mike turned his gaze toward the pasture where the horses pranced and played in the late-afternoon sun. "She's a *wunderbaar* teacher." *And I wish I could get to know her even better.*

"I'm so *froh* for you."

"What?" Mike turned toward his cousin.

"You finally found someone. Mandy wanted to introduce you to one of her *freinden,* but I told her to give you time. I knew you'd eventually find someone."

"No, no." Mike shook his head. "We're not seeing each other. I only went to see her so John could thank her. It was his idea."

"I knew that *bu* was *schmaert.* He even wants to see you *froh* and with a *gut maedel.*"

"It's not like that," Mike insisted. "John is attached to her because she's made a difference in his life. She's given him confidence he never had with his last teacher. That's all it is. It has nothing to do with me. I just enjoy talking to her. She's very sweet, and she's a *gut* listener. She's a *gut freind.*"

Sam wagged a finger at Mike. "You don't see it yet, but it's there."

"What's there?" Mike regretted ever discussing Rachel with Sam. His cousin was blowing Mike's friendship with Rachel out of proportion.

Sam tapped the fence. "I had a feeling the first time I saw you talking to her at the shop, and even when you told me about your argument, you had a sparkle in your eyes."

"What are you talking about?" Mike gave him a withering

look. "You didn't see us while we argued. We didn't like each other at all. Why would you have a feeling about a *maedel* who couldn't stand me?"

Sam grinned. "The attraction was there from the beginning. You just wait and see."

Mike shook his head and opened the gate. "You've got it all wrong. We're just *freinden*. Besides, I don't have time to even think about dating. You agree *mei dat* isn't doing well. I can't take my focus off him right now. The most important jobs I have are taking care of *Dat* and John. I can't jeopardize them by thinking about a *maedel*." He started toward the house, and Sam caught up with him to walk by his side.

"Mike, no one expects you to stop living," Sam said. "We're all helping you with your *dat* and John. Besides, you're doing a great job taking care of things. Your *mamm* and Vera would both be so proud of you."

Mike swallowed at the mention of his mother and stepmother. "I'm just doing what I'm supposed to do, and that's take care of my family."

The back door opened, and Mandy appeared on the porch. She was petite and pretty with light brown hair and hazel eyes. Her hands flew to her abdomen where they cradled a bump shielded by her royal blue dress. Mike was so happy for Sam and his growing family. Although Sam and Mandy had participated in different youth groups, they had met through mutual friends and quickly fallen in love. Mike hoped he could someday enjoy a happy marriage like his cousin had with his wife.

"Hi, Mike," Mandy called with a warm smile. "Are you hungry?"

"I'm always hungry."

Sam patted Mike's shoulder. "Let's get something to eat."

As Mike walked with Sam toward the back door, he wondered if his cousin had been right. Did Mike deserve to be happy or was he selfish to dream of having someone like Rachel by his side? Although doubt lingered in his mind, he also wondered if Rachel was developing feelings for him.

Could Rachel ever love someone like him? Would she consider taking on someone who already had so many responsibilities?

CHAPTER 16

"It's so nice to see you," Rachel said to Lena Zook's mother. "I'm so glad you could come to our school picnic today. It's a wonderful way to end the school week."

"I wouldn't miss it." Marian Zook smiled down at Lena, who had wrapped herself around her mother's arm. "Isn't it *schee* out today?"

"*Ya*, it is. It's difficult to believe next week will be May." Rachel glanced across the playground, where the rest of her class and the students in the larger schoolhouse ate lunch with family members. She saw John sitting with Mike, and her smile widened. She hadn't seen Mike since he'd visited her at her farm last Saturday.

"The school year will be over before we know it," Marian continued. "Lena has had a *gut* year with you and Malinda. I'm grateful for all you've done to help her."

"I have enjoyed it very much." Rachel smiled at the little girl. "I'm glad you're in my class."

Marian pointed to the blanket she'd spread out on the ground. "Let's sit and have our lunch. Do you want to join us, Rachel?"

Rachel turned back toward where John and Mike sat, and they both waved.

"Thank you so much for the invitation," Rachel said to Marian. "But I see someone I need to talk with." Marian nodded, and Rachel made her way through the knot of students and parents, smiling and nodding greetings as she worked her way toward the far end of the playground.

When she reached John and Mike, John patted the blanket beside him.

"Sit with us," John said.

"*Danki.*" Rachel sat down on the blanket and smoothed her green dress over her legs. The sun warmed her cheeks as she smiled at Mike. "I'm glad you could make it today. Your note said Janie would probably come in your place."

"I stayed late last night and was able to finish up my jobs so I could come today." Mike unwrapped a tuna fish sandwich. "Would you like half of my sandwich?"

"*Ya, danki.*" Rachel took the sandwich and noticed her basket sitting on the blanket beside Mike.

Mike followed her glance and pointed. "We used your basket to pack our lunch today. *Danki* for the meals you sent this week."

"*Gern gschehne.*" Rachel took a bite of the sandwich and then swallowed.

"You really don't have to send us meals," Mike said with a shy smile. "My cousins take care of most of the cooking, and I don't want you to feel as if you need to spend the money and the time cooking for us."

"I enjoy cooking for you." Rachel realized what she'd said, and her cheeks flamed with embarrassment. She hadn't meant to make it sound as if she wanted to cook for him permanently—like as his wife. Would Mike think she was being forward or assuming they were more than friends?

Mike continued to eat his sandwich, and she breathed a sigh of relief. He didn't seem to have gotten the wrong impression.

"How has your week been?" Mike asked before taking a drink of water. His bright eyes reminded her of the clear blue sky above them. He took another bottle of water from the basket, opened it, and handed it to her. John was watching some of the other children who had started a game of tag.

"It's been *gut*. How about yours?"

"It's been busy." He placed his bottle on the blanket beside him and crossed one of his long legs over the other. "I've made several wishing wells this week. A couple of local businesses asked for them. Apparently they are the new trend." He took another bite.

"That's great that you're keeping up with a trend."

John leaned over and yanked at Rachel's sleeve. "May I go play? I finished my sandwich." He held up his empty sandwich wrapper and pointed to a group of children gathered by the open area where they played softball. They had begun to divide up into teams.

Rachel looked at Mike, who nodded. "*Ya*, you may go."

John stuffed his wrapper and napkins in the basket and ran off toward the group of children. As Rachel chewed a bite from her sandwich, she saw a team captain choose John for her team.

"It looks like he's getting along with the other *kinner*," Mike said.

"*Ya*, he is. The other *kinner* like him. He does well when they play softball."

Relief softened his features. "I was worried he didn't have any *freinden*."

Rachel smiled. "He has *freinden*."

As Mike watched his brother play ball, Rachel saw Malinda talking to another parent on the other side of the playground. When Malinda looked her way, Rachel smiled and waved, but Malinda only gave Rachel a curious expression.

"What are you doing tomorrow?" Mike suddenly asked.

"What's that?" Rachel turned toward him, wondering if she had heard him correctly.

"I asked you what you're doing tomorrow," he explained as he rested his arm on his bent knee. "Do you have plans tomorrow afternoon?"

"No." Her mouth dried with anticipation. What was he going to ask her?

"Would you like to go on a picnic?" He gestured toward the blanket. "I mean a real picnic that's not in a playground." Then his eyes widened and his words came out in a rush. "Not that this hasn't been nice. It's been great. I was just wondering if you would like to go on a picnic with me." Embarrassment covered his handsome face. "And John will be there too, of course."

Rachel bit back a giggle. Mike looked adorable when he was flustered.

"I don't think that invitation came out quite right," he said. Then he grinned, and a giggle escaped her lips.

She clamped her hand over her mouth.

"Don't hold it back," he said. "You have a great laugh."

Rachel looked down at the worn blue blanket as the tips of her ears flamed.

"Let me try this again." Mike cleared his throat. "Would you please go on a picnic with John and me tomorrow? I thought we could go down to that pond I told you about where I fell out of the fishing boat."

Rachel met his gaze, and he gave her a hopeful expression. "What about your *dat*?" she asked.

"Marie is coming over to work on the garden tomorrow. She said she'll take care of him while we're gone." Mike fingered the bottle of water in his hands. "He'll be fine."

Had Mike asked his cousin to take care of his father so he could spend time with her? Rachel's stomach fluttered at the possibility of spending more time with Mike. She'd thought about him every day since they'd seen each other on Saturday.

"So what do you think?" Mike asked again, his eyes begging her to say yes.

"What would you like me to pack for our lunch?" she asked.

Mike grinned, and she prayed he wouldn't break her fragile heart.

RACHEL GRIPPED THE PICNIC BASKET HANDLES AS MIKE guided the horse down the rocky lane the following afternoon. Butterflies danced in her stomach as she glanced over at Mike's handsome profile. She'd been awake most of last night planning out what she'd pack in her mother's picnic basket and worrying about how Mike felt about her. Did Mike like her as more than a friend? If so, then was this their first official outing as a couple?

"The pond is straight ahead." John leaned over the bench from the rear of the buggy and pointed, breaking through Rachel's mental tirade. "Sometimes I go fishing there with Mike, *Onkel* Tim, and Sam. *Mei dat* can't fish anymore, but I went with him a couple of times when I was four."

"You remember that?" Mike gave him a sideways glance.

"*Ya.*" John looked incredulous. "Why wouldn't I?" He slipped into the back of the buggy.

Rachel and Mike exchanged smiles, and her heart felt like it was turning over in her chest as Mike turned his focus back on the road ahead of them.

Rachel had thought about their picnic all morning. She hurried through her morning chores before packing lunch and calling for a ride over to Mike's farm. When she arrived she talked to Marie for a few minutes before Mike hitched up the horse and they started off toward the pond.

"Maybe you can go fishing with us sometime," John said, leaning over the seat again. "*Onkel* Tim has a small boat. We could borrow it and go out some Saturday afternoon."

Rachel turned toward Mike, who raised his eyebrows. "That sounds nice," she said.

"Great." John clapped. "I haven't been fishing in a long time. It's so fun. I caught a fish that was bigger than my two hands." He held out his hands. "It was so big!"

Rachel grinned. "That's amazing! Maybe we can try to get a bigger one when we go."

"We'll see if we can work out a day sometime soon." Mike gave her a thankful smile. He guided the horse up another rocky path, and the pond came into view. He brought the horse to a stop by a small picnic table. "*Mei dat* and *onkel* put this picnic table here a few years ago. We always liked coming here, so we thought we'd make it more conducive to picnics."

They climbed out of the buggy, and Mike tied the horse to a nearby tree. Rachel set the picnic basket on the table and pulled out a tablecloth. Then she brought out three roast beef sandwiches, a bag of pretzels, and a thermos of lemonade.

"This is nice." Mike sidled up to her, and she breathed in his smell—this time soap mixed with earth and sunshine. He pulled the cups out of the basket. "*Danki* for bringing such delicious food."

"You're welcome."

"I could get used to this," Mike quipped as a grin slid across his face.

Rachel's pulse surged. *What does he mean by that? My food? Or spending time together?*

"John," Mike called. His younger brother was tossing stones into the pond. "Let's eat and then you can play."

John trotted over, and Rachel sat down across from them at the picnic table. After a silent prayer, they began eating.

"Do you like throwing stones into the pond?" Rachel asked.

John's head bobbed up and down as he chewed, then swallowed. "I like to make big splashes. I play a game where I try to make the splash bigger each time."

"That sounds like fun." Rachel swiped a pretzel from the bag. "*Mei schweschder* Veronica is an expert at skipping stones."

"Oh?" John tilted his head. "I don't know how to do that."

"I'll have to show you." Rachel lifted her sandwich. "I'm not an expert, but Veronica is."

"Maybe your *schweschder* can show me sometime." John turned toward Mike. "We should invite Rachel's whole family to come on a picnic, and Veronica can teach us all to skip stones."

Mike nodded. "We can talk about that."

Rachel studied John's excited face. She hoped she could continue her relationship with the boy. Would they still be friends after he returned to the schoolhouse in his district? Would she still be friends with Mike? Her hope blossomed at the question.

"So, John," Rachel began, "you've told me you like to fish, and I know you like to play softball. What else do you like to do?"

"Well . . ." John rubbed his chin. "I do like to climb trees. One time I climbed a tree that was as tall as the barn!"

Rachel and Mike finished their lunch as John launched into his tree-climbing story. Mike grinned and shook his head as his little brother spoke.

Soon John had finished his sandwich as well, plus a few handfuls of pretzels. Rachel pulled out a plate of brownies for dessert, and as they ate John told more stories about some of his outdoor adventures.

"I'm going to go play, okay?" John asked, brushing his hands together after finishing his brownie.

"*Ya.*" Mike dropped John's napkins into the basket. "Don't fall into the water."

John stood. "I wish we could do this all the time. I like it when the three of us are together. It's almost like we're a family."

Rachel turned toward Mike, and something that resembled panic flashed in his expression and then disappeared. Had John's comment made him uncomfortable?

John trotted off toward the water and began picking up stones.

Mike stood and then came around the table, slipping onto the bench beside Rachel. "You're so *gut* with him."

"*Danki*." Rachel shrugged casually, even though she was keenly aware of Mike sitting beside her. "I just try to talk to John at his level, but not be condescending. I try to remember what I was like when I was six and what I liked to talk about." His arm accidentally brushed hers, and she swallowed a gasp.

"You were born to be a teacher. It's your gift. I was watching the other *kinner* interact with you at the picnic yesterday, and they all gravitated to you, even the *kinner* from the big schoolhouse." Mike swiped a brownie from the plate and broke it in half, then offered her one of the halves.

Rachel took the brownie and broke off a smaller piece as she considered his words. He was watching her yesterday?

"You look stunned." Mike swiveled toward her.

"I just never considered myself a natural teacher." She popped the quarter of brownie into her mouth and watched John toss stones into the pond. Her thoughts drifted to David and how different her life would have been if they had stayed together and gotten engaged. For the first time since they broke up, she didn't feel sadness and regret. Instead, she felt as if she had a new beginning full of possibilities. A smile crept across her lips.

"You look like you're planning to do something devious."

Rachel turned to face Mike, who cocked an eyebrow. "I was just thinking."

"Oh?" He snatched another brownie. "These brownies are just too *appeditlich*. Are you trying to fatten me up?"

"Now why would I do that?" she teased and broke off a corner of the piece of brownie he had shared with her. She enjoyed joking around with Mike. David had always been so serious. He rarely understood her jokes, and if she teased him he would ignore her or become angry.

"So what were you thinking?" Mike asked.

Rachel brushed some crumbs off the tablecloth and onto the

ground as she thought about how much of her past she was ready to share. Then as she looked into Mike's warm eyes, she found the strength to share the truth about why she became a teacher.

"I told you I thought I'd be engaged by now and planning a wedding in the fall." He nodded, and she continued, "I was dating someone. His name was David, and we'd been together for four years."

Mike raised both of his eyebrows and studied her. "Four years. That's a long time."

"*Ya*, it is." Rachel rested her elbow on the table and her chin on her palm. "We went to school together, and we're in the same church district. I was certain we were going to be married and grow old together, but that wasn't what he wanted." She recalled the scene at Veronica's wedding, but it suddenly didn't feel as painful as it had a few weeks ago. "The breakup was completely unexpected. I overheard him talking with my best *freind* the day of my sister's wedding."

"What did you hear?" he asked.

"She asked him when he was going to break up with me so he could be with her."

"*Ach*, no." Mike looked pained. "I'm so sorry."

"Thanks." She brushed more crumbs off the tablecloth to avoid his concerned expression. "I was devastated, but my family took care of me. Malinda's former co-teacher had gotten married, and Malinda was looking for someone to help her out since John was going to join the class. She asked me if I would help her as a way to start fresh and get my mind off what David and Sharon had done." She looked to where John was playing with a couple of sticks. "I hadn't thought about teaching until Malinda asked me."

"I'm glad she did." Mike's voice was full of warmth, and Rachel's nerve endings tingled at the sound.

Rachel smiled at him. "I am too."

They were silent for a moment as they both turned toward

John. Rachel's mind spun with thoughts of Mike and his brother. She realized she was thankful David had changed his mind about her. He had unknowingly changed her life by setting her free.

"You were with David for four years," Mike said, more as a statement than a question.

Rachel nodded, wondering where Mike was going with his observation. "That's right."

"I dated a *maedel* for about two months when I was seventeen." Mike's smile seemed embarrassed as he leaned his elbow on the tabletop. "My stepmother passed away when I was eighteen, and I haven't dated anyone since then. After she died, my life changed completely, and I stopped going to youth group and spending time with other young people. My best *freinden* are my cousins. I have *freinden* at work, but my cousins are the ones who have been there for me in the tough times."

Rachel nodded slowly, taking in his words. "That had to be so difficult for you."

Mike broke another brownie in half. "Losing Vera, my stepmother, was one of the most difficult things I ever went through. I really never thought much about giving up my time with *mei freinden*. I was most concerned about John and *mei dat.*"

He flicked a pile of crumbs off the table. "*Mei dat* was broken when *mei mamm* died when I was ten, and it was just as bad when Vera died, if not worse. When he married Vera, he told me he felt like he'd finally gotten his life back. He'd wanted to give me a *mamm*, and he also wanted to have more *kinner*. Vera was the answer to his most fervent prayers, and then two years after they started their life together, just when they were going to have a child, he lost her. He was completely crushed." He shook his head, and his frown deepened. "I didn't know what to say to *mei dat*, so I just tried to take care of everything I could. I figured that by helping him, I was carrying some of his burden."

Rachel's chest constricted with sympathy. "I'm so sorry."

Mike looked out toward the pond.

"How has your *dat* been this week?" she asked, longing to read his thoughts.

"He gets weaker all the time." He stared off toward John as his expression became grimmer. "I'm really concerned, but I'm doing my best to shield my worry from John. I don't want to upset him."

Rachel fought the urge to place her hand on his arm to comfort him. "I'm sorry."

Mike gave a brisk nod and then glanced up toward the sky. "It's so *schee* out today. And next week it will be May. The year is passing quickly, *ya*?"

"*Ya*." Rachel suppressed a disappointing frown as she studied his sad eyes. She longed for Mike to share more of his feelings instead of discussing the weather and season to avoid what was truly in his heart.

"Rachel!" When she turned to look, she saw John tenting his hand over his eyes to block the bright sun. "Would you show me how to skip stones now?"

"I'll try." Rachel stood and smoothed the skirt of her blue dress. "Do you know how to skip stones?" she asked Mike.

"I'm not an expert like your *schweschder*, but I've been known to skip a few." He walked with her toward the pond.

"Okay, John." Rachel leaned down and perused the bank of the pond. "First, you find a flat stone."

"I HAD A *WUNDERBAAR* TIME." RACHEL STOOD WITH MIKE beside the passenger door of the van later that afternoon.

After skipping stones for nearly an hour, they had gone back to the house, where they talked on the porch for the rest of the afternoon. It had been such a wonderful afternoon that Rachel didn't want it to end. She had laughed until her side ached while they were skipping stones and then she enjoyed the quiet conversation with Mike. But now it was time to go home and help her mother and Emily.

"*Danki* for inviting me to go on the picnic with you and John."

"You know, it wasn't my idea to invite you. It was all John's idea." Mike's eyes twinkled with mischief as a smile played at the corners of his mouth.

"Oh, is that right?" Rachel enjoyed seeing this teasing side of Mike. She longed to see it more often. "Well, since John is doing his chores, I will thank him for the picnic when I see him at school on Monday."

"That's a *gut* idea." Mike paused and his expression became serious. "I had a great time. *Danki* for bringing more *appeditlich* food for us to eat. I still think you're trying to make me fat."

Rachel chuckled. "No, that's not true."

They studied each other, and something unspoken passed between them. Rachel's breath hitched in her chest. Did Mike like her, truly like her as more than a friend?

"Would you like to join me at my youth gathering tomorrow night?" The question burst from her lips before she could stop it. Then she held her breath, awaiting his response.

"I'm sorry." He shook his head and frowned. "I can't."

Rachel's hope deflated like a balloon. *Oh no. I've been too forward, just like I was with David.* "I understand." Her voice was soft and shaky. She gestured toward the van. "I need to get home and help *mei mamm* and Emily with chores. I'll see you soon."

Mike nodded and opened the passenger door for her. After greeting her driver, Charlotte Campbell, he turned toward Rachel. "Have a *gut* evening."

Rachel waved before he closed the door.

During the ride back to her house, Rachel stared out the

window and silently analyzed the events of the day. Had she misread Mike's teasing for flirting? Did he only want to be friends?

Regret boiled in her gut. She'd allowed herself to get too wrapped up in Mike's and John's lives, just as Malinda had warned her she might. When would she learn to stop trying to force love and marriage?

"Are you all right?" Charlotte asked, giving Rachel a sideways glance.

"*Ya*, I'm fine." Rachel forced a smile. "How is your family?"

Charlotte began to discuss her grandchildren, and Rachel smiled and nodded. Her thoughts, however, were still stuck with Mike and her confusion over their friendship. Had she done something wrong today or had she misinterpreted Mike's behavior toward her?

Rachel's mind whirled with questions as the van bumped down the road toward her farm. She longed to stop the familiar apprehension and dread that seized her chest. Mike was her friend, and she could be satisfied with only being his friend.

Rachel closed her eyes and sucked in a deep breath. She had to find a way to convince herself that any romantic feelings for Mike were immature and pointless.

Deep in her soul, however, that seemed like an impossible task.

CHAPTER 17

"HOW WAS YOUR PICNIC YESTERDAY?" SAM ASKED MIKE AS THEY converted benches into tables after the Sunday church service.

"How did you know about the picnic?" Mike was immediately aware of what a stupid question that was. Naturally, Marie told her *mamm* about the picnic, and then the news spread throughout the family as if a match had been dropped on the barn floor during a dry summer.

Sam shook his head as they lifted another bench. "Do you really have to ask how I know? Marie talked to Mandy, of course."

"Right. It was *gut*." Mike slipped his end of the bench into the stand. "We went out to the pond and talked, and then Rachel taught John how to skip stones. After that, we came back to the *haus* and sat on the porch and talked. It was nice." He shrugged, deliberately downplaying how wonderful the day had been.

As they lifted another bench, Sam grinned. "It was nice, huh?"

Mike ignored the smile and trained his eyes on the bench. "*Ya,* it was nice."

"Is that why you looked so distracted during the service?" Sam asked as they slid the bench into the stand.

"What do you mean?" Mike followed him to a corner of the barn. "I wasn't distracted. I was concentrating on the message."

Sam crossed his arms over his white shirt. "You looked like you were staring off into space. Were you thinking about Rachel instead of listening to the sermons?"

Mike blinked. Sam was right. As much as Mike had tried to concentrate on the minister's and bishop's holy words, his thoughts had remained with Rachel and how much he had enjoyed their afternoon together.

When he closed his eyes during the prayer, he found himself recalling every detail of her face and beautiful smile. After praying for his father's health, he thanked God for bringing Rachel into his and John's life. It was as if something warm and beautiful had taken root in Mike's soul, and a new sensation he'd never felt before seeped through his veins.

Was he in love with Rachel?

"So, I'm right, *ya?*" Sam's grin deepened.

Mike ran his hand down his face. "*Ya,* she has been on my mind." Had the rest of the congregation also noticed his lack of concentration? Worry overwhelmed him. He didn't want to embarrass *Dat* or the rest of his family.

Besides, he knew it would never work between him and Rachel. His life was too complicated.

"I think that's fantastic." Sam patted Mike's shoulder. "Rachel seems like a great *maedel.*" His smile collapsed. "*Was iss letz?*"

Mike glanced around to make certain no one was listening. "I really like her, Sam. I like her a lot."

"That's *wunderbaar.*" Sam stepped closer to him and lowered his voice. "Let's go outside and talk away from the others."

Mike followed him outside, smiling and nodding as women walked past them carrying trays piled high with food and supplies for the noon meal. They stood behind the barn, and Sam gave Mike a concerned expression.

"Why aren't you *froh* about Rachel?" he asked, keeping his voice low.

Mike leaned against the barn wall. "I'm not unhappy. I'm just realistic. It will never work between us."

"Rachel obviously likes you if she spent the afternoon with you." Sam rubbed his beard, a gesture Mike was accustomed to seeing when his cousin was trying to figure out a riddle. "I don't understand what the problem is."

"I don't have room in my life for a *maedel* right now." Mike glanced toward the pasture behind the barn. "*Dat* isn't doing well, and I don't think things are going to get much better. Didn't you notice how weak he was when you said good morning to him before the service? I need to focus on taking care of him and John, not trying to find a *fraa*."

"You don't need to feel rushed with Rachel," Sam said. "You can take your time. Let your relationship grow naturally. You don't need to decide today whether it's going to work. You should just get to know her and see where the relationship goes. If it's meant to be, then God will guide your path to her."

Mike pondered his cousin's words, but doubt continued to roil in his gut. "I care about her, but it's better if I let go of any romantic feelings and just be her *freind*."

"Have you ever felt this way about another *maedel* before?"

Mike shook his head. "No, but I've never really dated before."

"I think you're missing the bigger picture here," Sam insisted. "You told me she's wonderful with John. She's just what you and John need. You might regret letting her go."

"I didn't say I was going to let her go," Mike insisted. "I just need to find a way to stop thinking about her."

"Why would you want to stop thinking about her? That's just *narrisch*."

Mike folded his arms over his chest as the pieces clicked into place. "Yesterday she asked me to join her for a youth gathering, and I told her I couldn't."

"Why would you say no?" Sam asked.

"While we were eating lunch, John said he wanted the three

of us to spend more time together. He said it was as if we were a family." Mike blew out a long breath. "That was when I realized John and I have become too attached to Rachel. I can't risk getting any closer to her and then having things fall apart. John has already lost his *mamm*. I can't run the risk of dating Rachel and then breaking up. It would be too painful for John. That's why I have to take a step back from her. I can't let it go any further. I have to protect John."

Sam shook his head. "You can't let your fear get the best of you, Mike."

"Are you two going to eat?"

Mike turned and found Mandy watching them from the corner of the barn.

"The men are sitting down," she said, sounding insistent. "Your fathers are looking for you."

"We'll be right there," Sam said, his smile returning as he studied his wife.

"Okay." Mandy hesitated for a moment, and she absently rubbed her abdomen. "Is everything all right?"

"*Ya*," Sam said. "Everything is fine."

"We'll be right there," Mike promised, forcing a smile.

Mandy studied them for another moment longer and then disappeared around the corner.

"We'd better go eat," Sam said. "Just make me one promise."

Mike nodded. "Sure."

"Don't give up on Rachel just yet. God has a way of surprising us with his plans." Sam started toward the front of the barn. "I'm starved."

Mike lingered behind Sam for a moment as he considered his cousin's words. If being with Rachel was God's plan, then why did he feel such hesitation holding him back?

"Rach?" Emily appeared in Rachel's doorway dressed in a purple frock. "Are you ready? It's time to go."

"You go ahead without me." Rachel placed the devotional she'd been reading on her bedside table. "I'm going to stay home tonight."

"Why?" Emily's forehead puckered with concern as she crossed the large room and sat on the edge of Rachel's bed. "Are you ill?"

"No." Rachel ran her fingers over her maroon Log Cabin design quilt as she leaned back against the headboard. "I just feel like staying home today. You can tell me all about the youth gathering when you get home."

"There's something you're not telling me, Rach." Emily tilted her head. "Are you worried about running into David and Sharon? You don't need to feel embarrassed around them. You did nothing wrong. They're the ones who hurt you, so you don't have to hide at home and feel ashamed around them."

"It's not that." Rachel sighed. "I don't feel ashamed, and it doesn't bother me anymore when I see them. I just feel like staying home today." How could she admit she didn't want to go to the youth gathering if Mike wasn't there? Saying those words aloud would sound so immature.

"What's going on?" Emily touched her hand. "This isn't like you. You've never shied away from going to see our *freinden*."

Rachel gnawed her lower lip and met her sister's concerned expression. She couldn't keep the truth from Emily any longer. It was time to tell Emily how Mike had hurt her feelings yesterday. "I already told you I had a *gut* time with Mike and John yesterday."

Emily nodded, and concern filled her pretty face. "You said you and Mike really got to know each other."

"We had fun, but I made the mistake of asking him to go to youth group with me. He said no." Rachel turned her eyes to the quilt to avoid her sister's expression. "I just feel so stupid and imma-ture. I thought he liked me, and I misread his behavior, just as I did with David. I can't stand the idea of going to youth group and see-ing other couples talking. It will remind me of the mistakes I made with David and now with Mike. I get anxious and I mess things up. That's why I'm alone." Her voice quavered.

"You're too hard on yourself. Just because he said no to going to youth group doesn't necessarily mean he doesn't like you." Emily clucked her tongue. "I can't stand seeing you this unhappy. Come with me and we'll have fun. All our girlfriends will be there. You don't need to be with Mike to have fun. We have fun together too."

She took Rachel's hand and gave it a quick tug, but Rachel didn't move. "Let's go. We have to leave now or we're going to be late. I already have the buggy hitched up."

"No, I really don't want to go out tonight." Rachel shook her head and yanked her hand back. "I've been giving it a lot of thought since yesterday, and I feel like I have to figure some things out. I feel as if something isn't right. I don't know what's wrong with me. I guess I'm just too focused on getting married after all."

She sniffed as tears stung her eyes. "I need to stay away from the youth gatherings before I develop a crush on another man and then wind up with a broken heart again. I'm a detriment to myself."

"*Ach*, Rachel." Emily lightly squeezed her arm. "You don't really mean that. You haven't done anything wrong."

"Girls?" *Mamm* stepped into the doorway. "You're going to be late if you don't head out now." Her eyes widened as she studied Rachel. "*Was iss letz?*" She crossed the room and stood over Rachel. "Are you crying?"

"No." Rachel shook her head, but then wiped away more tears. "I don't feel like going tonight."

"Why not?" *Mamm* pulled a chair over to the bed.

Rachel repeated the conversation she'd had with Emily.

"*Ach, mei liewe,*" *Mamm* began with a sigh. "You worry too much. Mike may have his own reasons for not going to youth group, but that doesn't mean he doesn't like you. You have been a *gut freind* to him, and I'm certain he's thankful for your friendship. Just give him time."

Rachel cleared her throat and took a shuddering breath. "He told me he hasn't dated much. He dated a *maedel* for two months when he was seventeen. He was stunned to hear I dated David for four years."

"That's why you need to give him time," *Mamm* said. "Just be his *freind* and see where it leads. I imagine he'll eventually want to come to youth group, but you have to remember he has a lot of responsibilities with his *dat*. It's not as easy for him to go to youth group when he has to take care of his *dat* and John."

Rachel nodded. "I know. I just hoped we had become closer yesterday. I hoped maybe his cousin would take care of his father so he could come to the youth group, like his family did so we could go on the picnic." She grimaced, realizing how that had sounded. "I didn't mean to be so selfish. I just wanted more time with Mike."

Mamm rubbed her arm. "I understand. It's the excitement of new love. When you first fall in love, you want to spend every minute of every day together. It's natural."

Rachel's throat dried. "In love?" She gulped. "I don't love Mike." Did she love him?

Oh no.

Her chest tightened as the reality hit her. She was falling in love with Mike. All of the signs were there. Thoughts of him drifted through her mind during the day. No wonder she didn't want to go to youth group without him. She wanted to spend all her free time with him.

Rachel closed her eyes and swallowed a groan.

"You should go to youth group with Emily," *Mamm* continued. "Don't sit here alone and worry about how Mike feels about you. You're young, and you need to be with your *freinden*."

Rachel shook her head.

Emily scowled before grabbing Rachel's hand and pulling her to her feet. "Let's go. We're late as it is."

Rachel teetered and then righted herself.

"I can always count on you to get things done, Emily," *Mamm* quipped.

Rachel sighed with defeat. Emily wouldn't give up until she got the answer she wanted. "Fine. I'll go."

Emily gave a little cheer as she pulled Rachel into the hallway.

"You two have fun," *Mamm* said as she followed them down the stairs.

"We're going to have a great time," Emily said as they climbed into the buggy. "I can't wait to see Malinda. She told me after church that she met a *bu* from another youth group. I wonder if he'll be there. I can't remember his name. Did she tell you about him? He's someone's *bruder*, and apparently he's really handsome."

Rachel stared out the window as Emily talked on about their friends. She wondered what Mike was doing and if he was thinking about her. *Mamm* was right when she said Rachel was falling in love with Mike. A feeling of dread slithered through her. Rachel had been determined not to give her love away so quickly, but she'd managed to do it anyway.

Now what am I going to do?

As she turned back toward her smiling sister, Rachel hugged her arms to her chest as if to guard her heart. She longed to be more like Emily, the sister who smiled no matter what life threw her way.

If only Rachel could turn off her feelings for Mike. She bit her lower lip. Maybe she wasn't supposed to turn them off. What if she was meant to teach Mike how to love despite all the challenges he had in his life?

Her stomach fluttered as the thought came into focus. God could have brought Rachel into Mike's life for a reason, a reason that went beyond helping his brother. Rachel could be the one to show Mike what true love with a partner in life could be like.

She would take her mother's advice and give him time, but she would also continue to reach out to him and encourage him. She gripped the buggy door as excitement overtook her. Maybe, just maybe, she and Mike could find happiness together.

CHAPTER 18

"THANK YOU." MIKE PAID THE POST OFFICE CLERK AND pocketed the book of stamps. "Have a good afternoon."

As he walked toward the exit, he heard a familiar voice. He glanced toward the mail slots and saw Rachel and Emily talking as Emily placed stamps on envelopes. A smile spread across his lips. It had been two long weeks since he'd gone on the picnic with Rachel.

He'd missed her. Although they hadn't spoken, Rachel continued to send delicious meals to them in her basket and write encouraging notes in John's journal about his progress at school.

"Rachel," he said as he stepped toward her.

Rachel glanced up from the stack of mail, and her eyes widened with surprise. Was that also excitement he saw?

"Mike."

She looked beautiful in her teal frock and black apron. He'd forgotten how gorgeous her deep brown eyes were. Why hadn't he made the effort to see her during the past two weeks? He'd longed to spend time with her, but he'd been too preoccupied with keeping up at work and caring for *Dat* at home.

Or was it because he feared the deep emotions that had taken root inside of him the day of the picnic by the pond?

"Hi, Mike." Emily gave him a little wave, yanking him from his thoughts. He nodded a greeting, but his eyes were immediately pulled back to Rachel.

"How have you been?" he asked her, resting a hand on the counter where they were working.

Rachel smiled, and her face lit up. Oh, how he had missed her smile.

"I've been fine. How about you?"

"*Gut, gut.* We've enjoyed the meals you've sent home," he said. "*Danki.*"

A look passed between the sisters, and Rachel's cheeks blushed a bright pink. She was adorable.

"I'm glad you liked them," Rachel said. "Emily and I have had fun preparing them."

"You've done most of the cooking, Rach," Emily said. "Don't give me any credit."

Mike pointed toward the envelopes. "So are you here for stamps too?" He pulled the book from his pocket and held it up.

"*Ya,* that's right." Rachel nodded. "We were running a few errands, so we thought we'd mail the bills for our *mamm.*"

"I was doing errands too." He jammed a thumb toward the door. "I'm actually working today. Ever since it got warm, we've been overloaded with orders. The May weather has done wonders for our business. We can't seem to get caught up, so I'm working for the next few Saturdays."

"What time do you get off work?" Emily asked, and Rachel shot her an incredulous expression.

"I'm hoping to leave at four. Why?"

"You should come over for supper tonight," Emily said.

Rachel's eyebrows careened toward her hairline as she stared at her sister.

"Our *schweschder* Veronica and her husband are coming," Emily continued, ignoring her sister's alarmed expression. "You can meet them."

The sisters seemed to share a silent conversation with their eyes, and then Rachel suddenly smiled.

"That's a great idea," Rachel agreed. "Can you go home and

pick up your *dat* and John? We'd love to have your family meet our whole family."

Mike was surprised by Rachel's hopeful expression. "Are you sure? I don't want to impose on your family time."

"Don't be *gegisch*," Rachel said, waving off the comment. "It will be fun."

"*Ya*," Emily chimed in.

"All right. *Danki*." Mike rubbed his chin. "I'll arrange for my driver to bring us over to your farm. Do you need me to bring dessert or anything?"

"No," Rachel said. "We'll take care of all that. You just bring your family. We're going to eat around six."

"Sounds great." He stuck the book of stamps back in his pocket. "I'll see you then."

Mike walked out the door as a smile turned up the corners of his mouth. He couldn't wait to see Rachel later this evening. He was thankful their paths had crossed today. He just hoped *Dat* would feel well enough to go.

Rachel watched as Mike disappeared through the post office door and then turned toward Emily. "What made you invite him over for supper tonight?"

Emily shrugged as she stuck stamps on the remaining envelopes. "I'm tired of seeing you mope around the house, so I decided to take matters into my own hands."

"I haven't been moping," Rachel insisted. "I've just been giving Mike some space. And I've been busy sending the meals over so he sees I care about him and his family."

"That's great, but you have to see him too." Emily stamped the last letter and then slipped the pile into the slot.

"I know that," Rachel said with annoyance. "But I didn't want

THE COURTSHIP BASKET

to invite myself over to his *haus*. That would make me look too eager."

"That's why I did it. There's nothing wrong with inviting him to have supper with our family," Emily said. "And I invited him instead of you, so that makes you look like you're not too eager."

Rachel grinned. *"Danki."*

"Gern gschehne. That's what *schweschdere* are for." Emily shrugged. "I'm glad I can help you. I just want to see you *froh* like Veronica is."

Rachel tilted her head and studied her sister. "Why are you so worried about helping me get to know Mike if you aren't dating anyone? You always take care of everyone else, Em, but you never worry about yourself. Shouldn't I help you find someone special too?"

Emily shook her head. "I'm not really looking. I feel like it will happen when the time is right."

"But you've never had a boyfriend. There has to be someone you like at youth group," Rachel pressed.

"No, there really isn't anyone. I want a boyfriend I can really talk to, but I haven't met anyone at youth group I connect with. But it's okay. Like I said, I'll find the right person when it's my time to date." Emily looped her arm around Rachel's shoulder. "Now, let's get to the grocery store so we can pick up the ingredients for supper."

"Hello, hello!" Veronica's voice rang through the kitchen later that afternoon. She hefted a large tote bag onto the table.

"Veronica!" Rachel called from her place standing at the counter. *"Wie geht's!"*

"It's so *gut* to see you." *Mamm* rushed over to her and hugged her. "Where's Jason?"

"He went out to the shop to talk to *Dat*." Veronica gestured toward the bag. "I brought four pies. You have your choice of

209

chocolate, lemon meringue, shoofly, and rhubarb custard. I did quite a bit of baking this week now that my bake stand is up and running."

Emily began to unload the pies from the bag. "I'm glad you brought four. We're having company for supper."

"Oh *ya*?" Veronica looked surprised. "Who's coming?"

"Mike Lantz and his *dat* and *bruder*." Emily elbowed Rachel.

"Stop, Em." Rachel's cheeks were hot with embarrassment as Veronica placed her hand on her hip and her eyes twinkled.

"Do you have a new boyfriend, Rach?" Veronica touched Rachel's arm. "Tell me all about him."

"He's just a *freind*," Rachel said with a noncommittal shrug. "His *bruder* is in my class."

"They're really *gut freinden*," Emily said. "She's not telling you the whole story."

"I'll make tea," *Mamm* said, moving to the counter. "The pork roast is in the oven, so we can talk before we make the mashed potatoes."

Veronica dropped into a chair at the table and gestured for Rachel to sit beside her. "*Kumm*. Tell me all about Mike."

Rachel shot Emily an annoyed expression, but Emily only smiled as she brought four mugs to the table.

"Stop glaring at me, Rach," Emily said, handing her a mug. "Veronica is going to meet Mike tonight, so you might as well fill her in."

"Mike is a very nice young man," *Mamm* chimed in as she delivered the sweetener and cream to the table. "He's caring for his ill father and his little *bruder*, who is in Rachel's class."

"Oh," Veronica said with interest. "Where does Mike work?"

Rachel shared where Mike worked, explained his father's illness, and talked about working with John on his studies. "John has really improved on his schoolwork and his behavior. I enjoy having him in my class."

"It sounds like you really like teaching," Veronica commented.

"I do." Rachel sat up a little taller. "I want to keep teaching there next year. I'm so grateful Malinda asked me to work with her."

"I can't wait to meet Mike and his family." Veronica set her elbow on the table and rested her chin on her palm.

Emily brought the kettle to the table and filled their mugs. "I think Mike really likes Rachel. He seemed excited when I invited him over for supper."

Rachel's stomach pitched with both excitement and dread when she thought about supper. She hoped it would go well and Mike would want to continue their friendship. Had he missed her as much as she had missed him during the past two weeks?

"So how have you been?" Emily asked Veronica.

Rachel swallowed a sigh of relief when the focus was taken away from her. She stirred sweetener and cream into her cup. She was thankful to share tea with her mother and sisters.

"I've been *gut*." Veronica lifted her mug. "Jason has been really busy at the shop, and I've been baking lots of pies. Quite a few people have come by to give me orders. I'm really *froh* with the bake stand Jason and his *dat* built for me. I get a lot of traffic on Saturdays. I already have some regular customers."

As Veronica continued to talk about her bake stand, Rachel lost herself in thoughts of Mike. The sweet aroma of the spring breeze coming through the open windows mixed with the smell of the baking pork roast permeated the kitchen. She hoped Mike's father was well enough to come to supper tonight and that their families would enjoy their time together.

MIKE HURRIED UP THE BACK STEPS SHORTLY BEFORE FIVE o'clock. He had rushed through his projects at work as quickly as he could in hopes of getting home early. When a customer came in at a quarter to four to discuss ordering a set of planters for his business, however, Mike's plans to leave early went up in smoke.

He rushed through the mudroom and entered the kitchen, where Marie was sitting at the table and looking at a book with John.

"Hi, Mike," John called.

"How was work?" Marie asked.

"*Gut.*" Mike gestured toward the doorway behind her. "How's my *dat*?"

Marie frowned. "He's been napping all afternoon in his recliner."

"Oh," Mike said as dread settled heavily on his shoulders. "I ran into Rachel and Emily at the post office, and they invited us over for supper."

"Rachel invited us over for supper?" John asked, his expression brightening with excitement.

"*Ya*, she did. Do you think *Dat* is well enough to go, Marie?"

"I don't know." She looked skeptical. "I tried to talk him into sitting on the porch with me since it's so *schee* outside, but he insisted he was too weak."

Mike cupped his hand on the back of his neck. All afternoon he'd wondered if *Dat* would be well enough to go out to Rachel's house for supper. He didn't want to disappoint John, and he also didn't want to disappoint Rachel. And he'd been looking forward to seeing her ever since the day they'd gone on the picnic.

Of course he would never risk his father's health, but he wanted his family to enjoy an evening with Rachel's family too.

"I'm going to check on him," Mike said, crossing the kitchen floor. He stood in the doorway to the family room and found *Dat* with his eyes closed. "*Dat*," he said quietly. "Are you awake?"

"Michael." *Dat*'s voice was barely a whisper. "How was work?"

"It was *gut*. Busy." Mike sat in the chair across from his. "How are you doing?"

"Tired." *Dat* ran his hand over his graying beard. "I was

hoping to maybe sit outside. Marie wanted me to. But I just don't have the strength."

Mike scowled as his dream of having supper at Rachel's house dissolved. He tried to shove away the disappointment. He had to take care of *Dat*, which was why he had to stop dreaming of dating Rachel and having a future with her.

"What's on your mind?" *Dat* asked.

"Nothing." Mike shook his head and forced a smile. "What would you like me to make you for supper?"

"You're making supper?" Mike looked up to see John pouting in the doorway. "I thought we were all going to Rachel's *haus* for supper."

"John," Mike began, "what have I told you about eavesdropping? You shouldn't listen in to conversations when you're not invited."

"Why aren't we going to Rachel's *haus*?" John crossed the room and glared at Mike. "You said we would all go."

Mike blew out a frustrated sigh and rubbed the bridge of his nose. He couldn't stand disappointing his brother. "No, I didn't say that. I said we'd been invited. *Dat* isn't feeling well. We can have supper with Rachel and her family another time, all right?"

"You can go," *Dat* said. "You and John go and have a *gut* time. I can stay here."

"I'm not leaving you alone," Mike insisted. "We'll stay home with you."

"No." *Dat* shook his head. "I can't stand holding you back, Mike. Go and have supper with Rachel."

"Why can't you come, *Dat*?" John took *Dat*'s hand in his. "We'll bring your wheelchair with us. I can help you climb the steps into Rachel's *haus*." He tugged at *Dat*'s hand. "Let's go, *Dat*. I don't want to go without you."

Mike's chest constricted as his little brother pleaded with their father. How he longed for *Dat* to be healthy.

Dat's lower lip trembled, and Mike held his breath, hoping his father wouldn't cry. "I'll go," *Dat* whispered.

John jumped up and down and clapped his hands. "I'll get your shoes, *Dat*." He rushed out of the room, his own shoes pounding on the hardwood floors.

Dat turned toward Mike and wiped his fingers over his tired eyes. "I can't say no to that *bu*."

"I know the feeling," Mike said with a smile.

RACHEL'S PULSE SPED UP WHEN SHE HEARD THE CRUNCH OF tires on the rock driveway.

"I think they're here," Veronica said, peering out the window above the sink. "There's a white van in the driveway."

"You go greet them, and I'll finish setting the table," Emily said, shooing Rachel away with a wave of her hand.

"Thanks." Rachel placed the last dish on the table and then rushed out the back door. She wiped her hands down her black apron as she stood on the back steps.

Her father and her brother-in-law, Jason, walked over to the van. After shaking hands with Mike and his father, they helped Raymond out of the van and into his wheelchair, which the three men then lifted to the sidewalk leading to the back porch.

John hopped out of the van and rushed toward the house, waving. "Hi, Rachel!"

"Hi, John," she said. "I'm so glad you could come tonight."

"I am too. *Mei dat* wasn't feeling well, but I asked him to come. I told him I didn't want to come without him." He pointed toward his father.

Mike pushed the chair toward the house as he talked with Jason and her father. Raymond looked thin, but he smiled at Rachel. She waved, and he raised his hand.

"I'm so glad to see all three of you." Rachel gestured toward the house. "You can go inside and choose a seat in the kitchen. We put the leaf in the table so we have plenty of room for everyone."

John hurried into the house.

"Hi, Mike," Rachel said as they approached the porch. When Mike smiled at her, happiness washed over her. She turned her attention to his father. "Raymond, it's so *gut* to see you."

"It's *gut* to see you too," Raymond said, his voice quavering.

He seemed weaker and paler than the last time she'd seen him. Her chest compressed with concern for him.

"Can I help you up the stairs?" her father offered. "I'll take your arm."

"I'll help too," Jason offered.

Rachel took a step back as her father and brother-in-law helped Raymond slowly climb the stairs. She held her breath, hoping Raymond would make it to the porch without collapsing. His slim legs trembled, but her father and Jason held him up more steadily than his slight body could.

Mike stood behind them and watched his father intently. She could feel his unspoken concern. Once his father was safely on the porch, Mike carried the wheelchair up, and Jason and *Dat* helped Raymond sit down.

"We're so glad you came tonight, Raymond," *Dat* said. "Let's head inside. Mattie made a pork roast and mashed potatoes and the *haus* smells heavenly."

Jason held the door open, and *Dat* and Raymond disappeared inside. Jason followed, and the screen door clicked shut behind them. Their muffled voices sounded inside the house, and Rachel and Mike were left alone on the porch.

"Hi," Mike said, stepping toward her.

"Hi," she said with a smile as her pulse zipped through her with delight.

"*Danki* for inviting us tonight." He leaned against the porch railing, lifted his hat, and pushed his sandy blond hair back.

A grin taunted the corners of her mouth as she recalled the joke he made about the picnic. "It wasn't my idea. It was Emily's idea to invite you tonight."

He chuckled, and his eyes twinkled with mirth. "Is that so? Just like the picnic, huh?"

"That's right."

They stared at each other for a moment, still smiling, and she felt as if their friendship had suddenly deepened to a new level.

"I wasn't sure we were going to make it," he finally said. "*Mei dat* hasn't been feeling well, and he tried to convince John and me to come alone. But John insisted *Dat* come with us."

"John told me your *dat* wasn't feeling well." Rachel pondered sharing her concern over his father's health but decided to keep it to herself. She didn't want to add to Mike's anguish. "I'm thankful you're here. I wanted you to meet the rest of my family."

"Jason is very friendly," Mike observed.

"*Ya*, he's *wunderbaar* to Veronica. I'm grateful she has him."

Mike studied her with an unreadable expression, and Rachel moved her hands over her apron. She hoped she looked presentable.

"It's really *gut* to see you," he said softly.

Rachel gave him a tentative smile as a thrill buzzed through her. Had he missed her as much as she'd missed him?

"Rachel? Mike?" *Mamm* appeared in the doorway. "We're ready to eat. The food is on the table."

"Oh." Rachel's cheeks flushed with embarrassment. "We're coming now."

Mike moved ahead of her and greeted her mother before holding the door open for Rachel. They stepped through the mudroom and into the kitchen, where the two families were already seated and platters of food dotted the long table.

Rachel took a seat beside Veronica, and Mike sat next to his father on the opposite side of the table. After a silent prayer, arms resembling a large octopus reached for the platters. The clink of utensils scraping plates and conversations that broke out around the table overtook the room.

Rachel watched Mike fill his father's plate with food, and then her chest squeezed as he cut up the meat for his *dat*. Then he whispered something to his father, who nodded. Raymond lifted the fork, and his hand trembled as he stabbed at the meat. For a moment, Rachel wondered if Mike was going to have to feed Raymond, but he slowly fed himself.

"So, Mike," Jason began, "you do woodworking for a living. I build sheds."

Mike nodded. "Rachel told me that. I make lawn ornaments—lighthouses, planters, that sort of thing. How long have you done shed building?"

Rachel smiled as Mike and her brother-in-law discussed their work. She felt someone watching her, and she turned to find Emily grinning. At the far end of the table, John was talking to her father. Happiness flooded her soul. She'd hoped Mike and his family would enjoy spending time with hers, including Veronica and Jason, and they had blended in as if they had been friends with the Fishers for years.

If only Raymond could return to good health. The sorrow in Mike's eyes broke her heart.

CHAPTER 19

MIKE RUBBED HIS STOMACH AS HE SAT ON THE BACK PORCH with Jason, Leroy, and his father. A warm breeze saturated the air with the aroma of flowers and dirt as John tossed a ball up in the air on the driveway.

"I am stuffed," Mike announced. "Everything was *appeditlich*."

"I can't get enough of my *fraa*'s pies," Jason said, rocking in the chair beside Mike. "She thinks I built her a bake stand on our property so she can sell her pies. The real reason is I want her to feel inspired to keep making them for me." He chuckled.

Leroy joined in the laughter. "You're a *schmaert* man, Jason." He turned toward Mike's father. "Raymond, how long ago did you start Bird-in-Hand Builders?"

While the two fathers began discussing their businesses, Mike turned to Jason. "Do you work at the shed place just up on Old Philadelphia Pike?"

"*Ya*. It's close to your shop."

Mike nodded. "That's right. Where is your farm?"

"I live in Gordonville. How about you?"

"I live a few miles away in Ronks."

"Oh *ya*?" Jason smiled. "I go to a hardware store over there pretty often."

As the two men fell into an easy conversation, Mike's shoulders relaxed. He was thankful he and his family clicked with Rachel's family. He just hoped she felt the same way.

"MIKE IS SO NICE," VERONICA SAID AS SHE WASHED A PLATE in the frothy water. "John is adorable."

"*Ya*, I know." Rachel dried a bowl and set it on the counter.

Veronica smiled over at Rachel. "Mike really likes you too."

Rachel could feel the weight of her older sister's stare as she concentrated on drying another dish.

"Rach?" Veronica prodded her. "Did you see how he was watching you during supper?"

"Shh," Rachel hissed, glancing toward the open window. "They're all sitting on the porch. I don't want them to hear you."

"They won't," Emily insisted as she swept the floor. "They're talking about work. They're not paying any attention."

Rachel turned back toward her older sister. "You really think he likes me?" she whispered.

Veronica nodded. "Absolutely. He seemed to hang on your every word."

"I agree," *Mamm* chimed in as she wiped off the table. "He definitely likes you, Rachel. I don't know what you're worried about."

"What do you mean?" Veronica asked, her smile fading. "You've been worried he doesn't care about you?"

Rachel placed the dry dish on the pile on the counter. "I've been worried he doesn't care about me the same way I care about him."

"You love him," Veronica said quietly.

Rachel nodded. "*Ya*, I do. And I didn't want to fall in love so quickly after losing David."

"Mike is not like David," Emily said. "Mike is much warmer and more in tune with you. David was always so aloof and disconnected."

"I thought the same thing, but I never said it," *Mamm* commented, agreeing with Emily. "David always seemed as if he wanted different things than what you did, Rachel. I never saw David look at you with the love I saw in Mike's eyes tonight."

Rachel's throat dried. "Love?" she gasped.

Mamm nodded, and Emily grinned as she rushed over to Rachel.

"Shh!" Rachel shushed them again. "They're going to hear you."

"No, they won't," Emily insisted again, hugging her. "I'm so *froh* for you."

"Just take it slowly," Veronica warned. "Mike will eventually ask you to be his girlfriend, but give him time."

"And don't give up on him," Emily added. "He definitely has his hands full with his *dat*, but he cares about you. I'm sure of it."

Rachel's head spun like a buggy wheel as her mother and sisters continued to pepper her with unsolicited advice. *Doesn't Veronica remember how she felt when we were all giving her advice about Jason!*

She nodded as they talked, but her mind was stuck on one detail—they all agreed that Mike loved her. But did he really love her? And if so, would he tell her soon?

MIKE GLANCED OVER AT HIS FATHER, WHO WAS NODDING AS Leroy spoke to him. *Dat's* eyes looked dull, lacking the sparkle he'd witnessed earlier.

"Are you all right?" Jason asked. "You look upset."

"It looks like *mei dat* has had enough excitement for one night," Mike said. "As much as I hate to say it, I think I'd better get him home."

"*Ach, ya.*" Jason glanced toward Mike's father. "He does look tired. You'd better call your driver." He stood. "I'll show you where the phone is."

"*Danki.*" Mike followed Jason to the phone shanty next to the barn and called his driver.

After Mike hung up, Jason leaned his back against the shanty. "So you like Rachel, huh?"

Mike smiled. "*Ya,* I do."

"I'm *froh* to hear that." Jason pulled a toothpick from his pocket. "Did you hear what her former boyfriend did to her?"

Mike grimaced. "*Ya*, that was terrible." He rested his hand on the shanty door.

"Rachel was really heartbroken when he broke up with her, and Veronica was upset too. It was tough on the family because Rachel and David had been together a long time." Jason shook his head and rubbed the beard on his chin. "I can't believe David did that, but *mei mamm* said they probably grew apart. Four years is a long time to be together when you're so young, but that's the time to find out you're not right for each other."

Mike glanced toward the porch, where his father still sat beside Leroy, and absently wondered what it would be like to be a member of this family.

"I knew Veronica's former fiancé," Jason continued. "He and I were best *freinden*, and he told me how amazing Veronica was. We worked together, and then he died in an accident at work."

"He had an accident at work?" Mike asked with a gasp. "Was he building a shed?"

"*Ya*, that's right," Jason said. "I was there when he died."

"*Ach*, no," Mike said, shaking his head. "I remember now. I heard about that accident. It was horrible."

"It was." Jason's eyes flickered with sadness. "I saw Veronica at the funeral, but I hadn't officially met her. I met her a couple of months later when I came to her bake stand here. It was love at first sight. Well, at least it was for me." He rolled his eyes and laughed. "I know that sounds so lame."

Mike laughed along with him. "You two seem really *froh* together."

"We are." Jason grinned. "Veronica is the best thing that's ever happened to me."

Mike thought about Rachel and nodded. "I know the feeling.

I'm just trying to figure out how to work things out with Rachel and take care of my father at the same time. His health is failing faster than I ever imagined it would."

"I think Rachel would be willing to help you with your father if you gave her a chance. The Fisher *maed* are *wunderbaar*." Jason started walking toward the house. "I'll help you get your father down the stairs and into the van."

"I appreciate it." They climbed the porch steps, and Mike went inside. He stuck his head into the kitchen, where the women were still cleaning up. "*Danki* again for supper. Everything was *appeditlich*."

The women spun to face him.

"Are you leaving?" Rachel asked, her smile fading to a frown.

"*Ya*." Mike pointed toward the porch. "*Mei dat* is worn out. I need to get him home."

"Oh." Rachel walked toward him with apparent disappointment twisting her pretty face. "I'll walk outside with you." Was she as disappointed as he was that he had to leave?

Emily, Veronica, and Mattie said good-bye before he followed Rachel out to the porch.

"I'm sorry we didn't get to talk more," Rachel said. "If I had known you were going to leave, I would've come outside with you."

"It's okay," Mike replied. "I was enjoying getting to know Jason and your *dat*. Your family is great."

"They like you too," she said, her expression bashful. "*Danki* for coming over tonight. We need to do this again soon."

"Absolutely," he said. He wanted that more than he could say.

The hum of an engine drew his attention to the driveway, where the white van came to a stop. Why did his driver have to arrive so quickly?

"I guess you'd better get going," she said. Her expression seemed to be mirroring what he imagined was his own.

"Let me help you down the steps," Jason said, approaching Mike's father. "It was really nice meeting you, Raymond."

Mike touched Rachel's hand, and heat rushed to the place where their skin met. "*Danki* again. I won't let two weeks pass before I see you again."

Rachel's eyes widened as a smile found the corners of her pretty mouth. "I'm going to hold you to that promise."

"Mike, would you please get the wheelchair?" Jason asked.

"*Ya*," Mike called over his shoulder. Then he looked back at Rachel. "*Gut nacht*."

"*Gut nacht*," she whispered. Her eyes were warm, and his chest constricted. He was falling in love with her.

"I HAD A GUT TIME TONIGHT," DAT SAID AS MIKE HELPED him to his bed. "Rachel and her family are very nice."

"*Ya*, they are." Mike held *Dat*'s arm until he was settled on the edge of the bed. "I'm glad you came with us."

Dat gave him a weak smile. "You love Rachel."

Mike dropped into the chair beside the bed and breathed in deeply through his nose. "*Ya*, I do."

"I'm glad." *Dat* patted Mike's arm with his bony hand. "I remember when I met your *mamm*. We were younger than you. We met at a youth group gathering and became *freinden*, but really, when I saw her across the barn, I knew I would marry her."

Mike chuckled to himself remembering Jason's comment about love at first sight.

"Her *freinden* introduced us and we got to know each other enough to become *freinden* ourselves. But it wasn't too long before we started dating." *Dat* had a faraway look in his eyes. "We were married the following fall and then we had you a year later. It seems like it was only yesterday."

He turned to focus on Mike. "You should go to Rachel's youth group meeting and get to know her better. She's *gut* for you. She loves John, and she'll be *gut* to you both."

"I don't need to go to youth group," Mike insisted. "I'm fine here with you, and that's where I need to be."

Dat shook his head. "You're just as stubborn as your *mamm* was."

"You need your rest." Mike pointed toward the bed. "I'll see you in the morning."

After *Dat* lay down, Mike tucked him in. Then he extinguished the lanterns and climbed the stairs. After tucking John in, he trudged to his room next door. He changed into a fresh pair of boxers and a T-shirt, turned off his lanterns, and climbed into bed.

Mike stared at the ceiling as he contemplated the evening at Rachel's house. He tried to close his eyes and fall asleep, but his mind was stuck on her smile and her gorgeous, deep-chocolate eyes. He was definitely falling in love with her, but apprehension twisted in his gut. He was no longer worried about things falling apart if he and Rachel got together. He felt sure now that Rachel felt the same way about him.

But how could he make room in his life for Rachel when *Dat*'s health was failing?

"OKAY, SCHOLARS," RACHEL SAID AS SHE STOOD IN FRONT of the class. "Gather up your lunch pails and bags. It's time to go home. Have a nice evening. We'll see you tomorrow."

The students scurried out the door where Malinda stood saying good-bye to them. Rachel straightened the desk, fetched her favorite red pen, and picked up a stack of math worksheets to grade.

She was marking a worksheet when she heard a familiar voice

in the doorway. Glancing up, she saw Mike talking with Malinda, and Rachel's stomach twisted with anguish. Why was Mike off from work early to pick up John? Had something happened to Raymond?

"Mike," she said, rushing to the front of the classroom.

"Hi, Rachel." Mike greeted her with a warm smile. "How are you?"

"I'm fine," she said. "I'm surprised to see you here. Is everything all right?"

"*Ya*, everything is fine. I got off work early today and thought I'd surprise John." Mike mussed his brother's blond hair. "We were just talking about going out for ice cream. Would you like to come with us?"

"We're going to the Lapp farm," John said, rubbing his hands together. "Please come with us, Teacher Rachel."

Rachel grimaced. As much as she wanted to go, she didn't feel right leaving all the paperwork and cleanup to Malinda. "I would love to, John, but I have to grade papers and prepare the lessons for tomorrow."

Malinda placed her hand on Rachel's arm. "Go."

Rachel gave Malinda an incredulous expression. "I don't feel right leaving you with all the work. I can go out for ice cream with them another time."

"It's fine." Malinda gave her a knowing smile. "You can make up for it next week, and I'll let you plan the lessons."

Rachel smiled. "*Danki*."

"THIS WAS UNEXPECTED," RACHEL SAID AS SHE SAT AT A TABLE with John and Mike. She licked her vanilla cone, savoring the sweet taste.

"I wanted to do something fun with you and John today." Mike glanced down at John. "How's the chocolate?"

"Chocolaty!" John grinned, revealing his chocolate-covered teeth. His mouth was also outlined in the ice cream.

Rachel chuckled as she wiped her own mouth with a paper napkin. "You certainly do enjoy your ice cream."

Mike grinned and then licked his butter pecan treat. "It's been a long time since we've done something like this. *Mei dat* always loved Lapp's ice cream."

"Are we going to take him some?" John asked between licks.

"He's not supposed to have it, but I might take home a pint as a surprise." Mike took another lick.

John stood. "May I go look at the animals?" he asked.

"*Ya.*" Mike nodded. "We'll come and find you when we're done eating."

"Okay!" John trotted off toward the barns.

"How is your butter pecan?" Rachel asked.

"It's fantastic." Mike took another lick before speaking again. "*Danki* for the meals you sent Monday and Wednesday. We've really enjoyed them, and *mei dat* is still talking about how much fun he had at supper Saturday night."

"I'm glad you enjoyed them," Rachel said. "I was wondering if I could bring a meal over to you tomorrow night after school."

"You don't have to do that." Mike shook his head. "You've already done too much."

"I enjoy it," Rachel said. "I thought it would be easier if I brought the meal to you this week so your *dat* doesn't have to travel."

"Rachel," Mike began, "you've done so much for our family already. I don't feel right accepting another meal from you, especially during a weekday. You work all day and then you want to bring a meal to us. That's just too much."

Rachel shook her head. "I disagree. That's what we do in our community. We take care of each other. Besides, it's a Friday. I'll have the food already prepped, so I just have to stop at home and get it before coming over. It's not a problem."

She held her breath while he considered her offer. She and Emily had been planning a meal Rachel could take to the Lantz family Friday night. This time the meal was Rachel's idea, but Emily offered to help with the cooking since she would have time to prepare the food between her chores and her shift at the harness shop.

"I suppose it's all right if you bring a meal," Mike finally said. "But I feel like I need to do something for you."

"You already are. You're allowing me to spend time with you and your family." Rachel felt a blush begin at the base of her neck and move up to her ears.

"I feel like I owe you more than that," Mike said. "Spending time with me can't be nearly enough payment for all you've done for John and me." He licked his cone.

"It is." Rachel longed for her cheeks to cool down.

They ate their ice cream in silence for a few minutes, and then their cones were gone.

"Should we find John?" Mike offered.

"Okay."

They threw their paper napkins in the trash can and strolled toward the barns.

"It's such a *schee* day," Rachel said, walking beside him. "This was a special treat."

"It was for me too." Mike stopped and looked down at her, his eyes glittering with a mixture of appreciation and something resembling affection. "I promised you I wouldn't let two weeks go by before seeing you again."

"*Ya*, you did." Her heart raced as she studied the fondness in his eyes.

"Rachel," he began, his voice warm and smooth. "I'm really thankful for your friendship. I'm enjoying getting to know you."

Rachel's breath paused, and her eyes widened. "I'm enjoying getting to know you too."

"*Gut.*" He gave her a nervous smile before pointing toward the barns. "I suppose we'd better go."

As they walked, Rachel suppressed a cry of joy. Her mother and sisters had been right. Mike did like her. She looked forward to where their friendship would lead.

M<small>IKE SAT AT THE KITCHEN TABLE, SORTING THROUGH A STACK</small> of bills. The hum of the water running in the bathroom above him indicated John was taking his bath as he'd been instructed. The sweet smell of the spring breeze filtered through the kitchen from the window above the sink.

Gripping his pen, Mike sifted through the bills for the third time in an attempt to decide which bills to pay, but his mind wasn't concentrating on the due dates. Instead, he was contemplating the time he'd spent at the Lapp farm with Rachel. Picking up John and Rachel after school had been an impulsive decision after Sam insisted Mike leave work early. He'd longed to spend more time with Rachel after visiting her home Saturday night, and waiting until Thursday had been tough enough.

Every day that passed without seeing her felt like torture. He was falling in love with her. He longed to tell her how he felt about her, but he didn't know how to form the words. Something was holding him back from sharing his deepest thoughts and feelings.

It had taken every ounce of Mike's emotional strength just to tell Rachel he was enjoying getting to know her. He was thankful she hadn't rejected him. As they walked together toward the barns to find John, Mike had thought about holding her hand, but he didn't want to move too quickly or appear too forward. She seemed comfortable with him, and he hoped their friendship would continue to progress.

He tried in vain to turn his attention back to the bills, but his mind continued to recall his outing with Rachel. He was staring at the checkbook when a crash sounded from somewhere in the house.

Mike leapt up from the chair, knocking it over with a clatter as it hit the kitchen floor.

"*Dat!*" He ran into his father's bedroom. "*Dat!*"

"Michael." His father's shaky voice sounded from the small bathroom off the bedroom.

Mike hurried to the bathroom and opened the door. He gasped when he found his father sprawled on the floor with blood pooling under his right arm. *Dat* had fallen before, but he'd never seen that amount of blood. The sight sent terror clawing at his neck.

"Oh, *Dat*," he gasped. "You're bleeding! Should I call nine-one-one?"

"No, no." *Dat* shook his head. "Just help me up." He reached for Mike with his left arm.

Mike took his father's arm and hefted him onto the commode. "What hurts?" he asked, examining his bloodied arm.

"I think I scraped my arm." *Dat* slumped on the seat, placing his arm on the sink beside him. "I thought I could make it to the bathroom myself."

"You should have called me," Mike said gently. "I'll always help you."

"I know you will, but I want to do things for myself sometimes. I can't stand being a burden to you."

Mike met his father's expression. "You're not a burden." He examined the bloody arm and found a long gash. "This looks pretty bad. You may need stitches."

"Just put a bandage on it." *Dat* waved off Mike's concern. "We can get the nurses to look at it at the dialysis center tomorrow."

Mike cleaned the wound with peroxide and then applied salve to it before covering it with a bandage and taping it.

"Does anything else hurt?" he asked, studying his father's tired eyes.

"No." *Dat* gave him a grim smile. "Just my dignity."

Mike smiled, and some of the tension in his body eased. "Don't worry about your dignity. Just call me when you need something. I want you to be safe."

"You're a *gut bu.*" *Dat* patted Mike's arm. "John told me you took him and Rachel for ice cream earlier."

"*Ya.*" Mike stood and leaned his arm on the towel rack. "I brought home a pint of vanilla, but you have to ask your doctor if you can have it."

Dat gave him a sad puppy-dog expression. "Ice cream would make my scraped arm feel better."

A bark of laughter escaped Mike's throat. "I know it would, but we have to ask your doctor first. If he says your labs are *gut*, then you can probably have some when you get home from dialysis tomorrow." He lifted *Dat* to his feet. "Let's get you to your chair, and I'll wheel you out to the kitchen. You can have some pretzels instead."

Once *Dat* was settled at the kitchen table, Mike brought him a small bowl of pretzels and sat beside his father while he ate.

"What kind of ice cream did Rachel have?" *Dat* asked between bites of pretzels.

"Rachel likes vanilla," Mike said, absently tracing a finger over the tablecloth.

"She has *gut* taste."

"She's bringing supper over tomorrow night after she gets off work." Mike rested his arms on the table. "I tried to talk her out of it. I told her she's already done too much for us, but she insisted."

"Some people enjoy taking care of others." *Dat* lifted a pretzel from the bowl. "All you have to do is thank her, and she'll feel appreciated."

"I really do love her, *Dat*."

He patted Mike's hand and smiled. "That's obvious, Michael. What I want most is for you and John to be *froh*. Don't let Rachel get away."

Mike pondered *Dat's* words as he finished the pretzels. An unfamiliar sense of hope swelled within his gut, and he silently prayed he could find a way to make a life with Rachel.

CHAPTER 20

RACHEL CLIMBED THE STEPS AND KNOCKED ON MIKE'S BACK door the following evening. The delicious aromas of the creamy noodle and hamburger casserole and chocolate brownies drifted up from her mother's basket, which she held in her arms.

Muffled voices sounded from beyond the door, and Rachel glanced down at her best purple dress, which she'd changed into for the dinner tonight. She hoped everything would be perfect. Hopefully, she could steal a few private moments alone with Mike, and maybe, just maybe, he'd officially ask her to be his girlfriend. Her heart skipped a beat at the thought.

The door opened with a loud *whoosh*, and John stared at her, his eyes round with alarm.

"*Mei dat* is very sick," John said, his words rushed.

Rachel's breath caught in her throat. "*Ach*, no. I'm so sorry to hear this. Do you need me to run to the phone and call nine-one-one?"

"Rachel." Mike appeared behind John. "I'm so sorry. I tried to reach you by phone before you left your *haus*. *Mei dat* is violently ill with flu-like symptoms. He's been ill since he got home from his dialysis treatment earlier today. It would probably be best if you went home." He opened the door and craned his neck to see toward the driveway. "Is your driver still here?"

"No." Rachel shook her head as dread pooled in her belly. "She's already left."

"Oh." Mike's faced was lined with anguish and panic. "I'm sorry. It's just not a *gut* time."

"I made John's favorite." She held up the picnic basket. "It's creamy noodle and hamburger casserole. He told me at school that he loves it. I also made a pan of brownies. Could I at least leave it on the counter?"

"Can she eat with us, Mike?" John begged, folding his hands as if he were praying. "Please, Mike?"

Mike gave him a curt nod. "Fine." He turned and disappeared into the house.

Rachel stood there, feeling off balance. Her plans of spending a nice evening with Mike were ruined. Both regret and concern overwhelmed her. She prayed Raymond would be okay and his symptoms were the result of only minor stomach flu.

"Rachel?" Marie stepped into the doorway.

"Hi, Marie." The weight of the basket caused her arm to ache. "Could I please give you the dinner? Mike said I could come in, but I don't want to impose."

"Don't be *gegisch*." Marie held the screen door open. "You're always welcome here. John has been talking about your visit all afternoon."

"*Danki*." Rachel stepped into the house and followed Marie to the kitchen. She set the basket on the counter and took out the pan of brownies and casserole dish. Mike's muffled voice sounded from somewhere beyond the kitchen.

"*Onkel* Raymond's symptoms came on suddenly," Marie shared while pulling out utensils. "Mike called his doctor, and the doctor told him to give his father some over-the-counter medications. But he doesn't seem to be getting any better, so I'm not sure if he'll have to go to the hospital or not. Dehydration is so dangerous."

"*Ach*, no." Rachel set a stack of dishes on the table as she wondered if she was in the way. "Should I leave?"

"No," John said. "Please stay." He came up behind Rachel and wrapped his arms around her waist.

Rachel's eyes filled with tears. How she loved this little boy. "I'll stay if it's okay with Marie."

"Of course it's okay. Let's eat." Marie's smile seemed forced.

She must be so worried.

Rachel sat down at the table beside John, and Marie sat down across from them. After a silent prayer, they filled their plates with the casserole. The only sound in the room came from the scraping of their utensils on the dishes and the muffled voices in the nearby room. Rachel searched for something to say, but her mind whirled only with concern for Raymond. Her excitement about the meal fizzled out, and the casserole tasted bitter, much like her worry.

"Marie!" Mike's urgent voice bellowed from the hallway beyond the kitchen.

"Excuse me," Marie muttered before hurrying out.

Rachel glanced down at John and forced a smile. "How's your casserole?"

"*Gut.*" John speared another bite with his fork. "Do you think *mei dat* is going to be okay?"

The question hung in the air between them while Rachel searched for an appropriate answer. She couldn't possibly admit she didn't know if he would be okay. She didn't want to add to his apprehension.

"*Ya,*" she finally said, touching his slight shoulder. "I think after he gets the right medicine he'll be fine."

A door squeaked open, and Rachel saw Marie rushing through the hallway before returning with an armful of towels. A door slammed, and voices sounded beyond the walls.

Rachel and John ate in silence. When they were finished with the casserole, Rachel cut the brownies and stacked a few on a plate.

John devoured two brownies while she picked at one. She found herself staring at the doorway, awaiting Mike's return. When he didn't appear, she filled the sink with hot, soapy water and washed the dishes and utensils she and John had used.

"Oh, you don't need to do the dishes," Marie said, sidling up to her. "I can take care of that."

"I don't mind at all." Rachel tried to smile at Marie, but her frown refused to budge. "I'm *froh* to help."

"John, would you please go take your bath?" Marie asked as she dried a dish.

"Okay." John wrapped his arms around Rachel's middle and squeezed her in a tight hug. "*Danki* for supper, Rachel."

"You're welcome, *mei liewe*," Rachel whispered, touching his hair.

John raced out of the kitchen, and Rachel began to wash the utensils, worrying about Mike and Raymond as she worked.

"Mike asked me to tell you he's sorry," Marie said, breaking the silence between them.

"It's not his fault," Rachel said, her voice quavering with emotion.

"He's under a lot of pressure with his *dat*," Marie said, giving her a sideways glance. "I'm sorry we didn't think to call you earlier. We were just so concerned about Raymond."

"I understand." Rachel washed the last spoon and handed it to Marie. "I don't want to be in the way, so I'll get going." She pointed toward the table. "Could I leave the food for Mike?"

"Of course." Marie's lips formed a sad smile. "You've been a blessing to Mike and John. I'm so *froh* you came into their lives."

Rachel nodded as emotion seemed to clog the back of her throat. She didn't feel like much of a blessing. In fact, she felt more like a burden showing up at Mike's house at the most inopportune time. "John can bring the serving dishes to school whenever they finish the casserole and brownies. I'm going to use the phone."

Rachel called her driver and then finished helping Marie clean up the kitchen until the van arrived. During the ride home, Rachel held the basket in her lap and stared out the window while she thought about Mike and sent up prayers for Raymond.

MIKE RUBBED HIS HANDS DOWN HIS FACE AS HE STEPPED INTO the kitchen. "I finally got *Dat* settled into bed." He glanced around and found Marie sitting at the table eating. "Where's Rachel?"

"She went home." Marie sipped from her glass of water. "She washed the dishes she and John used and then called her driver."

Mike slumped into a chair across from Marie as guilt washed over him. "*Ach,* no." He covered his face in his hands. "I didn't mean to completely ignore her, but I was so worried about *mei dat.*"

"She knows that," Marie said, her voice full of empathy. "Don't worry about it. She left food for you." She pushed the casserole dish over to him. "It's amazing. You have to have some. The brownies are *gut* too. I stole a piece off one before I started on the casserole."

Mike stared at the food, but his appetite had evaporated once his father became ill. The thought of eating caused his stomach to sour. "She must be furious with me," he whispered, not meaning to say the words aloud.

"No, I don't think she's angry with you, but I do think she's disappointed." Marie scooped up more casserole with her fork. "She's an adult, Mike. She understands the situation." She tapped his plate with her fork. "You need to eat. We don't need you getting ill next."

He filled his plate and said a silent prayer. But he only pushed the food around on the plate as he thought about Rachel. He'd been looking forward to her visit all day, but *Dat*'s stomach problems had overshadowed the whole evening. He hoped Rachel really wasn't upset with him. He didn't want to hurt her.

Maybe this is the sign that I don't have room in my life for a special maedel *like her.*

The voice in his head startled him and sent more dread coiling in his gut.

"How is your *dat*?" Marie asked, her voice breaking through his worried thoughts.

"He fell asleep." Mike set his fork next to his plate. "He said he couldn't eat. I was glad his stomach settled down."

"Do you think he needs to go to the hospital?" Marie asked.

He shrugged. "I don't think so, but I'll keep an eye on him tonight. I'll sleep on the floor in his room."

Her eyes rounded. "You'll sleep on the floor?"

Mike nodded. "I don't mind it. If he's doing okay, then I'll move to the sofa."

"Don't you have to work tomorrow?"

"*Ya*, I do."

"You need your rest if you're working." Marie pointed to her chest. "I'll sleep on the sofa, and you sleep in your bed. That way you can function at work without accidentally cutting your arm off with a saw."

Mike gave a wry smile at her exaggerated worry. "All right. You can stay tonight, but you need to go home tomorrow and get your rest."

She waved off the comment. "I don't need as much sleep as my siblings do. I'll be fine." She carried her plate to the sink. "You need to eat, Michael. You need your strength for work tomorrow."

As Mike speared a forkful of casserole into his mouth, he reflected on how he could make things up to Rachel. He had to find a way to apologize for not spending time with her tonight.

"I SMELL RAIN IN THE AIR," EMILY SAID AS SHE LOOKED UP at the gray sky. She and Rachel were walking side by side down Old Philadelphia Pike.

Rachel glanced up and took in the dark, foreboding clouds. She breathed in the aroma of warm air and the hint of rain. "*Ya*, you're right. I hope it holds out until after we finish our grocery shopping."

"*Ya*, I do too. Rach, I meant to ask you if you've heard from Mike since last night. Did you check the messages this morning?"

Rachel scowled. "I checked the messages, but he didn't leave one. I've been worried about his *dat* ever since I left their *haus*."

"*Ya*, I was wondering how he's doing too." Emily pointed in front of them toward the Bird-in-Hand Builders sign. "Do you want to stop by and see if Mike's working? Didn't he say he would be working some Saturdays when we saw him at the post office?"

Rachel gnawed her lower lip and remembered her promise to herself not to appear eager or pushy toward men anymore. "Yes, he did. But I don't know . . ."

Emily stopped walking and faced her. "What are you worried about?"

Rachel took a deep breath, wondering how to best express her complicated feelings. "Mike was busy taking care of his *dat* last night, and I backed off and gave him his space. His father needed him, and that's important. If I go into his store to see him today, I don't want to seem like the overbearing and smothering girlfriend."

Emily raised an eyebrow. "Are you officially his girlfriend and you haven't told me?"

"No, no, no!" Rachel shook her head with emphasis. "He hasn't asked me to be his girlfriend, but it feels like he will soon. At least, I hope he will." She folded her arms over her middle. "If I go in to see him, will I seem like I'm too pushy?"

Emily gave her a withering smile. "No, you're just a *gut freind* who is concerned about his *dat*'s health." She took Rachel's hand and tugged. "Let's go see if he's there."

Before Rachel could protest, Emily steered her toward Bird-in-Hand Builders. Rachel couldn't help remembering her last visit there. When they stepped through the front door, the same bell rang, announcing their arrival. And when Rachel and Emily crossed the showroom to the counter, the same Amish man with a brown beard was talking on the phone. He placed his hand over the mouthpiece and raised his eyebrows, perhaps as if to ask what he could do for them.

"We're looking for Mike Lantz," Rachel said.

"Rachel, right?" he asked.

Rachel nodded with surprise. How did he know who she was? Had Mike told him when she was last here? *Oh no.*

"You can go on back." He pointed toward the door leading to the shop.

"*Danki,*" Rachel said. She glanced at Emily as they made their way toward the shop. Her sister was grinning.

"Do you want me to wait here?" Emily offered as they approached the door.

"You can come with me," Rachel insisted, motioning for Emily to follow her.

Rachel pushed the door open and moved through the hallway where she and Mike had argued. She wrenched open the shop door, but she stopped when she saw Mike talking to an Amish girl.

Rachel froze in place. Mike was standing close to the young woman, sharing an evident familiarity with her. Rachel's stomach twisted as Mike touched her arm and then leaned in close and whispered to her. The girl was beautiful, much more striking than Rachel could ever hope to be. Dressed in a dusty rose-colored frock, the young woman had clear porcelain skin, powder-blue eyes, and red hair peeking out from under her prayer cover. The girl touched Mike's arm and then whispered back to him as he nodded in response to whatever she said.

Rachel's stomach soured and bile rose in her throat. Mike

apparently cared about this beautiful young woman. He knew her well, and from the way he touched her arm, she shared more than Rachel could ever share with him.

Rachel hugged her arms around her middle as her body began to shake with a familiar betrayal. It was happening all over again. Mike was seeing another girl behind her back—just as David had done. Mike had taken her heart and smashed it into a million pieces. Their relationship was over before it ever really had a chance to begin.

"Rach," Emily whispered, placing her hand on Rachel's arm. "Calm down."

Rachel pulled away from Emily, turned around, and ran down the hallway and through the showroom. She wove her way through the knot of customers before she banged through the front door. As she hit the sidewalk outside the store, a cool spray of drizzle sprinkled her face, mixing with the warm tears pouring down her cheeks.

"Rachel!" Emily called, rushing after her. "Wait up!"

Rachel slowed her pace, allowing her sister to catch up with her. Emily grabbed Rachel's arm and spun her around.

"Hold on," Emily insisted, huffing and puffing to catch her breath. "You don't know who that woman is. You can't assume Mike is seeing someone else."

"Please, Emily." Rachel spat the words at her. "I'm not stupid." She pointed in the direction of the store. "He obviously is close to that *maedel*. He's never been that intimate with me. He's never whispered to me or touched my arm." She swiped at her angry tears. "He's seeing her. It's just like David. Only it's worse." She sniffed as her voice trembled. "I thought what Mike and I had was going to be something real, more real than what I had with David."

"Stop it." Emily placed her hands on Rachel's forearms. "You shouldn't assume the worst without talking to him first. That *maedel* could be a *gut freind* who is just as concerned as you are about his *dat.*"

"No," Rachel said, her voice louder than she expected. "That *maedel* is *schee.* He obviously cares about her. He cares about her more than he cares about me." Something painful twisted in her chest as she said the words. "She's the reason he hasn't called me to tell me how his *dat* is. He'd rather tell her and be with her instead of with me. I don't blame him."

"You don't know that," Emily said, her voice seeping with frustration. "You always jump to the worst conclusions without getting all the facts. You should give him a chance to explain."

"There's nothing to explain." Rachel yanked her arms out of Emily's grasp and marched toward the grocery store. "Let's get the groceries and go home."

"Rachel." Emily jogged to catch up. "You really should go back there and talk to him."

Rachel ignored her sister and stepped into the grocery store. Taking a deep breath, she poured herself into her shopping list and tried to ignore her fracturing emotions.

MIKE STUCK HIS PAINTBRUSH INTO THE PUNGENT CLEAR stain and moved it over the lighthouse. He worked mechanically as his mind swirled with thoughts of his father. Although *Dat* seemed stronger this morning, he still wasn't able to lift himself out of bed and had developed a cough overnight. Mike didn't like the sound of it. He planned to ask Marie to mention it to the nurses at dialysis on Monday.

Mike offered to stay home, but Marie insisted she could take care of everything. Mike finally agreed to go to work, but he instructed Marie to call him if she needed him to come home.

Mike thought about Rachel as well. He longed to call and

apologize to her, but he'd been so busy since he walked through the door this morning that he hadn't had a chance to get to the phone. He was catching up on his work when Janie stopped by to see him. She'd been worried about his father since she'd heard about his episode last night. Janie was going to head over to his farm to relieve Marie, but she wanted to check in with Mike before she went over there.

"Hey." Sam appeared behind him.

Mike spun to face him. He pushed his mask to the top of his head, placed the lid on the stain, and then balanced the brush on top. "I didn't see you there."

Sam sat on a stool beside Mike. "I was wondering how your visit went with Rachel. I didn't see her leave."

"Rachel?" Mike glanced around the shop. "Where is she? I haven't seen her."

Sam blinked and paused. "Isn't she a pretty brunette with brown eyes?"

Mike nodded. "That's right."

"She had a shorter blonde with her," Sam continued.

"That's her *schweschder* Emily." Mike looked around the shop again. "Where are they? Did you tell them to come back and see me?"

"*Ya*, I did." Sam gave him a befuddled expression. "So, you never saw her?"

"No." Mike shook his head. "I've been back here working. I've only spoken to Janie. When did Rachel stop by?"

Sam craned his neck, turning toward the large clock hanging at the back of the shop. "I guess it's been almost two hours. I wanted to check on you sooner, but it's been crazy up front."

Mike brushed his hands down his blue work shirt as bemusement overtook him. "Why didn't she come in here to talk to me?"

Sam shrugged as he slid off the stool. "I don't know. Maybe you should give her a call?"

"*Ya*, I will after I finish staining this lighthouse." Mike slipped the mask over his nose and mouth and then picked up the paintbrush. Sam waved before heading toward the showroom. While Mike finished staining the lighthouse, he tried to figure out why Rachel had come to the shop to see him but didn't speak to him.

Why would she leave without saying hello? Unless she had planned to tell him she was upset about his ignoring her last night or assumed he was too busy when she saw him working, it just didn't make sense.

CHAPTER 21

RACHEL LEANED DOWN AND WRENCHED ANOTHER HARDY, green weed from the garden. The hot midday sun beat down on her neck, burning into her skin. By the time Rachel and Emily had exited the grocery store, the rain had stopped and the sun had poked out from behind the gray clouds. Rachel refused to answer Emily when she tried to discuss the scene with Mike at the shop during the ride home. Instead, Rachel stared out the van window and held her breath to choke back more threatening tears.

When she arrived home, Rachel helped put away the groceries and then hurried outside. Despite the mud, she'd spent nearly an hour pulling weeds. The tedious task did little to drown her heartache or stop the despair that had taken root in her soul. She'd managed to avoid her mother's and Emily's concerned expressions by telling them she needed to work in her garden. Since then, she'd kept her back bent and her hands working. She didn't want to hear their platitudes or encouragement. Instead, she yearned to stay busy for now. She knew the tears would come as soon as she stopped moving.

"Rachel!" *Mamm* called from the phone shanty. "You have a phone call!"

Rachel brushed hands down her black apron as she stalked through the garden and toward the barn. "Who is it?" she called to her mother.

"It's Mike," *Mamm* said, gesturing to the small shed where the phone was. "I told him I'd get you."

Rachel's throat dried and anguish bit into her shoulder blades at the mention of his name. "Please tell him I can't come to the phone."

Mamm's eyebrows pinched together. "Why would you do that?"

"I can't talk to him." Rachel shook her head. "Please tell him I'm not available or that I went to the store." She squeezed *Mamm*'s arm. "I know it's a sin to lie, but I can't talk to him. Please, *Mamm*, I'm begging you to tell him I'm not here."

Mamm paused, studying Rachel. "Why won't you talk to him?"

"I don't want to get into it right now, *Mamm*." Rachel's voice shook. "I promise I'll explain everything later. Please tell him I can't come to the phone. Tell him I don't feel well and I'm going to my room to lie down. I'll go right now. Please, *Mamm*. I'm begging you."

Mamm shook her head. "I can't believe I have to do this for you. It's just like when Jason was trying so desperately to talk to Veronica, and she wanted me to shoo him away."

Rachel took a deep breath. "Please."

Mamm shook a finger at her as if she were a petulant child. "I'll tell him you're not feeling well, but you're not going to your room. You're going to sit down and explain everything to me when I get off the phone with him."

"All right." Rachel's voice trembled. She stood in the doorway as *Mamm* lifted the receiver to her ear.

"I'm sorry, Mike," *Mamm* said. "Rachel isn't feeling well. Could I give her a message for you?" She listened for a moment. "I will tell her. How's your *dat* doing today? Oh, *gut*. I'm glad he's feeling better. I will pass the message along to Rachel. Good-bye."

She hung up and faced Rachel, a frown turning down the corners of her mouth. "Mike was very disappointed you weren't able to speak with him. He said he was sorry he missed you at the shop."

Rachel gave a derisive snort while crossing her arms over her chest. "Is that right?"

"Rachel," *Mamm* said, shaking her head. "I don't understand what's going on. You said you loved him last Saturday night when he and his family came over for supper. What happened between you two?"

Rachel pointed toward the house. "Could we please go inside and discuss this over a cup of tea?"

Mamm nodded. "Of course."

Twenty minutes later, Rachel cradled a warm cup of tea in her hands as she finished explaining what had happened at the shop. *Mamm* sipped her tea and empathy glimmered in her blue eyes as she listened.

"He betrayed me the same way David did," Rachel said, her voice shaky with fresh emotion. "I thought Mike was different. I thought the friendship he and I were developing was stronger than what David and I had, but I was completely wrong." She sniffed and stared at the tea rippling in her cup like waves in a tiny lake. "I've spent all these weeks cultivating our friendship. I've sent meals over to him, and I've listened when he needed an ear. But in the end, all I've gained is another hole in my heart."

"Ach, mei liewe." *Mamm* reached across the table and rubbed Rachel's hand. "You've done nothing wrong. You have a loving spirit. You've helped his family, and that's what we're called to do."

Rachel blotted her teary eyes with a tissue from her pocket. "I know it's what we're called to do, but why does it hurt so much?"

"I still believe he loves you."

"What?" Rachel's eyes snapped to *Mamm*'s.

"He was truly disappointed when you wouldn't come to the phone," *Mamm* said. "He told me his cousin Sam said you'd stopped

by the shop, and he was sorry he didn't get to see you. He wanted
to apologize for missing you, and he wanted to apologize for not
getting to talk to you last night."

Rachel's thoughts turned to Raymond. "How is his *dat*?"

"He said his *dat* is still weak, but he's in better spirits."

"Oh, *gut*." Rachel cleared her throat while considering Mike's
sudden change in behavior. "I think I misread Mike. I believe he
only wants to be my *freind*. I'm going to still be the best teacher I
can to John, but I need to distance myself from the family. Malinda
warned me not to get too close, and I should've listened to her
from the beginning." She wiped away another wayward tear. "I'll
be all right. I just can't trust myself. I get too attached and then I
wind up hurt."

"You did nothing wrong," *Mamm* repeated while patting her
hand again. "I think you need to talk to him and tell him how
you're feeling. Don't give up on him so easily."

Rachel shook her head. "I can't put myself through any more
pain. I need to back away, at least for a little while."

Mamm nodded. "Fine. Do what feels right, but don't take your
frustration out on John. He's innocent in all of this."

Rachel gaped. "I would never do that. He's my student."

"*Gut*," *Mamm* said before drinking more of her tea.

As Rachel sipped her own tea, the warm liquid seemed a weak
balm for her aching soul. She longed to find comfort to wash away
the pain that tore at her heart.

LATER THAT AFTERNOON RACHEL PACED IN THE KITCHEN.
Although she'd finished washing the lunch dishes, her mind continued to whirl with images of Mike and the pretty redhead at the
shop. Her heart ached with pain over losing Mike, and she needed
something to take her mind off him. She remembered seeing a

stack of devotional books on her mother's dresser when she put clean laundry in her parents' bedroom the other day. She longed to push away the painful thoughts of Mike and his beautiful girlfriend. Maybe a good book would help.

Mamm had gone with Emily to the harness shop to help with the accounting books and she didn't want to bother her. She was sure *Mamm* wouldn't mind if she looked at the books. Rachel walked into her parents' bedroom next to the family room. She found the stack of books still on *Mamm*'s dresser and sifted through them in search of one that would somehow ease her heartache. None of the books piqued her interest, however, and she sank down onto the corner of her parents' bed and covered her face with her hands.

What could she do to keep her thoughts away from Mike? What could possibly take away the sadness that had drowned her the moment she saw Mike talking to that *maedel*?

She dropped her hands in her lap and looked around. Her eyes widened when she saw *Mamm*'s hope chest sitting under the window at the far side of the room. She suddenly remembered that the hope chest had been missing from the attic when she was up there looking for the basket. She wondered why *Mamm* had moved the hope chest downstairs.

This was the same chest where Veronica had found their grandmother's raspberry pie recipe. When had it been moved? *Dat* must have carried it down while Rachel was at school. She wondered if there were any books in the hope chest that could at least serve as a balm to her despair.

Rachel crossed the room and tried to lift the lid, but it was locked. She looked on *Mamm*'s dresser and found a key sitting in a small glass bowl. She slipped it into the lock, turned it, and the lock clicked open.

Rachel pushed up the lid and rummaged through the chest.

She lifted a quilt and saw a cross-stitch pattern in a loop at the bottom of the hope chest. The design had a colorful butterfly bathed in purple, blue, and pink, with words below.

> *Happiness is like a butterfly:*
> *The more you chase it, the more it will elude you,*
> *but if you turn your attention to other things,*
> *it will come and sit quietly on your shoulder.*

Rachel studied the words, taking in their meaning, and tears flooded her eyes. She flipped over the cross-stitch and found a note written in neat cursive writing:

> Mattie, May this warm your new home and your heart.
>
> All my love,
> *Mamm*

Rachel blinked as tears streamed down her cheek. Her grandmother had made this for her mother. Was it when *Mamm* first married *Dat*?

She closed the hope chest lid and then hugged the cross-stitch to her chest as she sat down on top of the hope chest.

"Rachel!" *Mamm* asked. "What are you doing?"

Rachel stood and spun. *Mamm* was standing in the doorway and studying her intently.

"I finished all the chores, and I thought I might find a book to read that would help me feel better. I looked through your books on your dresser and didn't find one, so then I thought there might be one in your hope chest." She held up the cross-stitch. "I didn't find a book, but I found this."

Mamm cupped her hand to her mouth. "I haven't seen that in years. It used to hang over by the back door."

"It's beautiful." Rachel studied the words again, letting them trickle through her mind. "*Mammi* made this for you?"

"*Ya*. She gave it to me when your *dat* and I were first married." *Mamm* walked over to her and ran her finger over the cross-stitch. "She said she was in a fabric store, and when she saw the pattern, she thought of me."

"It's *schee*," Rachel said. *And it's just what I need right now.* Was this *Mammi's* way of reaching out to her? Was *Mammi* trying to tell Rachel everything would be okay and happiness would eventually find its way back into her life? "May I keep it?"

"*Ya*, of course." *Mamm* gave her a sad smile. "How are you doing?"

Rachel shrugged. "I'll be okay." She looked down at the hope chest and then back up at *Mamm*. "When did you move the hope chest from the attic to here?"

Mamm shrugged. "I guess it was a couple of months ago."

"Why did you move it?"

Mamm sat on the edge of her bed and faced Rachel. "I felt like I needed to have it closer to me. Where did you find the key?"

Rachel pointed to the dresser. "It was over there in the glass bowl."

Mamm got up, locked the hope chest, and then slipped the key into the pocket of her apron. "Let me know before you go into it again."

"Oh." Rachel studied her *mamm's* expression, wondering if she'd upset her. "Okay. I will."

"I'm going to start supper soon." *Mamm* walked toward the doorway.

"I'll come with you." Rachel followed her out to the kitchen and wondered why *Mamm* wanted to keep the hope chest locked. Clearly she hadn't wanted Rachel to go through her things, but was there something else in it she didn't want anyone to find?

LATER THAT NIGHT, RACHEL PLACED THE CROSS-STITCH ON her dresser. After climbing into bed, she stared at the ceiling and pondered the quote on the cross-stitch. Her thoughts turned to her grandmother, and tears flooded her eyes. She longed to talk to *Mammi* again. She missed the days when she and her sisters would gather around *Mammi*'s kitchen table to eat grilled cheese sandwiches, drink chocolate milk, and talk. If only she could go to *Mammi*'s house now and tell her about Mike. What advice would *Mammi* give her?

Rachel rolled to her side and closed her eyes. With tears and anguish constricting her throat, she concentrated on the quote from the cross-stitch and fell asleep.

"RACHEL." MALINDA WHISPERED HER NAME AS THE STUDENTS took turns reading aloud at their desks Monday afternoon. "This note is for you." She pointed toward the stack of journals on her desk.

"Oh." Rachel moved to the desk. "I'll take over the journals, and you handle the reading assignment."

"All right." Malinda gave her a questioning expression as she handed her a journal.

Glancing down, Rachel immediately recognized the slanted cursive. The note was from Mike. Her stomach clenched as she lowered herself into the desk chair and took in the note.

Dear Rachel,

I left a message with your *mamm* on Saturday, and I was hoping you'd call me back. I'm sorry I missed you at the shop. I didn't realize you were looking for me. I would've met you out front if I'd known you were there.

I'm also sorry I didn't get to talk to you Friday night. *Mei dat* was very ill, but I never meant to neglect you.

I'd like to make it up to you. Would you please come over for supper Friday night? I'll cook. I promise we'll have a *gut* time. We can sit on the porch and eat ice cream sundaes. Let me know if this sounds *gut* to you. I miss you.

Sincerely,

Mike

Rachel's breath hitched as she studied the words "I miss you." The note sounded so genuine. It was as if he'd written it from his heart. So then why was Mike having an intimate conversation with a pretty redhead when Rachel had seen him at the shop?

She closed her eyes and took deep breaths in through her nose. She couldn't allow Mike to manipulate her any longer. She had to be strong. She had to be John's teacher, not Mike's close friend. It was time to be professional.

Rachel gripped her pen and wrote a response.

Mike,

Thank you for your note. I apologize for missing your call on Saturday. I wasn't feeling well.

John had a *gut* day today. He's improving his work on multiplication, and he's starting to read at a higher level. I've told him to take his time while completing his math worksheets. I'm certain he'll master the multiplication before school ends next month.

Thank you for the supper invitation. Unfortunately, I won't be able to come Friday night. I have plans with my family.

I hope your *dat* is feeling better. I'm sorry he's had such a tough time lately.

Sincerely,

Rachel

She closed the journal and nibbled on the end of her pen. Why was it so painful to turn down Mike's invitation? She looked across the room to John, who was reading aloud from his primer. She'd felt guilty for not bringing a meal for his family today. Why did she allow herself to become so attached to John? Her chest ached when she thought of Mike, John, and Raymond sitting down to supper tonight and not having one of her meals.

Rachel knew it was silly to feel guilty when John had his family members to care for him. Maybe the pretty redhead would prepare a meal for them tonight. The thought caused her shoulders to tense, but she had to let it go. She had to concentrate on her students and not worry about the Lantz family.

But if Rachel's feelings for Mike were wrong, then why was it so difficult for her to let go of them?

MIKE'S CHEST CONSTRICTED AS HE STUDIED RACHEL'S NOTE. He read it for the fourth time, taking in the cold and disconnected way she responded to his invitation to supper. She also hadn't sent home a meal tonight, which was unusual. He didn't expect the meals, but she had insisted on preparing them.

Mike was also surprised Rachel hadn't returned his phone call from Saturday. Was she angry he didn't spend more time with her on Friday? If so, then why hadn't she accepted his apology? Rachel didn't seem like the kind of *maedel* who would hold a grudge. They were taught to forgive at an early age, so then why hadn't she forgiven him?

Questions and worry swirled through Mike's mind. He'd thought he and Rachel had formed a close relationship. Where had the sweet Rachel gone? What had Mike done wrong?

"*Was iss letz?*" John asked, his little voice startling him from his thoughts.

"Nothing, nothing." Mike forced a smile as he set the journal beside his dinner plate.

"Did Rachel write something about me in the journal?" John's eyes were wide with concern.

"She didn't write anything negative about you at all." Mike lifted his piece of fried chicken. "The note was all positive today. You're doing well with the lessons on multiplication."

"Oh." John studied Mike with suspicion. That boy never missed a beat.

"Eat your supper," Janie instructed. Then she pushed a loose lock of her red hair behind her ear.

"Is Rachel coming for supper Friday night?" John asked with a mouthful of chicken.

"Please don't talk with your mouth full, John. No, she said she has plans with her family." Mike's words were hollow and cold, much like his soul. "We'll invite her again another time."

"Why don't we invite her for a picnic on Saturday?" John suggested, choosing another chicken thigh from the platter in the center of the table. "She seemed to like that, right?"

Mike paused to take a sip of water. From the tone of Rachel's note, Mike assumed she would turn down any invitation he made. Deep within his soul, however, Mike hoped he'd misread the tone of Rachel's note. Perhaps she'd had a bad day or she didn't want to write anything personal in the school journal because Malinda might see it.

"I can take care of your *dat* on Saturday if that will help," Janie offered while spooning some peas and carrots. "You can go on a picnic, and I'll be here. I'll see if Marie can come over, too, so we can continue working in the garden."

"*Danki*, Janie," John said. "Let's invite Rachel for a picnic again. That was so fun. Maybe her *schweschder* can come and teach

254

us how to skip stones. Maybe *Onkel* Tim can also come and we can fish. Wouldn't that be fun?"

"That would be fun, but I don't know if we can get everything together on such short notice." Mike felt a pang of regret as enthusiasm glimmered in his brother's eyes. This was exactly why Mike had been afraid to get close to Rachel; he had feared John would wind up hurt if their relationship didn't work out. He couldn't stand the thought of disappointing John, but he also couldn't force Rachel to spend time with them.

Everything Mike had tried to avoid had come true. Things hadn't worked out between Rachel and him, and now John was disappointed.

"I really want to go fishing," John continued.

While John prattled on, Mike heard his father's deep, chesty cough rattling from his bedroom. He looked at Janie, and her brow furrowed with concern.

"I had hoped the antibiotics were working," Janie said softly. "The doctor said he gave him the strongest oral medication he could. If that cough continues, I'll call him."

"*Danki.*" Mike gave her a curt nod. He thought *Dat* would sound better by now. Why was the illness lingering?

"What are you talking about?" John glanced between Janie and Mike.

"The doctor gave your *dat* medication for his cough," Janie explained. "He has what's called an upper respiratory infection, which means it's affecting how he breathes and gives him that cough. But the doctor will take care of him."

"Oh." John's forehead crinkled with concern.

"You don't need to worry, *mei liewe*," Janie said, placing her hand on John's slight shoulder. "I'll make sure the doctor is doing everything he has to for your *dat*."

John smiled up at Janie, and Mike's stomach eased slightly. He could do enough worrying for both of them; he didn't want John to worry too.

John spent the rest of supper talking about school and how much he enjoyed math. When they were finished eating, John climbed the stairs to take his bath. As Mike took dirty dishes to the counter, Janie started filling the sink with water.

"Is there anything you want to talk about?" Janie glanced over her shoulder at Mike as he gathered utensils from the table. "I can tell something is bothering you besides your *dat*'s health."

Mike stacked the utensils on a serving platter as running bath water hummed above him. He considered telling Janie nothing was wrong, but his cousins knew him too well to let something like this go.

"I think I've lost Rachel's friendship," he admitted. "Her note in the journal was cold and distant, and she never returned my call over the weekend." He explained what had happened Friday night and then how he'd missed her on Saturday. "I don't know how to explain to John that Rachel may not want to go on picnics with us anymore. It's going to be difficult for him."

"And also difficult for you." Janie gave him a sympathetic but knowing smile. "I can tell you care about her. I think you should write her a note and invite her for a picnic. Maybe she had an off day."

"That's what I was thinking." Mike's shoulders relaxed at her suggestion. He brought the platter to the counter. "I'll write another note."

"*Gut*. Don't give up hope." Janie nodded toward the table. "I'll finish cleaning up. You can write your note."

"*Danki*." Mike sat at one end of the table and opened the journal to a blank page. He hoped he still had a chance with Rachel.

"Do you think you can go on a picnic with us on Saturday?" John's expression was full of hope as Rachel stood with him on the playground the following afternoon. "Mike wrote you a note and asked you, but I thought I'd ask you too. We can go fishing, and maybe your *schweschder* can teach us how to skip stones."

Rachel fingered the skirt of her dress while John talked on about his hopes for a large family picnic on Saturday. She couldn't stomach the notion of turning him down, but she also couldn't stand the idea of not being Mike's only girlfriend.

"My cousin Janie said she'd stay with *mei dat* while we go on our picnic," John continued. "*Mei dat* has a bad infection, but she said she'll make sure the doctors take *gut* care of him."

"Wait," Rachel said, holding up her hand, stopping his explanation. "What did you say? What's wrong with your father?"

"He has a bad infection," John repeated. "I heard Mike say he was up most of last night with him because he was coughing."

Concern washed over her. "I'm so sorry to hear that."

"*Danki.*" His eyes pleaded with her. "So will you come on a picnic with us and see if your *schweschder* can come too?"

Rachel paused. She didn't want to hurt John, but she also didn't want to cause herself more pain. "I'm sorry, John, but this weekend is going to be very busy for me. Maybe I can come another time."

John blanched and then took a step back. "All right." He trotted off toward the swing set.

Rachel shook her head and leaned back against the fence.

"What was that about?" Malinda appeared at her side.

"John asked me to go on a picnic with him and Mike on Saturday. I told him no." Rachel hugged her arms to her middle. "I can't stand hurting him, but I have to take a step back." She turned toward Malinda. "You were right."

"I was right about what?" Malinda searched her face for an answer.

"I never should've gotten so involved with Mike and John."

"Why? Did something happen?"

Rachel breathed in the warm May air while gathering her thoughts. Then she told Marie about taking dinner over to the Lantz farm Friday night and what she saw when she went to see Mike at work on Saturday.

"You told me not to get too close to John and his family, but I didn't listen," Rachel said. "I followed my heart instead of my head."

"I'm sorry." Malinda placed a hand on Rachel's arm. "I was hoping I was wrong. You seemed so *froh* when Mike picked you up last week and took you out for ice cream."

"*Ya*, I was, but when I saw him with another *maedel* on Saturday, I realized I had let myself fall in love with him too quickly." Rachel shook her head as she gazed across the playground where John was swinging with two other children. "I have a bad habit of thinking with my emotions instead of my head. That's how I wound up with a broken heart with David. I've done it again, but at least I know the truth this time. I just have to pick myself up and move on. I'll find the right person. It will just take time."

She saw a gold-and-orange butterfly fluttering nearby, and her breath caught in her throat. *If I turn my attention to other things, happiness will come and sit quietly on my shoulder . . .*

Malinda gave her a sad smile. "*Ya*, just give it time. Don't rush yourself."

"I won't." A sharp stab of sadness pierced Rachel's heart as she watched John talk to the boy on the swing beside him. She'd hoped to be a big part of his life, but instead, she would only enjoy being his teacher until he transferred back to the school in his district.

Still, she couldn't shake the feeling at the back of her mind that God had brought her into John's life for a purpose beyond only being his teacher. But what could that purpose be if her relationship with Mike had ended so abruptly?

CHAPTER 22

MIKE SAT UP RAMROD STRAIGHT ON THE SOFA AND SCANNED the family room, which was cloaked in darkness. He turned toward his battery-operated digital clock on the end table and read two thirty-seven. The room was deathly silent, but something had jolted him out of a deep sleep. What was it?

He shoved the blankets from his legs and stood, the cool wooden floor creaking under his weight. As he moved toward the doorway leading to his father's bedroom, Mike shrugged his shoulders and moved his neck side to side in an attempt to release the aches and twinges. Sleeping on the sofa was tough on his back and neck, but Mike couldn't risk sleeping in his room upstairs and missing *Dat's* calls for help. Not when he'd been so ill.

Mike leaned into the bedroom doorway and saw the outline of *Dat's* thin body under the sheet. A loud, rattling cough was followed by a sputter and then gasping sound, and Mike ran to his father's bedside. Crouching down, Mike touched *Dat's* face. His skin was hot and clammy. Mike flipped on the lantern and saw that *Dat's* lips were tinted blue. His heart nearly exploded with fear. *Dat* needed help.

"*Dat, Dat,*" Mike whispered with urgency. "Can you hear me?"

Dat wheezed and gasped again. He was having trouble breathing.

"I'm going to call for some help," Mike said, his words rushed.

Mike dashed up the stairs and knocked on the guest room door. "Marie, Marie! *Dummle!* Wake up! I need help!"

A rustling noise followed by footsteps sounded and then the

door swung open, revealing Marie clad in a robe, her brown hair mussed.

In an instant, her brown eyes were wide with alarm. *"Was iss letz?* Is it *Onkel* Raymond?"

"Ya," Mike said, adrenaline roaring through his veins. "He's having trouble breathing. I'm going to call nine-one-one. Would you sit with my *dat?"*

"Ya, ya. Of course."

Marie followed Mike down the stairs. As she veered off into his father's room, Mike grabbed a lantern from the mudroom and ran out the back door to the barn.

When his feet hit the cold ground, he realized he'd forgotten his shoes. He dialed nine-one-one and begged the operator to send an ambulance as soon as possible. When he jogged back into the house, he found Marie applying a compress to *Dat's* forehead.

"He's burning up with fever," she said softly, her face creased with anguish. "I thought this might help."

Dat's skin was gray and his eyes were closed. He shuddered and then convulsed with another deep, rattled cough and wheeze.

Mike paced at the end of the bed. "I should've called the doctor last night. I should've insisted the doctor admit him to the hospital." He shoved his hand through his hair. "I thought he was getting better."

"It's not your fault," Marie insisted. "The rescue squad will be here soon."

Sirens sounded in the distance, and Mike ran out the front door. He stood on the porch and directed the ambulance to the back of the house, glad that John was such a sound sleeper.

The next thirty minutes were a blur. As the EMTs took vital signs, Mike stood at the back of the room beside Marie. He felt as if he were eighteen again and the EMTs were working on his stepmother instead of his father.

He hugged his arms to his middle as his body shook with fear. *How could this be happening again?*

As if reading his mind, Marie placed her hand on Mike's arm.

"Everything will be fine." She leveled her gaze with his, but apprehension flickered in her eyes. "You get dressed. You'll need to ride in the ambulance with him, and I'll stay here with John. I'll bring John to the hospital tomorrow if you let me know when that's okay."

Mike nodded. "All right." As the EMTs prepared to load *Dat* onto a gurney, he ran up the stairs, praying *Dat* would make it through this and not leave him and John orphaned.

"MR. LANTZ?" A MAN CLAD IN GREEN SCRUBS AND A WHITE coat approached Mike as he sat on a cold, vinyl chair in the emergency room waiting area.

Mike had been absently staring at a news program flickering on a large flat-screen television attached to the wall above him. It seemed as if it had been hours since *Dat* had been deposited in the emergency room. The sky had been pitch black when Mike entered the waiting room, but now the sun was starting to rise, bathing the sky in vivid streaks of orange, pink, and yellow.

"*Ya*," Mike said, running his hand down his face. "I'm Michael Lantz."

The man sat across from Mike and folded his hands in his lap. The rest of the waiting area was quiet except for a middle-aged couple sitting huddled together on the other side of the room. The only sound was the occasional telephone ringing and the *whoosh* of the electric doors when someone walked in or out. The aroma of cleaning solution assaulted Mike's nose.

"I'm Dr. Richmond," the doctor said, the corners of his mouth turned down in a frown. "Your father is very ill. He has pneumonia.

You gave us permission to do whatever is necessary, and we've had to put him on a ventilator to help him breathe."

"A ventilator?" Mike's eyes misted with tears. "This is serious." The words were more a statement than a question.

"Yes, I'm afraid it is." Dr. Richmond sighed. "Your father is very weak. The kidney failure has taken a toll on his body."

For a moment, Mike's words were trapped in his dry throat. He nodded slowly to avoid breaking down in front of this stranger. Then he took a deep breath and cleared his throat. "Can I see him?"

"Yes." The doctor nodded. "Once we have him comfortable, you can see him. We've moved him to the intensive care unit." He tilted his head. "Do you have any other questions?"

Mike cleared his throat again. "How long do you think he'll be in the hospital?"

Dr. Richmond shook his head. "I'm not sure. It depends on how he responds to treatment."

Mike wiped away an errant tear. "Thank you for your help."

"You're welcome." The doctor pointed toward the desk. "I'll have one of the nurses come to get you and take you to see your father."

Once the doctor was gone, Mike stared out the window, taking in the beauty of the brightening sky. The promise of a gorgeous spring day seemed to mock his bleak mood. He wondered if Marie had told John about Dat. How had John taken the news? He hoped his family would arrive soon. He longed for companionship.

He longed for Rachel.

But why would he think of her when Dat was lying in a hospital bed with a ventilator helping him to breathe? Rachel's notes from school remained cold and professional, proving she had rejected his friendship, but he still missed her. He missed the closeness they had shared the day they went on the picnic and the day they went for ice cream.

If only he had a loving girlfriend or wife to hold his hand and tell him everything was going to be all right. If only that person could be Rachel.

He sagged in the uncomfortable chair, closed his eyes, and tried to push those thoughts away as the low hum of the television penetrated the waiting room.

"Michael?"

Mike turned toward the exit doors as his aunt Sylvia and uncle Timothy rushed toward him. Relief overwhelmed him as he stood and his aunt pulled him into a hug.

"We got here as soon as we got Marie's phone message," *Onkel* Tim said, squeezing Mike's arm.

Mike sniffed as tears threatened his eyes. "I'm so glad you're here."

They sat down, facing each other in a circle of chairs.

"How is he?" *Aenti* Sylvia's eyes sparkled with tears.

"It's pneumonia." Mike shared the doctor's diagnosis, and his aunt choked back a sob, covering her mouth with her hand.

"We'll go with you to see him," Tim said.

"*Danki*," Mike said. "How's John?"

"Marie said John wanted to go on a picnic, but she convinced him to have one in the backyard so they can stay near the phone. She said she'd wait to hear from you before calling a driver to bring them here." Sylvia touched his arm.

Mike shook his head. "I don't think John should see *mei dat* hooked up to a ventilator. It would be too confusing and frightening for him."

"I agree." *Aenti* Sylvia studied Mike's eyes. "You look exhausted. You should have our driver take you home so you can get some sleep. Tim and I can stay and wait to hear more news."

Onkel Tim nodded. "That's a *gut* idea. You need your rest."

"No." Mike shook his head. "I can't leave him." He covered his face with his hands. "What am I going to tell John? I have to find a way to be strong for him."

"We'll help you, Michael," *Aenti* Sylvia said gently. "You're not in this alone. We're your family, and we'll help you through this."

Mike met his aunt's warm expression, and he gave her a sad smile. He was thankful he didn't have to bear this alone.

MIKE STUDIED THE FRONT PAGE OF THE LOCAL NEWSPAPER as machines hummed and clicked beside him. Every few minutes he glanced over at *Dat*, who lay silently in the hospital bed, his eyes closed and his skin still a grayish color.

The door opened, and his uncle Tim entered.

"Any change?" he asked, sinking into the chair across from Mike.

"No," Mike said softly. "I keep waiting for him to wake up and let me know he feels better."

"Have you seen the doctor yet this morning?"

"No." Mike held up the paper. "I just keep staring at the front page and reading the same article. I'm not retaining anything. I can't think straight."

"That's because you need rest," *Onkel* Tim said, placing his ankle on his opposite knee. "You need to go home and get some sleep. You've been here more than twenty-four hours. Go home and come back tomorrow."

"I can't leave him," Mike repeated for what felt like the hundredth time. He hadn't left *Dat*'s side except to go to the cafeteria to pick up something to eat or to go sit in the ICU waiting room while the nurses took care of his father. He was waiting impatiently for *Dat* to open his eyes and at least acknowledge him.

"How is John?"

"He's fine. Janie and Sylvia are with him now. He enjoyed the picnic in the backyard with Marie yesterday, and he went to church with Janie and Sylvia today." *Onkel* Tim absently ran his hand over his trouser leg. "He misses you, and he wants to see your *dat*."

"I know. I talked to him on the phone last night." Mike turned toward *Dat*. "I don't know if I should let John see *Dat*. I don't want to scare him."

"He needs to know the truth."

Mike opened his mouth to protest, but the door clicked open again. Dr. Richmond stepped into the room and greeted Mike and Tim before pulling the clipboard out from the slot at the end of the bed.

"How does it look for my father?" Mike asked, his voice thin and shaky. "I keep waiting for him to wake up and look at me, but he hasn't responded at all since he was admitted to the hospital yesterday."

Dr. Richmond leaned against the wall and frowned. His expression sent a shiver of alarm through Mike. Something was wrong. Very wrong.

"We've run several tests, and I'm sorry to tell you that your father is in a coma." The doctor's expression became grimmer. "I told you yesterday that the kidney failure has taken a toll on his body. Well, the toxins in his blood stream have caused his organs to start to shut down, which caused the coma." Dr. Richmond paused before going on. "I'm afraid I don't have good news. He most likely won't wake up, and you'll have to make some tough decisions."

Mike blinked back tears. He turned toward *Onkel* Tim, who shook his head in dismay.

"That can't be," Tim insisted. "My brother has always been determined. He'll fight this. He'll wake up."

"What kind of decisions?" Mike asked, wiping his wet eyes.

"You'll have to decide if you want to turn off the ventilator." Dr. Richmond hugged the clipboard to his chest.

Onkel Tim gasped. "Turn off the ventilator? And let him die?"

Mike swallowed a sob. *This has to be a bad dream. This can't be happening. I can't lose* Dat. *Not now.* He stared down at his lap as dread grabbed hold of his throat and squeezed.

"I'm sorry," Dr. Richmond said softly, his voice full of empathy. "My prayers are with you and your family."

"We need to give Raymond more time," *Onkel* Tim said. "We can't give up just yet."

Mike wiped his eyes again and met his uncle's gaze. "I need to talk to John. I have to bring him up to see *Dat* one last time." He looked at the doctor. "I know children aren't allowed in the ICU, but would you allow my six-year-old brother to come and see him?"

"Of course," the doctor said. "We always make exceptions in situations like this."

"Thank you." Mike turned toward his uncle. "I need to go home and see John. Will you stay tonight?"

"Of course." *Onkel* Tim took a handkerchief from his pocket and wiped his eyes.

"I HAD FUN WITH *AENTI* SYLVIA, JANIE, AND MARIE TODAY," John said as he sat on his bed. "We went to church and then we visited their neighbors. They have a barn full of cats and kittens. I sat with the kittens and rubbed their bellies." He started to laugh and then stopped, the corners of his mouth turning down. "*Was iss letz?* You look *bedauerlich.*"

Mike took a deep breath and then touched John's hair. He didn't know how to tell John that their father was dying when he couldn't accept it himself.

"You know *Dat* is very ill, right?" Mike asked, his voice sounding foreign to him. When John nodded, he continued, "*Dat* is in what's called a coma. It's when you're sleeping, and you can't wake up. A machine is helping him breathe because he can't breathe on his own."

John's eyes widened and sparkled with tears. "Is he going to die?" His voice was tiny as if he were much younger than six.

"I don't know." Mike sniffed. "Right now all we can do is pray for him."

John nodded. "I have been praying for him, and I'll pray harder tonight."

"*Gut*." Mike touched John's cheek. "I want you to come to the hospital with me tomorrow so you can see *Dat*." *And then you can say good-bye to him.* He couldn't say the words aloud because he hoped they weren't true. He hoped that through a miracle, *Dat* was going to rally back to them.

"Okay." John nodded with emphasis. "I want to see him. I want to tell him how much we want him to come home."

"That's a *gut* idea." Mike hugged John. They said prayers together before Mike tucked him in and left his room.

Mike went downstairs and stood in *Dat's* bedroom doorway for a few moments, trying to imagine him asleep in the bed. Fresh sheets covered the mattress, evidence that one of his cousins had taken the time to clean for him. He was grateful for them.

As he made his way to the kitchen, Mike's thoughts turned to Rachel. How he longed to hear her voice. He'd thought about calling her more than once while he was at the hospital, but he couldn't bear the thought of her rejecting him again. What if she refused his call or didn't bother to call him back if he left a message? His heart was too tender to survive another blow.

Mike stepped out onto the back porch and breathed in the warm, sweet, spring air. He needed strength to face tomorrow. He couldn't imagine saying good-bye to his father, and he didn't know how to explain the gravity of the situation to John.

Mike prayed God would give him the right words.

CHAPTER 23

"Rachel." Malinda stepped into the classroom and dropped her tote bag on one of the students' desks. "We have to talk before the *kinner* get here. It's urgent."

"*Was iss letz?*" Rachel's stomach twisted with alarm as she looked up from the stack of papers she was grading at the front of the classroom.

"Sylvia Lantz called me last night." Malinda sat on a desk at the front of the classroom.

"Sylvia Lantz?" Rachel tilted her head. The name was familiar, but she couldn't place it.

"She's John and Mike Lantz's *aenti*." Malinda took a deep breath. "Raymond Lantz is in the hospital. He was admitted Friday night with pneumonia, but he's gotten worse. He's in a coma now."

Rachel gasped and cupped her hand to her mouth. "No."

Malinda nodded, her expression grim. "She said it doesn't look *gut* at all. John won't be at school today. Mike is taking him to the hospital to see his father."

Rachel blinked as tears blurred her vision. Mike and John had been on her mind nearly nonstop over the weekend, and she longed to call Mike to talk to him. She'd walked over to the phone shanty and picked up the receiver on Saturday, but her stubborn pride kept her from dialing his number. Why hadn't she called him? She missed Mike, and for some unknown reason, she had a feeling he'd needed her too. Now she knew why.

"Sylvia isn't sure when John will be back at school," Malinda continued. "She wanted us to know why he was gone."

Rachel nodded and sniffed as anguish and regret washed over her. She needed to do something for Mike. He needed her friendship now, and she couldn't walk away from him, even if he was seeing the pretty redheaded girl behind her back.

RACHEL CLIMBED THE BACK STEPS OF MIKE'S HOUSE THAT afternoon. She held the basket handles in one hand as she knocked on the door, grateful Malinda hadn't minded her leaving school a little early so she could go home and prepare some food for Mike and his family.

She looked down at the basket and recalled her mother telling her that her father had used the basket to bring meals to her. *Mamm* said the basket had served as a kind of mediator between her parents when they were having problems. Rachel prayed the basket could bring her and Mike together just as it had worked to bring her parents together so many years ago.

Although Emily had offered to come with her, Rachel insisted she needed to make this visit alone. She had to face Mike and apologize for not being a friend when he needed one most.

The back door opened, and the pretty redheaded woman Rachel had seen at Bird-in-Hand Builders smiled at her. Rachel bit back a frown as jealousy surged through her veins.

"Hello," the girl said, opening the door wide.

"Hi," Rachel said, gripping the basket with both of her hands. "I'm Rachel Fisher. I brought a meal for Mike and John."

"Oh, *danki*. That is so kind of you." The woman motioned for Rachel to step into the house. "I'm their cousin, Janie Lantz."

Rachel's stomach lurched, and shame shoved away her jealousy. The pretty girl was Mike's cousin, not his secret girlfriend.

How could she have been so distrustful? Once again, her quick temper and stubbornness had gotten the best of her. How could she have been so stupid?

Shaking herself back to the present, Rachel followed Janie into the kitchen and set the basket on the counter.

"Mike is still at the hospital, and John is finishing his chores." Janie took two mugs from the cabinet. "I just made some tea. Would you like some?"

"*Ya, danki.*" Rachel pointed to the basket. "I brought meatballs and pasta. I also made brownies. John enjoys them."

"That's *wunderbaar.*" Janie gestured toward the table where she had set the mugs and was about to pour the tea. "Please sit. I've heard a lot about you from John. You've helped him immensely at school. We're very grateful for you."

"*Danki.*" Rachel didn't feel worthy of the compliments. "I enjoy having John in the class." Her thoughts swirled with trepidation for Raymond and Mike as Janie handed her a mug. "How is Raymond?"

Janie shook her head as tears glimmered in her eyes. "It's not going well. Mike took John to the hospital today so he could see their *dat.* Raymond is still in a coma, and his organs are shutting down. The doctor said they have to make a decision about turning off the ventilator."

"*Ach*, no." Rachel bit back a sob. "I'm so sorry."

Janie grabbed the tissue box on the counter and set it on the table. She pulled out a tissue and blotted her eyes with it. "I was at the hospital this morning. Mike took John into the room alone so they could spend some time with Raymond. Mike said John just talked to Raymond as if he were awake." She sniffed.

"John had talked all week about going on a picnic, but *mei schweschder* convinced him they could have one in the backyard so she could stay close to the phone in case Mike called from the

271

hospital. Even though they never left the backyard, John thought it was fun, and he told his *dat* all about it."

Rachel's hands trembled as regret choked her throat. She should've been on that picnic with them. No, she should've been at the hospital holding Mike's hand when he needed her most. She grabbed a tissue as tears flowed from her eyes. How could she have turned her back on Mike and John?

"Mike asked me to bring John home," Janie continued, her voice thick with emotion as tears traced her cheeks. "He didn't want to overwhelm John too much. He just wanted him to have a chance to see their *dat* again."

"How is Mike doing?" Rachel asked, her voice quaking.

"I think he's just trying to hold it together at this point. *Mei dat* and *mamm* have been encouraging him to get some rest. They finally got him to come home last night, but he went right back to the hospital today with John and me, of course, and he wouldn't come home with us."

Janie wiped away more tears and then gripped her mug. "I hope he comes home tonight. I'm afraid he's going to collapse from the exhaustion, but I also understand his reasons for wanting to stay at the hospital. He doesn't want to miss any changes."

Rachel stared down at her mug as her tears began to flow again. She took a deep shuddering breath in an attempt to stop crying, but she couldn't.

"*Ach*, Rachel." Janie touched her hand. "I know you're close to John and Mike. It's difficult for all of us to face this."

Rachel nodded and picked up another tissue to dry her face. "I just feel terrible I haven't been here for Mike."

"It's not your fault. The illness came on quickly." Janie pointed toward the basket. "They will appreciate the meal you made."

"It's the least I could do," Rachel said. She sniffed and rubbed at her eyes again.

The door opened and clicked shut, and then John burst into the kitchen.

"Rachel!" He ran up and hugged her.

"Hi, John," Rachel said, forcing a smile. "We missed you in school today."

"I was at the hospital with my *dat*," he said. "He's really, really sick. He's hooked up to a machine to help him breathe, and he's asleep. Mike says *Dat's* in a coma."

Rachel nodded. "I'm so sorry to hear that. How are you?"

"I'm *bedauerlich*." John dropped into the chair beside her. "But I'm praying for *mei dat*. I'm hoping he'll get better soon."

Rachel willed herself not to cry as she studied John's big, blue eyes. Oh, how she longed to wrap him in her protective arms like a mother would. Her bottom lip trembled. "We can't ever stop praying."

John nodded. "I know."

Rachel looked at Janie, whose eyes were still full of tears. "I should go. I told my driver I would be only a few minutes."

Janie stood and walked her to the door. "*Danki* for coming by."

"Would you please tell Mike I stopped by and that I'm thinking of him?" Rachel asked.

"I will," Janie promised. "*Gut nacht*."

During the ride home, Rachel closed her eyes and prayed for everyone in the Lantz family.

MIKE STOOD BY THE WALL-LENGTH HOSPITAL WINDOWS IN the ICU waiting room and stared out at the setting sun. Although he preferred to stay with *Dat*, the nurse had told Mike he had to leave so they could run tests and administer medicine.

It had been a long and grueling day. He'd brought John to the hospital this morning to see *Dat*, but he didn't tell John it was to

273

say good-bye. Instead, he explained that it would help *Dat* if he heard their voices while he was sleeping. John talked to *Dat* as if they were sharing a meal. The enthusiasm in John's voice had broken Mike's heart.

After John visited with *Dat*, Mike asked Janie to take John home, away from the anxiety and sadness that hung over the family like a dark cloud. Then he spent the day sitting with his father, hoping for a sign that he was going to wake up. Although the doctor insisted things weren't going to get any better, Mike couldn't agree to turning off the ventilator. He couldn't give up hope for a miracle. Not yet.

Urgent voices and footsteps sounded in the hallway, and Mike tried to tune them out. He leaned his forehead against the cool glass and closed his eyes. Even though he hadn't slept much since Friday night, his body continued to buzz with adrenaline. He felt as if he were walking through a horrible dream and couldn't wake up.

"Mike." Sam appeared at Mike's shoulder. "How are you?"

Mike opened his eyes and stood up straight. "I'm not sure how to answer that question." He rubbed his eyes. "I guess I'm numb."

Sam's frown deepened. "I think you need to go home and get some sleep."

Mike gritted his teeth as frustration coursed through him. "I really wish everyone would stop saying that to me. I need to be here. If I'm at home, then I'll want to be here."

"Fine." Sam blew out a sigh. "Then let me buy you something to eat. You have to be hungry. When was the last time you ate?"

Mike rubbed his chin where stubble had appeared. He couldn't remember the last time he'd eaten a full meal or the last time he'd shaved. He was certain he looked like a derelict. "I had a few bites of oatmeal this morning."

"My point exactly." Sam made a sweeping gesture toward the hallway. "Let's go get something to eat."

Mike glanced over to where *Aenti* Sylvia, *Onkel* Tim, Mandy, and Marie sat staring absently at the evening news coming from the television above them.

"They'll let us know if we need to come back." Sam grabbed Mike's arm and began to nudge him toward the doorway.

As they stepped into the hallway, Mike heard a commotion and loud voices sounding from the other end of the hallway. A loud noise like a blaring alarm sounded.

Someone hollered, "Clear!"

He heard more noise and voices, and then the commotion suddenly stopped.

The floor dropped out from under Mike as icy chills slithered up his spine. He bolted for his father's room.

"Michael!" Sam called after him. "Mike!"

Mike skidded to a stop just inside his father's room. A couple of nurses and a doctor were standing by his father's bed. The loud alarm seared into Mike's skull and bile rose in his throat. Then he saw the flat line on his father's monitor, which he knew must have been the source of the alarm he'd heard.

When the nurses turned toward Mike, one of them had tears in her eyes.

Dr. Richmond stepped over and touched Mike's shoulder. "I'm sorry, Michael, but he's gone."

The world tilted, and Mike's heart was lodged in his throat, making it difficult to breathe.

"No," he said in a strangled whisper, backing out of the room. "No!"

His spine collided hard with the wall behind him, and he sagged down into a sitting position on the floor. Pulling his knees up to his chest, he buried his face in his hands and sobbed.

MIKE FOUND JOHN SITTING ON A SWING IN THEIR YARD. HE swallowed a deep, ragged breath and then made his way toward his younger brother. He had to find a way to tell John their father had passed away. His hands trembled with a combination of grief and anxiety.

John smiled and waved as Mike approached. "Hi!"

"Hi, Johnny." Mike pointed at the swing beside him. "May I join you?"

"Of course." John pushed his swing back and forth. "How's Dat?"

Mike dropped onto the swing and attempted to clear his dry throat. "John, I need to tell you something."

John's smile faded. "What is it? Did something happen to Dat?"

"Ya." Mike nodded as fresh tears spilled down his cheeks. "Dat passed away this afternoon."

John gasped and then a sob broke from his throat. He leapt out of the swing and threw himself into Mike's arms.

Closing his eyes, Mike rested his cheek on his brother's head and held him close. "I'm so sorry," Mike whispered.

"What's going to happen to me?" John wailed. "Where will I go now?"

"What do you mean?" Mike looked down at John's little face.

"I don't have a mamm or a dat," John said between sobs. "Where will I live?"

Mike stared into John's eyes. "John, you will always have me. You and I are a family, and we will always be a family, no matter what. I will never, ever leave you. You will always have me. Do you understand that?"

John nodded. "Okay." Then he buried his face in Mike's shoulder, and Mike held him close while he sobbed.

R ACHEL WAS WALKING OUT OF THE CHICKEN COOP WHEN SHE heard the phone ringing. She set the basket of eggs on the ground and rushed toward the shanty.

"Hello?" she asked, working to catch her breath.

"Rachel. It's Malinda." Her cousin's voice was grave.

"Malinda." Rachel leaned against the desk. *"Was iss letz?"*

"I just heard some terrible news. Raymond Lantz passed away last night."

Rachel swallowed a sob as tears saturated her eyes. *"Ach,* no."

"I had to call you as soon as I got the news. I knew you'd want to know." Her voice quavered with emotion.

"Danki." Rachel sniffed as tears poured from her eyes.

"We're going to cancel school."

"Of course." Rachel's voice quavered. "I need to go."

"I'll talk to you soon."

Rachel hung up and hugged her abdomen as sobs consumed her. Memories of Mike, John, and Raymond during their dinners together drowned her as tears clouded her vision.

CHAPTER 24

MIKE FELT AS IF HE WERE IN A DAZE AS HE STOOD BETWEEN *Onkel* Tim and Marie and mechanically shook hands with the community members who filed through his house to offer condolences and pay their respects to his father. From there the visitors moved to the open casket, which sat at the other end of the family room.

Mike's mind had registered that *Dat* had passed away, but his heart refused to admit it. Although two days had passed, Mike still expected to hear *Dat* call his name or laugh. But the house remained hollow and desolate, despite the flurry of visitors.

Many of the community members had also dropped off meals. Even though his kitchen table, counters, and refrigerator were cluttered with various dishes and desserts, Mike hadn't been able to eat. He also hadn't slept. Instead, he'd numbly floated through the days, hoping to wake up from this horrific nightmare.

His glance moved to the opposite side of the room where Janie stood with John. Holding his hand, Janie bent down and whispered something in his ear. A wave of grief doused Mike as he recalled how difficult it was for him to tell John that *Dat* had passed away. His spirit crumbled at the memory of the sound of his brother's sobs.

Hand in hand, Janie and John walked over to Mike.

"We're going for a walk," Janie said. "We've decided we need to get some fresh air."

"That sounds *gut*." Mike smiled at John. "I'll see you in a little bit."

John nodded before Janie led him through the crowd of people.

Janie and Marie continued to be a tremendous help to Mike. Not only had they handled the household chores, but they had also kept John occupied while Mike and *Onkel* Tim took care of the funeral arrangements and paperwork.

"You should get something to eat," Marie whispered after a new line of mourners disappeared. "You haven't eaten all day."

Mike nodded, realizing the cold and hollow feeling in his stomach wasn't only grief—it was also hunger. His stomach rumbled in response. "I'll eat something on one condition."

"What's that?" she asked, raising an eyebrow.

"I can take the food out to my woodshop." Mike breathed in the humid air. Janie was on the right track when she said she and John needed some fresh air. Despite having the windows open, the house remained hot and stuffy. "I need to get some air, and I need to get away from the crowd for a while."

"Fine," Marie whispered. "Go on and take a break. My parents and I will handle the crowd."

"*Danki*." Mike touched Marie's arm before weaving through the knot of people, only stopping to shake hands when familiar faces blocked his path. He filled a plate with food and started for the back door, again stopping only when prompted by well-meaning members of the community.

After nearly twenty minutes, Mike finally made it out onto the porch. He was greeted by dark, threatening clouds, which seemed appropriate the day of *Dat*'s wake. He rushed down the path, through the barn, and into the solace of his woodshop. He breathed a deep, cleansing breath, enjoying the quiet and the smell of animals and wood. He was thankful to be alone with his thoughts.

Mike sat on the stool in front of the workbench and moved the food around on his plate. Despite the delicious aroma wafting up from the various casseroles and pasta dishes and his earlier pangs of hunger, the food didn't appeal to him. He placed the plate on the workbench and picked up a block of wood. After turning it over in his hand, he began to sand it.

The tedious work felt like a balm to his soul, and for the first time since *Dat* passed away, Mike was able to clear his mind.

RACHEL'S BODY TREMBLED AS SHE SCANNED THE KNOT OF PEOPLE milling around the room. Mike's handsome face was nowhere to be found.

"I don't see him," Rachel whispered to Emily. She looked toward the far end of the room, where she found Marie standing with a middle-aged couple. "He should be standing with his cousin." She nodded toward Marie.

"Maybe he stepped outside for a minute?" Emily suggested. "Let's go ask her." She took Rachel's hand in hers and steered her toward Marie.

Rachel shook the man's and woman's hands, assuming they were Mike's *aenti* and *onkel*. When she stepped over to Marie, Rachel pulled her into a hug.

"I'm so sorry," Rachel whispered, her voice trembling.

"*Danki.*" Marie gave her a bleak smile.

"Where are Mike and John?" she asked.

"*Mei schweschder* took John for a walk." Marie gestured toward the doorway. "Mike said he needed some air, so he took a plate of food out to his shop in the barn. He wanted to get away for a bit."

Rachel bit her lower lip while debating if she should go talk to him. Would it be rude to barge in on him, or would he want to see her? The questions whirled in her mind as her stomach tightened.

"You can go see him." Marie gave her a knowing smile. "His shop is in the back of the largest barn."

Yes, I remember.

"*Danki.*" Rachel touched Emily's arm. "I'll be back."

Emily nodded. Rachel slipped through the kitchen and waved to her parents, who were talking with another couple. Then she hustled out the back door.

Cool raindrops sprayed her face as she hurried across the lush grass to the barn. The aroma of dirt and animals assaulted her nostrils as she entered the barn and walked to the woodshop.

She stopped in the doorway. Her hands shook and her back stiffened as she took in Mike's handsome profile. Her eyes prickled with fresh tears as he sanded the piece of wood as if it were the most important task in the world.

Several minutes passed, and she wondered if he didn't see her in his peripheral vision or if he was ignoring her. The rain beat on the roof above them. The window was open just enough that its sweet smell blended with the scent of animals and dirt.

When Rachel thought the silence between them might suffocate her, she finally spoke. "Mike," her voice croaked.

Mike slowly turned toward her, but his face remained stoic. Violet circles outlined his dull eyes, and his mouth was turned down in a deep frown. He didn't speak. Instead, he held the block of wood and sandpaper in his hands as his cool, blue eyes assessed her, as if she were a stranger. His icy stare caused her breath to hitch in her chest.

"I'm so sorry about your *dat*," she said, her voice still trembling with grief and regret.

Mike placed the wood and sandpaper on the workbench behind him and then turned toward her again. "I'm surprised to see you." He gave her a murderous look.

She shivered. "Why are you surprised? You didn't think I would come to your father's wake?"

"No, I really didn't think you'd come." He folded his arms over his chest.

281

His cruel words stabbed at her chest. "Why not?" she asked.

"You stopped speaking to me," he said, holding up his hands. "You just dropped me as if I didn't matter to you. I've been trying to figure out what changed between us. Did you get back together with David?"

"No," she said quickly, stepping into the small woodshop. "I didn't get back together with David. I was wrong not to call you back last week. I'm so sorry."

He studied her again, and her mouth dried. "Why did you suddenly stop talking to me?"

"It was a misunderstanding," she said, her words tumbling out of her mouth in a rush. "I went to visit you at work a couple of weeks ago because I was worried about your *dat*. When I went back in the shop to see you, you were talking to a pretty *maedel*, and I misunderstood your body language. Your conversation seemed so intimate, and I thought she was your girlfriend. I thought you were seeing someone behind my back. I was so hurt that I left without talking to you."

"You saw me talking to a *maedel*?" Mike paused for a moment, and then realization flickered in his eyes. "Did you see me talking to my cousin Janie?"

"*Ya*." She cleared her throat. "I didn't know who Janie was, and I wasn't just hurt because I thought you were seeing someone behind my back. I was also jealous. I know jealousy is a sin, but . . . she was so pretty. I was so wrong not to trust you. I'm sorry, Mike. Please forgive me."

"You saw me talking to a *maedel* you didn't know, and you immediately jumped to the wrong conclusion?" His voice was acidic. "You didn't even give me a chance to explain. You just assumed I was betraying you, just as David did. When did I ever give you the impression that I was like David?"

A tear escaped her eye. "You never gave me a reason not to

trust you." She pointed to her chest. "It was my fault. I let my temper and my insecurities get the best of me, and I was wrong, completely wrong."

"You didn't even give me a chance to explain myself," Mike repeated, his voice rising with anger. "Janie and I were talking about *mei dat* and how worried we were about him. I asked Janie how I should talk to John about *mei dat* since *mei dat* seemed to be getting worse. That's all it was—a conversation between cousins. Janie and Marie are more like my *schweschdere* than my cousins."

His expression darkened. "Sam told me you stopped by, and I couldn't understand why you didn't come to see me. I was worried about you. I tried to call you and I wrote notes to you in the school journal, but you just threw our friendship away as if it were nothing."

"Your friendship means a lot to me, and I miss you." Rachel took a step toward him as more tears flowed down her face. "I made a terrible mistake."

"I needed you this week," he continued. "I just went through the most difficult week of my life, and I truly needed a *freind*. There were so many times when I wished I could talk to you, but you had rejected me as if I were nothing." He cleared his throat. "You broke my heart." His voice quavered, and his eyes sparkled with tears.

"I'm so sorry," she whispered, reaching for him. "I wish I had been there for you. I wish I had been in the hospital with you to hold your hand."

Mike leaned back on the stool, away from her touch.

"Let me make it up to you," she whispered. "Please forgive me."

"Of course I forgive you," he said, scowling. "But nothing will ever be the same between us." He turned away from her, and facing his workbench, he began sanding the block of wood again.

Rachel wiped away the tears with her fingertips as he worked. "What are you making?" she asked, her voice thin and shaky.

"I'm not sure yet." He kept his back to her.

She silently racked her brain for what she could say to make things right between them. Several minutes passed, the rain still beating on the roof above them.

"Mike," she began, hugging her arms to her middle. "When I met you, I wasn't looking for a relationship. I had just lost my boyfriend and my best friend, and my heart was shattered. As I got to know you, I could feel myself getting attached to you, and it scared me. I had assumed it would take years for me to meet someone special." She took a deep breath. "But as much as I tried to resist my feelings for you, they blossomed like the daffodils in the spring."

She took another shaky breath. "So when I saw you with Janie last week, I panicked. I thought our friendship was too *gut* to be true, and I thought I had misread how you felt about me. I was afraid I had fallen in love too soon, and the best thing I could do was pull away before you hurt me. The problem was, I had already given you my heart, and I wound up hurt anyway."

While she talked, Mike had stopped sanding and turned toward her. Now he closed his eyes for a moment. She waited for him to speak, but he remained silent.

"I can't tell you how sorry I am," she said, her voice becoming thinner and shakier as she continued. "I understand why you can never trust me again, but I'm going to miss you. I'm going to miss our talks and picnics and ice cream. And I'm going to miss spending time with John. I'm sorry I messed this up."

Mike bent his head and resumed sanding. She waited a few moments, and when he didn't respond, she took it as a sign that she should leave.

"Good-bye." Rachel choked back a sob and then ran out of the barn and into the rain. She hid around the side of the barn and leaned against it as she fought to stop her tears.

MIKE PUT DOWN THE WOOD AND SANDPAPER. HE COVERED his face with his hands and took a deep, shuddering breath. When he first saw Rachel, he'd longed to wrap his arms around her, bury his face in her neck, and cry, releasing all the grief he'd held in since he'd lost his father. Mike craved her friendship and her stability, but he couldn't bring himself to allow her to hurt him any more than she already had.

His stomach had churned with anger when she told him she'd thought he was cheating on her, all because she saw him with Janie. How could she not trust him when he'd opened up his heart to her? To make matters worse, why hadn't she asked him who Janie was? It seemed the misunderstanding could have been remedied with a simple conversation. Instead, Rachel had completely shut him out when he'd needed her most.

Mike looked toward the corner of the small woodshop, where he saw the shelf he'd been working on the first time Rachel visited him here. They'd barely known each other back then, but now they weren't even friends. If only he could go back to that first day she'd tutored John so he could start fresh with her.

Mike missed Rachel. He missed their talks. He missed her beautiful smile and the sound of her laughter. He missed the way she interacted with John. If only they could make things right, but it was too late. Mike's soul was shredded, and he couldn't allow Rachel or any other *maedel* back into his life.

RACHEL MANAGED TO KEEP HER EMOTIONS IN CHECK UNTIL she arrived home later that evening. As she climbed the porch steps, her eyes moved to the small planter Mike and John had given her, and a pang of sadness and regret slammed into her chest. The cheerful pink Gerber daisies seemed to heckle the anguish flooding her. When a butterfly flittered near the planter, Rachel gasped as tears prickled her eyes.

"Let's make some tea," Emily said, touching Rachel's shoulder. "We need to talk."

"*Ya*," Rachel whispered, her voice caught in her throat. She was thankful her sister knew just what she needed.

As *Dat* disappeared into the barn to care for the animals, Rachel stepped into the kitchen behind *Mamm* and Emily.

"I've lost him forever," Rachel managed to say as she flopped into a chair at the table. "I apologized to him over and over again, but he said things will never be the same between us."

"*Ach*, no," *Mamm* said, slipping into the chair beside her.

"What happened?" Emily sat down on Rachel's other side.

Rachel blotted her eyes with a tissue from her pocket as she shared the conversation she'd had with Mike. *Mamm* and Emily shook their heads as empathy gleamed in their eyes.

"I should've asked him who Janie was instead of assuming he was seeing another *maedel* behind my back," Rachel said, her voice shaky. "I let my stubbornness get the best of me again."

Mamm pulled Rachel into a warm hug. "Don't give up on him. He just lost his *dat*, and his emotions are a jumbled mess. You can reach out to him again in a couple of weeks."

"*Mamm* is right," Emily chimed in. "We can send meals over to him, and we can even visit him." She stood. "We can start cooking now." She glanced around the kitchen. "Where's the basket?"

Rachel sniffed. "I left it at his *haus* Monday when I went to see him. I'll have to leave him a message and ask him to have John bring it to school."

"That's a great idea," *Mamm* said with an encouraging smile. "You can show Mike how much he and John mean to you, and he'll realize you made a mistake. Just be patient with him. I know what it's like to go through a devastating loss, and it sometimes takes awhile before you can think clearly again."

Rachel nodded, but deep in her soul, she doubted any number of meals could make Mike realize how much she loved and missed him.

MIKE GLANCED AROUND THE KITCHEN AND RUBBED THE BACK of his aching neck. "I appreciate everyone who came by today, but I'm also relieved it's over."

Janie and Marie nodded in unison as they sat across from him at the kitchen table that evening.

"I can't believe all the food you have." Janie pointed her fork toward her plate full of a variety of casseroles. "We should probably freeze some of it so it doesn't go bad."

Mike finished chewing what he thought was a chicken casserole and then swallowed. The casserole tasted more like sawdust to him than chicken. "That's a *gut* idea. Before I go to bed, I'll sort through it and see what I can take to the big freezer next door."

Mike peered down at the plate Janie had filled for him, but his appetite was still nonexistent. He glanced over at the counter, still full of casserole dishes, and his eyes locked on Rachel's basket. He got up and walked over to the basket, studying it as if seeing it for the first time.

"When did Rachel bring this over?" he asked his cousins.

A look of alarm appeared on Janie's face.

"I can't believe I forgot to tell you! I was just so distracted by everything that was happening with your *dat*. Rachel came to see you Monday when she heard he was in the hospital."

She shook her head, her expression becoming grim. "She was so upset. She cried when I told her your father was in a coma, and she looked as if she was trying not to cry again when she talked to John." Her eyes were full of warmth. "I know you've been upset with Rachel, but she truly cares about you, Mike. She was devastated when we talked about your *dat*. I could tell she really cares about John, and he adores her too. He wrapped his arms around her when he found us talking in the kitchen."

"Janie is right," Marie chimed in. "I talked to Rachel during the visitation, and she was really upset. She hugged me when she saw me, and she immediately asked where you and John were. Did you get to talk to her? I told her you were out in your shop."

"*Ya*, I did." Guilt stole his breath as he picked up the basket. He recalled their painful conversation and the grief in Rachel's eyes. Had he been wrong to push her away when she reached out to him?

He lifted the basket lid and his eyes took in the Scripture verse written on the wood: *And our hope for you is firm, because we know that just as you share in our sufferings, so also you share in our comfort.*

Mike closed his eyes as the Scripture verse echoed through his mind. And then something in his mind and heart seemed to click.

God had sent Rachel to Mike and John when they needed a friend. Rachel had broken down the barriers around Mike's heart and showed him what true love could mean.

Mike's chest squeezed with a further revelation—he loved Rachel, and he didn't want to lose her. He and John both needed her.

His breath came in quick bursts. "I need to go see Rachel. I have to take her the basket. Are your parents still here? Did their driver leave?"

"I think they're still here, but don't you think you should wait?" Marie asked, giving Janie a look of confusion. "It's late."

"You shouldn't go out now," Janie protested. "You need some sleep. Wait until the morning."

"No, I have to go now." He peered out the kitchen window and saw his uncle's driver's van parked out there. "Warren is still here.

I'm going to see if I can get a ride." He started for the door with the basket and then turned back toward his cousins. "Will you stay with John?"

The sisters shared another incredulous expression before nodding in unison.

"Thanks." Mike darted out the back door. His aunt and uncle were standing on the steps and talking to their driver. The rain had stopped and the air smelled like wet grass.

"Warren," Mike said. "Would you please give me a ride to Bird-in-Hand?"

Warren nodded. "Sure. I can drop you off on my way to your uncle's farm. Let's go."

Mike's pulse quickened as he climbed into the van and set the basket on his lap. He hoped Rachel would talk to him, but more than anything, he hoped she would forgive him.

RACHEL CLOSED THE CHRISTIAN NOVEL SHE'D BEEN READING. She'd hoped reading would help clear her mind and ease some of the anguish that continued to swell inside of her. The book, however, didn't provide the diversion she needed, and she knew she wouldn't sleep tonight.

"Rachel!" *Dat* called from downstairs. "You have a visitor!"

Rachel turned toward the battery-operated digital clock on her nightstand and found it was nearly eight thirty. *Who would visit at this time of the night?*

She slipped on her robe, pushing her waist-length dark hair over her shoulder, and hurried down the stairs as her mind raced with questions.

"I'm sorry for coming this late," a familiar voice said. "I promise I won't keep her up long."

"It's fine," *Dat* said.

Rachel's heartbeat quickened when she realized the voice belonged to Mike. She clutched her robe tighter to her body as she entered the kitchen. Mike was holding her basket.

As his gaze met hers, he held out the basket.

"I wanted to bring you this," he said. "I hadn't realized you'd left it."

Rachel searched his eyes. The icy anger she'd seen earlier was gone and replaced with grief and exhaustion.

"*Danki*," she said softly, her body trembling with anxiety and regret. She took the basket from him and set it on the counter. "You didn't need to bring it out here tonight. I was going to send a message home with John once he's back at school, asking that he return it to me there."

"It's not a problem." Mike stuffed his hands in his pocket and cleared his throat. "Could we possibly sit on the porch and talk for a few minutes?" His blue eyes pleaded with her to say yes.

Rachel turned to *Dat*, who nodded.

"*Ya*, but only for a few minutes," *Dat* said. "You need to get to bed, Rachel." Then he gave Mike a sympathetic expression. "You need your rest too, Mike. You look exhausted. *Gut nacht*."

As *Dat* ambled toward his bedroom, Rachel grabbed a lantern from the mudroom and followed Mike out to the porch, where they sat next to each other on the glider. Rachel set the lantern on the floor so that it bathed the porch in a soft yellow glow.

She glanced toward the pasture and didn't see a buggy. "How did you get here?"

"*Mei onkel's* driver brought me here. He offered to wait, but I told him to give me thirty minutes." Mike gave her a dark smile. "I took a chance that you'd talk to me."

"Oh." Rachel was thankful to see his smile again. She smoothed her hands over her pink robe, and when her leg brushed his, she jumped slightly.

They sat in strained silence for a few moments, and she wondered if she should say something. Instead, she listened to the cicadas and took in the stars sparkling above them. The rain clouds that had pressed down on them earlier were long gone and replaced by a gorgeous, clear sky.

"I'm sorry," he finally said, his voice stricken. "I shouldn't have been so cold and cruel to you earlier."

"You don't need to apologize," she said quickly, angling her body toward him. "I was wrong. I should have asked you who—"

"Please," Mike said, holding up a hand to shush her. "Let me finish." He trained his eyes on the pasture. "I wasn't thinking clearly earlier. I haven't had a clear thought in days. I've just been so lost and distraught. I can't believe my *dat* is gone, and—" His voice broke.

Rachel placed her hand on his. He met her gaze with tears pooling in his eyes.

"I need you," he whispered.

"I'm right here. I'm not going anywhere." His wounded expression shattered her heart.

Before she could react, Mike wrapped his arms around her and pulled her to him. She closed her eyes and breathed in his scent—soap and musk combined with just a hint of the outdoors. She felt his body relax against her.

"I've wanted to hug you all week." His voice croaked softly. "This is just what I needed."

She closed her eyes and leaned in to him. "I feel the same way."

He choked back a sob.

"It's okay," she whispered, her voice wobbly. "You don't have to hold it in any longer."

His breathing hitched, and then his body shook as he sobbed. His warm tears trickled through her hair and down her neck, leaving shivers in their wake. Her fingers traced the length of his muscular back. She cherished the comfort and intimacy of his embrace.

"I'm so sorry," Mike finally whispered, pain creeping into his voice. "I was so hurt when you rejected me that I didn't know what to do. I was afraid to let you back into my heart."

She raked her fingers through his thick hair, enjoying the soft texture. "You don't need to apologize."

He released her and rubbed his eyes with the heel of his hands. "I looked at the scripture in the basket earlier, and everything made sense."

"What do you mean?"

"When I met you, I only knew how to take care of *mei dat* and John," he said, clasping her hand in his. "I didn't know how to accept help from others, except for my cousins. You helped me realize it's okay to accept help from people outside of my family. God puts special people in our lives for a reason, and he sent you to me and John when we needed you most."

Rachel nodded as tears prickled her eyes. "The basket did just what I'd hoped it would do."

"What do you mean?"

"*Mei mamm* told me *mei dat* brought her meals in that basket when they were going through a difficult time," Rachel explained. "*Mamm* said the basket was sort of like a mediator and helped them work out their problems. *Mei dat* wrote that Scripture verse on the lid for *mei mamm*. I had hoped the basket would help us work out our problems too, and it did."

"*Ya*, the basket did help us, but you helped me too. You taught me how to love. You reminded me that I am worthy of having someone special in my life." He paused, and his lip trembled. "I can't imagine losing you again. I need you by my side."

"I need you too," she whispered, her voice quavering with emotion. "I'm so sorry for doubting you. You taught me how to trust again, and you renewed my faith in love. I need you and John just as much as you need me."

"I want to go to youth group meetings with you. I want to get to know you better." He trailed the tip of his finger down her cheek. "John and I need you in our lives. *Ich liebe dich*, Rachel."

A single tear escaped her eye, and Mike wiped it away with his thumb. "I love you too," she whispered.

Mike leaned down and gently brushed his lips across hers, and heat thrummed through her veins. She closed her eyes and savored the feeling of his lips against hers, sending her stomach into a wild swirl.

As Mike pulled Rachel to him and wrapped her into a warm hug, she rested her head on his chest and opened her heart to him. The sound of his heartbeat filled her ears. Rachel's smile deepened, and she silently thanked God for sending happiness to sit quietly on her shoulder.

EPILOGUE

"MAMM," RACHEL CALLED FROM THE KITCHEN. "HAVE YOU seen *Mammi's* lace tablecloth?"

Mamm poked her head into the doorway. "I'm not sure. You should ask Emily. I think she used it one night when Veronica came over for supper."

"Oh, that's right." Rachel stepped out to the porch, where Emily was hanging laundry. The hot July air hit Rachel like a wall as she walked over to her sister. "Have you seen *Mammi's* lace tablecloth?"

Emily pinned a pair of their father's trousers to the line. "I think I washed it and put it back in *Mamm's* closet." She fished another pair of trousers from the large wicker laundry basket. "What do you need it for?"

"Mike and John are coming over for supper tonight, and I want to make the kitchen look nice."

Emily grinned. "Things are going well with Mike, *ya?*"

"*Ya.*" Rachel fingered her black apron as heat stained her cheeks. "It's going really well. I'm so *froh* he started coming to youth group meetings. We're getting to know each other better."

"*Gut.*" Emily pinned the trousers to the line. "Check *Mamm's* closet for the tablecloth. After I finish hanging out the clothes, we can talk to make sure we've planned everything we need for supper."

"*Danki.*" Rachel gave a sigh of relief. Emily was a much better cook than she was. "I'll need your help."

Rachel walked back into the house and found her mother sweeping the family room. "Em said I should look in your closet for the tablecloth. Is it okay if look there?"

"Sure," *Mamm* said, leaning the broom against the wall. "I'll come with you."

Once there, Rachel peeked in the closet but didn't see the tablecloth stacked with the towels and sheets. "It's not in here." Rachel looked toward the far end of the room and saw the chest. "Could it possibly be in your hope chest?"

Mamm hesitated and then shrugged. "I don't remember putting it back in there, but I might have another tablecloth in there that you can use."

"That would be great."

"I'll check for you." *Mamm* fished around in the top drawer of her dresser and then pulled out the brass key. She bent over the hope chest, turned the key, and the lock clicked.

Rachel stood by *Mamm* as she opened the chest, and she breathed in the sweet aroma of cedar. *Mamm* sifted through the linens, a quilt, and a few small boxes, then lifted a small wooden box at the bottom of the chest and placed it on the edge of a nearby chair. As she continued searching through the hope chest, the wooden box fell to the floor and a stack of envelopes spilled out.

Rachel picked up the envelopes and realized they were letters. They were addressed to her mother, and the slanted penmanship looked like her father's handwriting.

She pulled out the top envelope, took out the letter, and unfolded it.

Dear Mattie,

     I know you're upset with me. It seems that no matter what I say, it's the wrong thing. I hope you know I care about you.

Please come home. We're married now, and we need to build a life together. We can't work things out if you continue to stay at your parents' *haus*.

"Here you go," *Mamm* said. "This isn't the tablecloth Emily used recently, but it did belong to your *mammi*."

Rachel looked up and found *Mamm* standing in front of her, holding a white lace tablecloth. She held up the letter and envelope as questions and confusion crowded her mind. "What is this?"

Mamm tilted her head with question as she climbed over the boxes and moved toward her. "What are you reading?"

"It's a letter *Dat* wrote to you a long time ago." She held up the box. "This is a box of letters addressed to you from *Dat*. Why did *Dat* write to you and ask you to come home? Why were you living with *Mammi* and *Daadi* when you were already married to *Dat*? Does this have something to do with the rocky start you said you had with *Dat* when he sent you meals in the basket?"

"Please give me that." *Mamm* took the letter and envelope out of Rachel's hands. She folded the letter, placed it in the envelope, and looked around for the small box. When she found it, she put the letter inside and closed the lid. "It's not important. That was a long time ago." She set the box back in the hope chest and locked it.

As Rachel watched *Mamm* slip the key into her pocket, her mind still raced with questions about the letter she'd found. That letter didn't make any sense. Her parents always seemed to enjoy a happy marriage, so why would *Mamm* move out and leave *Dat* alone?

"We'd better start cooking," *Mamm* said, and she turned and walked out of the bedroom.

Rachel pushed the questions about the letter out of her mind as she followed her mother to the kitchen. Her heart felt as if it would burst with excitement as she thought about her special dinner tonight with Mike. The days of needing the basket to help them along in their courtship were over.

She was so thankful God had led her into Mike's and John's life, and she couldn't wait to see what the future held for all of them.

Don't miss the next installment to the Amish Heirloom novels— The Cherished Quilt!

When Christopher Hostettler comes from Ohio to work at his uncle's shop in Bird-in-Hand, Pennsylvania, he gets off on the wrong foot with Emily Fisher. But when he finally opens up to her about his tragic reasons for leaving home, her heart begins to change.

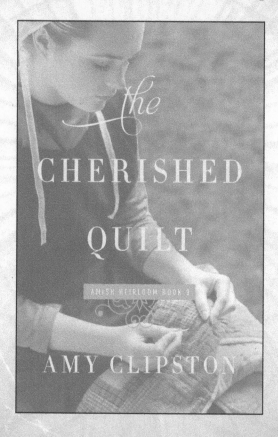

AVAILABLE IN PRINT AND E-BOOK NOVEMBER 2016

ACKNOWLEDGMENTS

AS ALWAYS, I'M THANKFUL FOR MY LOVING FAMILY, INCLUD-ing my mother, Lola Goebelbecker; my husband, Joe; and my sons, Zac and Matt. I'm blessed to have such an awesome and amazing family that puts up with me when I'm stressed out on a book deadline. Special thanks to Matt, aka Mr. Thesaurus, for helping me find synonyms. I couldn't ask for a more adorable wordsmith!

I'm more grateful than words can express to Janet Pecorella and my mother for proofreading for me. I truly appreciate the time you take out of your busy lives to help me polish my books. Special thanks to my Amish friends who patiently answer my endless stream of questions. Thank you also to Stacey Barbalace for her research assistance. Thank you also to Jessica Miller, RN, for her medical research in this book.

Thank you to my wonderful church family at Morning Star Lutheran in Matthews, North Carolina, for your encouragement, prayers, love, and friendship. You all mean so much to my family and me.

To my agent, Sue Brower—I can't thank you enough for your guidance, advice, and friendship. You are a tremendous blessing in my life.

Thank you to my amazing editor, Becky Philpott, for your friendship and guidance. Love you, girl!

I'm grateful to Jean Bloom, who helped me polish and refine the story. Thank you also for connecting the dots between my books. You're a blessing! I also would like to thank Kristen Golden for tirelessly working to promote my books. I'm grateful to each and every person at HarperCollins Christian Publishing who helped make this book a reality.

Thank you to the Bakery Bunch, my awesome Street Team! I appreciate your friendship, loyalty, and willingness to help promote my books. Special thanks to Jamie Mendoza! I'm so grateful for your expertise and guidance with marketing and promotion.

To my readers—thank you for choosing my novels. My books are a blessing in my life for many reasons, including the special friendships I've formed with my readers. Thank you for your e-mail messages, Facebook notes, and letters.

Thank you most of all to God—for giving me the inspiration and the words to glorify You. I'm grateful and humbled You've chosen this path for me.

Special thanks to Cathy and Dennis Zimmermann for their hospitality and research assistance in Lancaster County, Pennsylvania.

Cathy & Dennis Zimmermann, Innkeepers

The Creekside Inn

44 Leacock Road—PO Box 435

Paradise, PA 17562

Toll Free: (866) 604-2574

Local Phone: (717) 687-0333

The author and publisher gratefully acknowledge the following resource used to research information for this book:

C. Richard Beam, *Revised Pennsylvania German Dictionary* (Lancaster: Brookshire Publications, Inc., 1991).

DISCUSSION QUESTIONS

1. Rachel is devastated when her boyfriend breaks up with her to date her best friend. Have you faced a difficult loss? What Bible verses helped you? Share this with the group.
2. Mike is afraid of opening his heart to Rachel at the beginning of the book. By the end of the story, he realizes he's ready to love her and also accept help from others outside of his family. What do you think caused him to change his point of view on love throughout the story?
3. The basket Rachel finds in the attic is inscribed with 2 Corinthians 1:7: "And our hope for you is firm, because we know that just as you share in our sufferings, so also you share in our comfort." What does this verse mean to you?
4. Rachel pours herself into teaching as a way to deal with breaking up with her boyfriend and losing her best friend. Think of a time when you felt hurt or betrayed. Where did you find strength? What Bible verses would help with this?
5. Rachel misinterprets Mike's conversation with his cousin at the shop, and she turns her back on Mike instead of having an honest conversation with him. In the end, it's painful when Rachel learns the truth and tries to explain her behavior to Mike. Have you ever found yourself in a similar situation? If so, how did it turn out? Share this with the group.

6. At the beginning of the book, Raymond is in kidney failure and on dialysis, but he is too weak to undergo a kidney transplant. What are your feelings about organ donation? Have you known someone who was an organ donor or recipient? Share this with the group.

7. Rachel feels God is giving her a second chance when she falls in love with Mike. Have you ever experienced a second chance? What was it?

8. Which character can you identify with the most? Which character seemed to carry the most emotional stake in the story? Was it Rachel, Mike, John, or someone else?

9. What role did the basket play in Rachel and Mike's relationship? Can you relate the basket to an object that was pivotal in a relationship you've experienced in your life?

10. What did you know about the Amish before reading this book? What did you learn?

Four women working at the
Lancaster Grand Hotel find their
way through life and love.

The *Kauffman*
Amish Bakery Series

ABOUT THE AUTHOR

Photo by Dan Davis Photography

AMY CLIPSTON IS THE AWARD-WINNING AND BESTSELLING author of more than a dozen novels, including the Kauffman Amish Bakery series and the Hearts of the Lancaster Grand Hotel series. Her novels have hit multiple bestseller lists including CBD, CBA, and ECPA. Amy holds a degree in communication from Virginia Wesleyan College and works full time for the City of Charlotte, North Carolina. Amy lives in North Carolina with her husband, two sons, and three spoiled rotten cats.

Visit her website: amyclipston.com
Facebook: Amy Clipston
Twitter: @AmyClipston
Instagram: Amy_Clipston